Multinationals, Technology and National Competitiveness

NEW HORIZONS IN INTERNATIONAL BUSINESS

General Editor: Peter J. Buckley
Centre for International Business,
University of Leeds (CIBUL), UK

The New Horizons in International Business series has established itself as the world's leading forum for the presentation of new ideas in international business research. It offers pre-eminent contributions in the areas of multinational enterprise – including foreign direct investment, business strategy and corporate alliances, global competitive strategies, and entrepreneurship. In short, this series constitutes essential reading for academics, business strategists and policy makers alike.

Titles in the series include:

Global Competitive Strategies in the New World Economy
Multilateralism, Regionalization and the Transnational Firm
Edited by Hafiz Mirza

Foreign Direct Investment and Corporate Networking
A Framework for Spatial Analysis of Investment Conditions
Robert L.A. Morsink

Structural Change and Cooperation in the Global Economy
Edited by Gavin Boyd and John H. Dunning

Managing the Multinationals
An International Study of Control Mechanisms
Anne-Wil Käthe Harzing

The Origins of the International Competitiveness of Firms
The Impact of Location and Ownership in the Professional Service Industries
Lilach Nachum

Deepening Integration in the Pacific Economies
Corporate Alliances, Contestable Markets and Free Trade
Edited by Alan M. Rugman and Gavin Boyd

The Global Integration of Europe and East Asia
Studies of International Trade and Investment
Edited by Sang-Gon Lee and Pierre-Bruno Ruffini

Foreign Direct Investment and Economic Growth in China
Edited by Yanrui Wu

Multinationals, Technology and National Competitiveness
Marina Papanastassiou and Robert Pearce

Globalizing America
The USA in World Integration
Edited by Thomas L. Brewer and Gavin Boyd

Information Technology in Multinational Enterprises
Edited by Edward Mozley Roche and Michael James Blaine

Multinationals, Technology and National Competitiveness

Marina Papanastassiou
Athens University of Economics and Business, Greece

and

Robert Pearce
Department of Economics, University of Reading, UK

NEW HORIZONS IN INTERNATIONAL BUSINESS

Edward Elgar
Cheltenham, UK • Northampton, MA, USA

Published by
Edward Elgar Publishing Limited
Glensanda House
Montpellier Parade
Cheltenham
Glos GL50 1UA
UK

Edward Elgar Publishing, Inc.
136 West Street
Suite 202
Northampton
Massachusetts 01060
USA

A catalogue record for this book
is available from the British Library

Library of Congress Cataloguing in Publication Data

Papanastassiou, Marina.
    Multinationals, technology, and national competitiveness / Marina
Papanastassiou, Robert Pearce.
        — (New horizons in international business)
    Includes bibliographical references and index.
        1. International business enterprises—Great Britain.
2. Corporations, Foreign—Great Britain. 3. Research, Industrial–
–Economic aspects—Great Britain. 4. Technological innovations-
–Economic aspects—Great Britain. 5. Competition, International.
I. Pearce, Robert D., 1943–   . II. Title. III. Series.
HD2845.P35   1999
338.8'8841—dc21   99–31590
                                                                 CIP

ISBN 1 85898 822 5

Printed and bound in Great Britain by MPG Books Ltd, Bodmin, Cornwall

To Ioannis and Augustina-Maria and to Tony and Dawn

Contents

List of tables   ix
Acknowledgement   xiii

1.   Multinationals and industrialisation   1

2.   Roles of subsidiaries and MNE evolution   20

3.   Roles and markets of subsidiaries in the UK   55

4.   Technology in subsidiaries   89

5.   Multinationals' research and development in the UK   120

6.   Roles and motivations of MNE laboratories   146

7.   Scientific collaborations of MNE research laboratories in the UK   189

8.   Subsidiaries' linkages with UK input suppliers   208

9.   Multinationals and national competitiveness   224

References   241

Index   255

Tables

1.1	Composition, by industry and home country, of respondents to the subsidiary survey	15
2.1	Roles of foreign MNE subsidiaries in the UK, 1989 and 1994	33
3.1	Roles of subsidiaries in the UK, by home country	60
3.2	Previous roles of MNE subsidiaries in the UK, by current role	64
3.3	Likely future roles of MNE subsidiaries in the UK, by current role	65
3.4	Proportion of production that is exported by MNE subsidiaries in the UK	66
3.5	Regression tests of export characteristics of MNE subsidiaries in the UK	67
3.6	Proportion of exports of MNE subsidiaries in the UK that are intra-group trade	71
3.7	Proportion of exports of MNE subsidiaries in the UK that are intermediate products	72
3.8	Relative importance of markets supplied by MNE subsidiaries in the UK	74
3.9	Regression tests of markets supplied by MNE subsidiaries in the UK	77
3.10	Dates of establishment of UK subsidiaries	80
3.11	Size of subsidiaries in the UK	82
3.12	Share of subsidiaries in the UK of the global sales of their MNE group	84
3.13	Means of establishment of subsidiaries in the UK	86
4.1	Relative importance of sources of technology in MNE subsidiaries in the UK	99
4.2	Regressions with subsidiaries' sources of technology as dependent variable	104
4.3	Approaches to product development in subsidiaries	111
4.4	Extent of adaptation of technology by MNE subsidiaries in the UK	114
4.5	Reasons for adaptation of existing products by MNE subsidiaries in the UK	115
4.6	Reasons for adaptation of existing production processes by MNE subsidiaries	116
5.1	In-house R&D (OWNLAB) as a source of technology in MNE subsidiaries in the UK	125

5.2   Importance of in-house R&D (OWNLAB) as a source of   127
       technology in MNE subsidiaries in the UK
5.3   Regressions with OWNLAB as dependent variable–home country   129
       sub–samples
5.4   Anticipated changes in size of R&D laboratories of MNE   131
       subsidiaries in the UK
5.5   Regressions with anticipated changes in size of R&D   132
       laboratories as dependent variables
5.6   Dates of establishment of R&D laboratories of MNE   133
       subsidiaries in the UK
5.7   Dates of establishment of MNE laboratories in the UK.   135
5.8   Budgets of MNE laboratories in the UK   135
5.9   R&D budgets of MNE laboratories in the UK as a percentage   136
       of the total R&D expenditure of their groups
5.10   Regressions with R&D budget as dependent variable   137
5.11   Level of employment of scientific personnel in MNE   139
       subsidiaries' laboratories in the UK
5.12   Sources of recruitment of scientific personnel of MNE   141
       laboratories in the UK
6.1   Roles of R&D laboratories of MNE subsidiaries in the UK   150
6.2   Roles of MNE laboratories in the UK   151
6.3   Relative strength of roles in MNEs' R&D laboratories in the UK   152
6.4   Types of scientific work carried out in MNE laboratories in 161
       the UK
6.5   Evaluation of influences on the decision to set up an MNE   169
       laboratory in the UK, or on its recent growth or evolution
6.6   Evaluation of factors that might influence the growing roles 172
       of MNE laboratories in the UK
6.7   Evaluation of factors that might cause a diminished role in 173
       MNE laboratories in the UK
6.8   Evaluation by MNE subsidiaries in the UK without an R&D   176
       laboratory of reasons for not having one
6.9   Evaluation by MNE subsidiaries in the UK without an R&D   179
       laboratory of factors that could influence them to set one up
6.10   Sources of funding for MNE laboratories in the UK   181
7.1   Extent of collaboration between MNE laboratories in the UK   191
       and other scientific institutions
7.2   Types of work involved in collaborations of MNE laboratories 197
       in the UK with other UK scientific institutions

Tables

7.3	Reasons for collaboration of MNE laboratories in the UK with other scientific institutions	200
7.4	Nature of collaborations with UK universities of MNE laboratories in the UK	203
8.1	Relative importance of sources of inputs in MNE subsidiaries in the UK	210
8.2	Regressions with sources of inputs as dependent variable	212
8.3	Prevalence of provision of technological advice by MNE subsidiaries to UK input suppliers	217
8.4	Prevalence of different types of advice to UK input suppliers by MNE subsidiaries	219

Acknowledgement

We would like to express our considerable gratitude to Jill Turner, who produced the camera-ready manuscript with great competence and heroic patience and good humour.

1. Multinationals and industrialisation

Creativity remains a core imperative of enterprise and industry. Firms seeking sustained competitiveness need to pursue revitalised core technologies, from which they fuel a constant drive to new products, improved production processes and better organisational practices. National industries need to evolve, in a similar and complementary fashion, around higher-value-added sources of comparative advantage. An important area of public policy and debate in which these apparently mundane and routine truisms have often been damagingly neglected is that described as 'inward investment'. The headline representations of foreign direct investment (FDI) usually focus on homogeneous and quantitative flows, of capital and technology, resulting in numbers of jobs created. In established industrial economies, in particular, FDI often seems to be represented as a defensive salvation for short-term problems that in fact result from longer-term forces of structural decline.

The central analysis of foreign firms' manufacturing and technological operations in the UK, which forms the core of this book, indicates that an excessively monochrome or uni-dimensional view of the nature and motivation of the contemporary multinational enterprise (MNE) can lead to the neglect of the full scope of its contribution to the economies of host countries. The potential of MNE investments can realistically be seen as extending beyond the short-term gap filling (the ability to take up the slack in utilisation of existing standardised industrial inputs, notably labour) into dynamic processes that can embody the upgrading of local resources and the regeneration of the industrial sector itself.

Early analysis of the MNE (implemented initially to pursue a more complete and rounded explanation of the determinants of FDI[1]) provided two insights that are relevant to the development of the arguments and investigations of later chapters. Firstly, it was initially accepted that the primary motive for the international expansion of production operations of MNEs (mainly during the interwar years and into the early 1960s) was market seeking.[2] Thus firms set up plants within foreign countries in order to supply the national market of those countries in the best (most profitable) way available. The key factors determining these market-seeking investments (the relevant location advantages, in Dunning's terminology)[3] were the size, quality (income per capita) and expected growth of the local market and those protective barriers that precluded its supply (through trade) from potentially more efficient plants elsewhere. Although the cost and quality of local inputs was not irrelevant to the performance of subsidiaries set up in this context, and could sometimes

1

influence investment decisions in the case of marginal markets, an efficiency-seeking motivation was considered to be very secondary.

Also of considerable relevance, from the retrospective viewpoint of our contemporary perception of the MNE, was the lack in the early analysis of any motivation for manufacturing enterprises to respond in a positive way to idiosyncratic characteristics of local inputs (technology, skills, marketing perceptions). Standardised inputs that could be operationalised effectively to support the requirements of the MNEs' existing means of producing established products was assumed to define the full extent of the supply-side needs of these early local-market subsidiaries. However, Hymer's pioneering analysis (1960/76) provided a crucial negative basis for the influence of idiosyncratic elements of the host-country economy. Certain distinctive elements of the local economic, political and institutional infrastructure (the nature of practices in the labour market; the most acceptable and effective means of marketing goods; the best way to deal with various local bureaucracies; the legal and financial systems, and so on) were familiar to local enterprises and alien to newcomer MNE subsidiaries. To overcome such innate costs of foreignness and compete effectively with local firms, the MNE's operations needed to be based around a compensating source of advantage. Thus some source of ownership advantage (in Dunning's terminology) that is unique to the MNE (for example, a technology embodied in its products and/or production processes; distinctive and effective managerial skills; already renowned trade-marks backed by high-quality marketing expertise) provides its subsidiaries with the ability to out-compete indigenous firms, even where the latter can gain significant benefits from being fully at home with those elements of the local institutional environment that alienate and compromise the foreign firm's operations. This early perception thus provides the vision of a horizontally-integrated MNE[4] replicating its core behaviour in many separate national economies by producing a standardised range of goods in a manner that is widely competitive due to the possession of high-quality and distinctive competences.

The second vastly influential early contribution to the conceptualisation of the MNE was Vernon's (1966) description of the manner in which the product life cycle could be expected to determine investment and trade patterns. In terms of the issues of greatest concern here we can characterise Vernon's contribution as asserting that manufacturing companies that would become MNEs did so on the basis of knowledge-based ownership advantages that were created in (and entirely motivated by) that enterprise's home country. Thus for these proto-MNEs, innovation was fully centralised in the company's country of origin. As Vernon's analysis was based mainly on observation of US companies in the two decades after the Second World War, one factor supporting this home-country dominance of innovation was that new knowledge inputs would be vastly more readily available there than elsewhere. This reflected the relatively unimpeded availability of research infrastructure (extensively damaged elsewhere during the War) and the increasing accessibility for commercial application of new technologies recently generated for military purposes. A second relevant factor was that the US was the highest income market in the world, and thus most likely to reward (and perhaps provide indicative taste trends to) a successful innovation process.

Also of considerable (albeit initially mainly academic) significance was the implicit assumption that the enterprises active in the first (product innovation) stage of Vernon's product cycle had no overseas production or marketing operations. This is relevant as it means that even where important sources of new technology or taste trends were emerging in other countries the companies would have no intra-firm means of detecting and communicating these. Although, in theory, the monitoring for possible decentralised knowledge inputs into a centralised innovation process could be secured by, for example, commissioning local consultants in other countries, this would be too unlikely to be effective to divert the focus away from home-country inputs in practice. Even where the overseas agents in such an arrangement do not behave opportunistically, and do seek to achieve their principal's commission as effectively as possible, communication problems would severely compromise the process. Thus where the knowledge sought is itself inherently speculative and ill-defined, the commissioning firm could provide only a very imprecise specification of the information or ideas that might be relevant[5] and, even when accessing results that it believes could be suitable, the foreign agent will find it difficult to communicate the full scope of these possibilities back to the principal. The first phase of Vernon's product cycle thus explains the derivation of ownership advantages which were very location specific, in terms of reflecting their origins in the firm's home country. The sheer competitive strength of these advantages, however, led in the second phase of the cycle to the emergence of markets for the products in other high-income countries and eventually to the establishment of production facilities there (that is, market-seeking expansion of the firm's competitive horizons in response to location factors of the type discussed earlier). In the third phase, when the technology has become highly standardised and the market for the product intensely competitive globally, the company was expected to extend its horizons further by relocating production into particular low-cost supply locations (moving to an efficiency-seeking motivation).

From the early theorising we thus have a stylised view of the post-war MNE as a decisively hierarchical organisation in which a dominant parent (home-country) company creates and controls those sources of competitive advantage through which a number of quite homogeneous subsidiaries overseas operate successfully in their respective national markets. However, the nature of the global competitive environment at this stage in the evolution of MNEs meant that in practice the parent companies rarely needed to exercise their scope for control in a 'hands-on' (continually interventionist) fashion. Once a subsidiary had assimilated the centrally-generated technologies that it was expected to use, it was normally allowed to operationalise them in a fairly autonomous fashion. This could involve a certain degree of creativity in terms of responding to local tastes or production conditions. This creative scope would normally, however, have been constrained by the parameters of the existing group-level core technology and the distinctive needs of the local market. Subsidiary-level creativity at this stage could not intrude into the wider technological or product evolution of the parent MNE group.

Against this background much recent theorising on the nature of the contemporary MNE, and much of the analysis and documentation in this book, relates to the need to reconcile two divergent trends provoked by subsequent changes in the global economy. Firstly, movements towards freer trade (and more recently the full scope of 'globalisation') have led MNEs away from the local-market-focused multidomestic strategy towards some variant of a global strategy (Porter, 1986), in which the activities of national subsidiaries become less isolated and are increasingly expected to complement and support operations in other parts of the group. The need to coordinate ever more integrated networks of international operations then indicates a trend towards MNEs needing to activate much more decisively the potentials of centralised control.

However, a second emerging influence is that many countries that host subsidiaries of MNEs are becoming increasingly important as sources of distinctive and creative inputs, in the form of new technologies, taste patterns and so on. Thus a second key trend in the evolution of MNEs is to use their subsidiaries as means of detecting and operationalising these dispersed sources of knowledge and ideas.[6] But subsidiaries that are encouraged to contribute new elements to the creative scope of the MNE cannot be subjected to continual and close centralised control. To build new competences out of elements of their local (host-country) environment can only be a full-time responsibility of those subsidiary-level decision makers who have close ongoing experience of these possibilities. Important facets of strategic decision making (greatly transcending that available in old multidomestic units) need to devolve to the subsidiary level once dispersed contributions to the group's learning processes and knowledge generation become significant possibilities. Yet such subsidiary-level generation of new competences is ultimately still activated to support the development of group-wide competitiveness. As key elements of functional scope are increasingly dispersed in the modern MNE the importance of centralised *comprehension* of the full range of activities and emerging potentials becomes ever more vital, even where active *control* of the immediate implementation of some quite strategic parts of the global programmes is best ceded to the subsidiaries.

The tension between centralised control and decentralised responsibilities in the modern MNE both results from and can, in part, be resolved by acceptance of, various elements of heterogeneity. In terms of the external environment these include market heterogeneity (many national or regional markets still sustain and perhaps, with greater prosperity, further enhance, distinctive taste patterns) and input heterogeneity (diversity of skills, knowledge and technology available in different host countries). In terms of internal organisation the response of MNEs is to use a heterogeneous range of subsidiary types in order to encompass an extended set of strategic motivations within their pursuit of sustained global competitiveness. In the light of our earlier discussions we can discern three forces that have underpinned these evolutionary patterns in MNE response to the emergence of the global economy as an intense, but diverse, competitive environment.

We have already observed the relevance of increasing freedom of trade (responding to both General Agreement on Tariffs and Trade/World Trade Organisation (GATT/WTO) rounds and the emergence of regional trade blocs) as a factor motivating changes in the strategic orientation of MNEs. Thus the lowering of protective barriers to trade in the host countries of traditional market-seeking subsidiaries removed one of the relevant location advantages and thereby opened the other (a profitable market) to the competition of a much wider range of sources of supply. This was expected to expose inefficiency in many of these protected subsidiaries, which targeted individual national markets that might not allow the full realisation of economies of scale. For MNEs as groups, the situation was redeemed by the utilisation of the new freedom of trade, and the restructuring of global or regional supply profiles so that individual goods were produced in a limited number of locations and exported to wider markets. Each subsidiary was thereby opened to a fully competitive market situation, which was now usually extensive enough to realise economies of scale so that optimal efficiency in production could be achieved.

For an individual subsidiary seeking to survive within such an MNE restructuring programme, it becomes necessary to claim the right to continue to produce (now for export markets) some of the goods it previously supplied to the local market. Assuming the subsidiary's ability to use the existing technologies effectively, which goods, if any, it retains the right to supply then depends on which input factors the host country can supply most cost effectively. The standardised product and process technologies that comprise the current ownership advantages of an MNE are assumed to be perfectly mobile within the group (and output is now freely transferable between countries) so that where particular goods are manufactured relates to the location advantages of host countries (which now become, primarily, their ability to supply particular inputs at internationally competitive prices). For the MNEs this phase of their evolution (in response mainly to the problems and potentials of freer trade) represents a redistribution of unchanged ownership advantages, in order to create an international network of production subsidiaries which optimises the supply of the established range of products that represents the current commercial embodiment of their existing knowledge capabilities. Thus the driving imperative of these companies moves from market seeking to efficiency seeking. For host countries this process of MNE restructuring should contribute to the effective transformation of the competitiveness of their industry through the improved operationalisation of their existing sources of static comparative advantage.

The second key force that we perceive as undermining the hegemony of the leading MNEs of the immediate post-war era is an increasing international dispersion of the sources of stimulating and original creative inputs. A crucial element in the effective rehabilitation of many traditional industrial economies (notably in Europe) and in the emergence of major new players (especially in East Asia) was the increasing ability to access local sources of distinctive technology and idiosyncratic market needs and trends. The emergence of new globally-competing enterprises building their competences outwards from these origins in their home-country capabilities became a major factor in the intensification of international competition. This development carried two vital implications for firms (ultimately both well-established MNEs and the new entrants) seeking sustained competitiveness in the global marketplace. Firstly, it reconfirmed the crucial importance of not just using existing ownership advantages efficiently but of a continual and emphatic commitment to their regeneration. Development of better products from an existing core technology, and the reinforcement and revitalisation of that knowledge stock itself, were both key imperatives. Secondly, it became clear that to an evermore significant degree the most effective derivation of a globally-competitive product range, and the most complete strengthening of core technology, could be achieved only by accessing the heterogeneous scientific capabilities and product ideas available from an expanding range of countries (in effect tapping into a variety of national systems of innovation).[7] Hence innovation remains central to global competitiveness, but in the new situation can no longer be adequately achieved from centralised perspectives or by using only home-country inputs.

Thus the second significant trend in the organisational evolution of MNEs has been the interjection of an increasingly *knowledge-seeking* motivation into their overseas operations. Our analysis in subsequent chapters deals in detail with two manifestations of this new imperative, the emergence of subsidiaries that themselves develop products (as, in effect, part of increasingly globalised approaches to innovation itself) and the greatly extended and deepened use of decentralised research and development (R&D) facilities. These knowledge-seeking elements in the international scope of the contemporary MNE aim to use particular host-country location advantages to help to expand the ownership advantages available to the group. The location advantages operationalised in this case are clearly very different from those relevant to market- or efficiency-seekers since they represent emerging, and not yet fully or optimally articulated, sources of creativity in the local economy (that is, emerging aspects of dynamic comparative advantage).

Because these creative types of location advantage can be seen as, in the first instance, enhancing the ownership advantages of MNEs it then becomes a crucial issue as to where these new sources of firm-level competitiveness are actually applied commercially. In much of the behaviour we will discuss in later chapters the result *is* direct support of the competitiveness of industry located in the host country (in this study the UK). This is by no means the inevitable outcome, however, and some forms of MNE knowledge-generating activity that build on local technology, product concepts, and so on (notably that of certain types of R&D laboratory) can flow out to fuel the wider competitiveness of the MNE group, in ways that may then provide only an indirect and moderate stimulus to local industry. This mode of MNE behaviour may greatly assist the generation of new and unique sources of higher-value-added industrial competitiveness that derive distinctively from a country's own knowledge and creativity. Alternatively it may divert the benefits from a country's most powerful potential sources of future comparative advantage into other parts of MNE operations located in rival economies. The implications of the ways in which MNEs operationalise *national* sources of knowledge development for *international* competitiveness are central to our analysis.

The third perspective on the organisational evolution of the MNE builds on the previous point in the light of our description of the product cycle. In the original formulation of the product cycle, we suggested, one reason for home-country location of innovation was the lack of reliable access to creative inputs from elsewhere due to the absence of overseas operations that could properly monitor useful developments. Even if a company suspected that more appropriate new technologies, or more stimulatory and original market perspectives, might be emerging elsewhere, it would accept that it did not possess the means to acquire them in adequate and reliable detail. However the eventual establishment, in the second phase of the original cycle, of producing subsidiaries in the more prosperous and advanced of overseas markets provides the institutional solution to the problem. Now subsidiaries that initiate their operations around a detailed knowledge of the company's existing products and technologies also seek to embed them in the different taste conditions, and production and knowledge circumstances, of other economies (which may be in the process of manifesting the increasingly distinctive attributes suggested by the previous point).

But where subsidiaries come to possess the in-house abilities to discern and articulate valuably distinctive dimensions of local attributes and conditions, they are likely to be reluctant to then merely act as conduits through which such original perceptions flow back to parent-company creative operations. They can often suggest convincing reasons why they can themselves provide the most effective operationalisation of the local potentials in support of the wider competitive needs of the whole group (for example, as product mandate subsidiaries). Once the working through of the original product cycle process has led to the initiation of overseas sales and production facilities, an increasing propensity for these subsidiaries to become involved in the innovation process tends to dissolve the distinction between the first two stages.[8] As the firms become true MNEs, the innovation process becomes informed by, and responsive to, various aspects of global heterogeneity. How such differentiated innovation programmes are developed, and how individual subsidiaries (and/or laboratories) assert their positions in them, are crucial elements in the internal dynamics of the modern MNE. Understanding the MNE as a differentiated entity in perpetual flux is, we shall argue, vital for host countries that aim to upgrade the competitiveness of an industrial sector (and of a technological scope) which embodies a foreign-controlled component.

It is, therefore, an innate propensity for change in MNEs as differentiated networks that provides their greatest potential and challenge to host countries. All countries that are willing to host manufacturing MNEs can be assumed to themselves have an acceptance of the need for industrial change. Even the most successful of current industrial economies will be aware of the need for continual evolution of the competitiveness of the manufacturing sector, and many of them are willing to host MNE subsidiaries as a source of stimulation and challenge towards the achievement of further progress. Here there is an acknowledgement that the current possession of significant sources of comparative advantage can only be the basis of sustained competitiveness if the underlying technologies, skills and commercial ideas are continually reinforced and reoriented in the light of globalised changes in knowledge and markets. Such an orderly evolution of current success can, in at least some elements of a country's industry and capabilities, be stimulated by the involvement of foreign MNE subsidiaries, activating locally new sources of complementary knowledge and competitive perception.

At the other end of the development scale many countries seeking to initiate industrialisation have sought the involvement of MNEs as a means of providing the inputs (technology, management, international market access) that can activate unrealised sources of competitiveness (for example, cost-effective unskilled labour, raw materials and cheap energy). Whilst in the case of the already highly-competitive industrialised countries MNEs may expect to learn from (as well as help further strengthen the knowledge scope of) their host economies, here the flow of intangible resources is assumed to be essentially one way. How host-country learning can spread out from (and ultimately complement, rather than remain dependent on) knowledge assets that are imported by MNEs to initiate their manufacturing activities[9] is one of the great challenges in harnessing these globally-competing companies to true national development and sustained industrial progress.[10]

Between the extremes of contributions to orderly progress and evolution in already successful and balanced industrial economies and of providing substantial initiating inputs into the startup of industrialisation in poor countries, we can perceive various contexts that can involve MNEs in processes of industrial restructuring or revitalisation. An obviously very important contemporary context for this is the countries that are in the process of transition from centrally-planned economic systems. Here the need is not only simply to overcome decades of industrial inefficiency, which reflect the lack of a truly competitive environment, but also to confront an inherited industrial structure that is very unlikely to reflect adequately those sources of comparative advantage that would be most relevant to asserting the economy's position internationally. The role of MNEs in speeding up the processes of industrial transformation, and of operationalising the most effective local attributes towards early international competitiveness, can be vital.

Another intermediate context that may provide particular scope for MNE dynamism is that faced by established industrial countries whose manufacturing sectors have discernibly lost ground in terms of international competitiveness. The fact that the situation is less dramatic (not involving fundamental ideological reformulation or basic institutional restructuring) may also make it more insidious. Rarely in such countries is there sufficient public consensus on the extent or nature of industrial decline to allow for the formulation of a cohesive package of measures that can be convincingly presented as, for example, a 'programme of industrial renewal'.[11] Nevertheless, attempts to halt decline and provide a revitalised status in global industrial competition can be addressed at various levels. This may involve not only enhanced public policy commitment to education, training and science (as well as aspects of physical infrastructure), but also the generation of improved support mechanisms for the embodiment of the output of this in long-term development programmes in industrial enterprises. More discriminating (though not obviously *discriminatory*) attitudes towards inward investment can support this, through a recognition of the variegated roles accessible to subsidiaries and the scope for evolution thereby available. New investments can be attracted in forms (that is, to play roles) that build on, and specifically benefit from, the emerging revitalised location advantages, whilst existing subsidiaries that may have been dangerously alienated by discerned local decline may now be induced to restructure in ways that again activate the regenerated sources of local competitiveness. Host-country commitment to, in effect, the renewal and restructuring of location advantages, needs to be accompanied by an active encouragement of MNEs to benefit from the application of upgraded ownership advantages.

Most discussion of the potential contribution of MNEs to host-country industrialisation has tended to address those scenarios which are motivated by a need for its initiation or invigoration (for example, the latter three above) and analyse the implications of new inflows of FDI. The favourable interpretation is then that such FDI brings new firm-level competitive attributes (ownership advantages) that are able to activate certain under-utilised local factors (location advantages) more effectively than indigenous enterprises would be capable of doing. However, it then becomes of equal relevance to explain how MNE operations can become embedded in, and generate continued support for, the sustained processes of industrial development that should follow the successful origination or restructuring of a manufacturing sector. Crucially, a challenge is likely to emerge to host-country policy, since part of the impact of growth and development will be to change the nature of its comparative advantage and therefore the location advantages faced by MNEs. The location advantages that initially serve to attract MNE subsidiaries cannot also serve as the basis for a sustained contribution to a progressive industrial sector that retains its competitive status as global markets develop and intensify. In an established industrial economy (such as the UK in our investigation) inward investment policy needs to understand not only how to attract new projects but also how to secure persistent contributions from those already in place. Viewing the modern MNE as a continuously evolving differentiated network provides a basis for comprehending a scope for endogenous dynamism in subsidiary/host-country relations.

It is now widely accepted that industrial development and economic progress in general benefit much more from the qualitative improvement of inputs (intensified or deepened use of resources) than from their quantitative expansion (extensive or widened sources of growth). A complementary perception is then that governments should, at least, support certain aspects of this through the provision of public goods that can facilitate the upgrading of inputs. These may include physical infrastructure, but increasingly relate to knowledge in the form of education, training and retraining, generation of commercial skills (management, marketing, financial expertise, and so on) and support for pure research. The reaction of MNEs to the knowledge-based elements of such policies is crucial and central to our analysis.

The host country is actively seeking to change the nature of its location advantages. One possibility is that to the extent that the local input changes (restructured location advantages) means the removal of those factors that were supporting the subsidiary's activity, the MNE may reject the new (higher-cost but upgraded) factors as inappropriate to its overall strategic portfolio and shut down its operation. More hopeful is a positive response in terms of refocusing the subsidiary (presumably into a higher-value-added status) in a way that utilises the new location advantages. This would be expected to involve a complementary application of upgraded ownership advantages by the MNE in the revised subsidiary role. One version of this would involve the subsidiary importing new ownership advantages (for example, more advanced product technologies) from elsewhere in the group. Here a higher-value-added role emerges in the subsidiary because the host country unilaterally initiates the upgrading of its location advantages enough to attract more advanced parts of the MNE's knowledge scope (and therefore secure production of more sophisticated parts of its existing product range).[12]

Of even greater potential, but perhaps also more contentious, is the possibility of an interdependence between the commitment of an MNE subsidiary and the ways in which a host-country's factor base is upgraded. The intra-group ambition of a subsidiary in a country that already provides very competent skills and a distinctive science base may lead it to involve itself proactively in training and localised R&D (both by internalising elements of the scientific community in an in-house laboratory and through externalised collaborations with local universities, and so on). This may then complement host-government aims for knowledge and skill development, and interject distinctive (hopefully, but not inevitably, beneficial) facets into the reformulated location advantages. This type of subsidiary behaviour can then also be seen as responding to the aims of host-country location advantage improvement not just through the application (import) of *better* ownership advantages, but as an attempt to actively involve such local knowledge attributes in the actual process of generation of *new* ownership advantages. Once MNE subsidiaries become involved creatively with such local attributes in this way there is, to some degree, a dissolution of the distinction between ownership advantages and location advantages. The ownership advantage now exercised by a subsidiary is still likely to have a strong group-level component (available to other subsidiaries elsewhere), but also possesses a unique (locally-generated) element that provides it with a distinctive intra-group competitive status. The location advantages that attract MNEs can thus sometimes be operationalised in forms that become specific attributes of individual subsidiaries.

The way in which MNE subsidiaries operationalise technology in the context of an industrialisation process is seen as open to substantial change as the host country's development progresses. Successful development involves closing the gap in relative technological competence between the country and other more advanced economies (from which FDI inflows might be expected). When the gap is large (the country is relatively underdeveloped) FDI transfers technology in large net amounts. The expectation is that this is mainly standardised technology of the MNE, whose effectiveness for the group is enhanced through improved access to relevant low-cost inputs. The host country benefits through the effective activation of previously unemployed (or underemployed) local factors that had represented an unrealised source of comparative advantage. Apart from very routine and process-specific training of labour there is no motivation for the MNE to seek systematic change in the local inputs it employs. Thus at this stage of the MNE involvement the mutual benefits derive from a complementarity between standardised ownership advantages and location advantages, neither of which are expected to be changed by forces endogenous to the immediate operation. Successful industrialisation, however, does invoke exogenous forces for change in that it will lead to factor price increases (higher wages, and so on) that would render such unimproved location advantages less attractive, and therefore com-promise the efficiency of the MNE/host country relationship. As already noted, retention of MNEs as effective contributors to sustained industrial-isation needs their positive response to processes of upgrading and renewal of the country's location advantages.

Once a country has significantly closed the development gap it will itself possess an enhanced level of technological competence, through a substantial commitment to education and the emergence of an effective local scientific community (including a distinctive R&D capacity). However, the effective commercial application of parts of the output of this science base may be best secured within MNE subsidiaries, through the application of complementary technologies and other aspects of product development expertise. The local technology (and the factors that generate it) now becomes (as a source of dynamic comparative advantage) part of the location advantages that attract MNEs. But it is then a key part of the MNE subsidiary's responsibility to complete the commercial development of the local technology in ways that make it a distinctive part of the competitive scope of the group. To do this the subsidiary will initially bring (as ownership advantages) parts of the existing technology stock of its MNE and explicit product development skills (for example, in marketing, engineering and planning). These existing group competences (ownership advantages) are then themselves enhanced by the application of local technology (location advantages), with the latter securing a more effective commercial implementation than could otherwise have been achieved. The subsidiary's operation thus embodies a *creative* inter-dependence between MNE group resources and those of the host country, which provides it with a distinctive competitive status within the global-competitive network of its parent company and also interjects a new facet to the local industrial sector.

The latter scenario discerns important technological elements in both ownership advantages and location advantages, and finds scope for unique subsidiary-level activity to generate new knowledge (in a process of localised product development) which represents an enhancement of both the MNE's ownership advantages and the country's location advantages. However, we shall argue in later chapters that this does not provide a subsidiary with substantial autonomy in its MNE group. Its individualising activity, though deriving from local technology and skills, is only fully effective when also built into group interdependencies. This can lead to situations where the subsidiary's creative success (operationalising local technology) may benefit the MNE group it is part of more than it enhances the competitiveness of local industry. Substantial production of an internationally competitive good developed in one country may be carried out in other locations, and an MNE's operations may serve as a conduit for the underrewarded export of local technology in other ways. An example of the latter may reside in the activity of stand-alone MNE laboratories in a particular country, which carry out precompetitive (basic or applied) research as part of these groups' programmes to regenerate their core technologies. These may supply a vital stimulus to the evolution of the country's scientific and research capacity, but provide no direct mechanism through which technologies generated move through to support new competitiveness in the *local* industrial sector.

The core analysis contained in this book investigates the behaviour and implications of foreign MNE operations in the UK, building on the perceptions and issues outlined earlier. Two broad, but overlapping, areas of discussion are addressed. The first of these uses the material on the foreign companies' UK operations to elucidate a range of issues relating to the nature of the contemporary MNE, with a notable focus on the range and evolutionary potential of subsidiaries' roles and the key status of dispersed technological activity (both the application and generation of knowledge and expertise) in these companies. The second, parallel, line of investigation addresses the effects of such operations by MNEs on the competitive dynamics of a host country's (here the UK) industrial sector and technological scope. Thus the overall agenda derives from the view that an adequate policy towards 'inward investment', in the context of the positioning of national industrial competitiveness in the current international economy, can be achieved only through a full comprehension of the global perspectives of the companies implementing and developing such projects (that is, the modern MNEs).

The detailed investigation proceeds through the interlinking of materials from two complementary survey analyses, carried out in 1993–94 as part of a study supported by the Economic and Social Research Council (ESRC). The first survey involved a questionnaire that was sent to manufacturing subsidiaries of MNEs located in the UK. In addition to organisational characteristics (age, means of establishment, size and so on) this survey targeted three crucial aspects of these subsidiaries' positioning and status. The first of these was their market orientation, looking closely at the degree to which they play roles that are essentially part of the company's European strategy. Secondly, evidence on the technologies used by the subsidiaries was sought, in the belief that this would crucially define the subsidiary's access to (or scope to pursue) higher-value-added positioning. These first two issues then coalesce into the third, which seeks to delineate the precise current strategic status of the UK subsidiaries and the presence of evolutionary scope within this. In total the questionnaire was sent to 812 subsidiaries of foreign companies operating in the UK, with satisfactory replies being received from 190 of them.[13] The composition of this sample, by home country and industry, is presented in Table 1.1.

The second survey focused on the work of foreign MNE R&D laboratories in the UK, and used a questionnaire that was sent directly to such facilities. This sought evidence on the positioning of such R&D units in terms of both their direct support of UK production operations of the parent companies and the wider dimensions of the technological creativity of these MNE groups. Thus this survey encompassed both 'associated' laboratories that worked directly in collaboration with UK production subsidiaries, and 'stand–alone' laboratories that are mostly independent of such operations and are more oriented towards positions in the group's precompetitive R&D programmes.

Table 1.1 Composition, by industry and home country, of respondents to the subsidiary survey

	Home country				
Industry	USA	Japan	Europe	Other	Total
Food	5		2	2	9
Automobiles	9	7	2		18
Aerospace	5			1	6
Electronics and electrical appliances	11	32	7	1	51
Mechanical engineering	8	9	9		26
Instruments	8	3	1		12
Industrial and agricultural chemicals	12	4	12	1	29
Pharmaceuticals and consumer chemicals	6	1	5		12
Metal manufacture and products	4	4	1	2	11
Other manufacturing	1	9	6		16
Total	69	69	45	7	190

The questionnaire was sent to 180 MNE laboratories in the UK and 48 satisfactory replies were obtained.[14]

The next chapter elaborates on those aspects of the modern MNE that provide the crucial underpinning of our analysis. In line with the vital importance of understanding the MNE as a network of variegated subsidiaries, the chapter provides a detailed review of the most influential typologies of subsidiary roles that have emerged in the literature over the past fifteen years. At this point we also introduce a detailed discussion of the typology that provides the foundations for our own subsequent analysis. This is a variant of the scope typology, and our description of its antecedents includes the presentation of the results of several very valuable earlier studies of MNE operations in the UK that adopted this approach. The emergence of differentiated roles for MNEs is clearly seen as a crucial facet of the way these companies have moved from hierarchical structures to ones that can effectively operationalise aspects of global heterogeneity. The chapter thus ends by reviewing the concept of heterarchy, and other approaches to the conceptualisation of the modern MNE, which provides a basis for understanding these companies as differentiated networks that pursue organisational flexibility in order to compete globally.

Chapter 3 is the first that brings our own evidence to the fore. The first section analyses subsidiaries' replies to a question that sought to define their strategic status in terms of an operationalised version of the scope typology. Here we investigate the expectation that these subsidiaries are undergoing a reorientation away from a focus on the UK market, towards more open supply positions in their parent group's wider operations. Two alternatives for such repositioning are then delineated, one of which is a cost-based role that involves supply of already established products of the MNE group to export (as well as local) markets, whilst the other seeks a higher-value-added status by activating more dynamic elements of comparative advantage into a product development role. The next section of the chapter then looks at market orientation more directly. Firstly, evidence is presented on the overall export orientation of the subsidiaries, and on the position in this of intra-group trade (a key element of increased supply networking in MNEs) and of intermediate goods. Secondly, the particular markets supplied are analysed, with the key issues here relating to the role of Europe in the positioning of these subsidiaries. Overall this chapter provides an introduction to key aspects of the strategic status of MNE subsidiaries in the UK.

The following chapter then picks up the other central facet of strategic positioning of subsidiaries, namely the sources of the technology that they use. The chapter starts, however, by elaborating on two important issues already alluded to. Firstly, it is observed that where subsidiaries (or indeed laboratories) develop individualised competences out of unique local technology, the exercise of these should support the orderly and cohesive evolution of the group's overall knowledge capacity and product scope. We suggest ways in which such decentralised technology generation should support, but usually operate within, the group's coherent technology trajectory and not serve to unbalance, or interject anarchic forces into, its progress. Secondly, we look more systematically at the moves towards a decentralised approach to innovation in the contemporary MNE, suggesting the possible characteristics of a global innovation strategy. Chapter 4 then moves forward to review the relevance of seven sources of technology in the operations of UK subsidiaries, relating the prevalence of these to strategic position as represented by the roles discussed in the previous chapter.

Chapters 5 and 6 provide the core of our analysis of foreign MNE R&D operations in the UK. We observe that the current status of such decentralised R&D laboratories provides them with very much a key role in the evolution of the strategic competitiveness of MNEs. Both in support of localised programmes of product development (part of the emerging globalised approach to innovation) and as part of precompetitive networks seeking to reinforce the core scientific scope of the group (helping extend the technological trajectory) we find potentially crucial roles for MNE UK-based R&D. Another facet of the investigation of these chapters is to evaluate the influences on the decision to locate these R&D laboratories in the UK, with a particular emphasis on supply-side factors such as a distinctive and high-quality technological heritage embodied in the current research base and scientific labour force. This points back to our earlier argument that a mutually-supportive interface can be generated between MNE creative operations and these created types of national comparative advantage.

The two chapters that analyse MNE in-house R&D laboratories are, in effect, dealing with ways in which parts of local scientific capacity are internalised by these companies to support particular facets of the development of their own technological scope. Chapter 7 looks at a complementary externalised mechanism that pursues part of the same objective, in the form of MNE collaborative arrangements with independent UK scientific institutions such as universities. The extent, content and motivation of such research associations are documented in order to indicate the nature of this facet of MNE attempts to monitor and access new knowledge trends worldwide in support of their continuing technological evolution. Chapter 8 looks at another crucial linkage of subsidiaries, namely that with their suppliers of inputs. From the point of view of the host country, creative and forward-looking relationships with local suppliers is a vital potential. Thus the chapter assesses the relevance of particular supply sources (within the UK or outside the UK; intra MNE group or independent) and investigates the extent and content of information transfers to local suppliers.

The final chapter returns to the themes outlined at the start of this introduction. From an understanding of the nature of contemporary MNEs, and of the form of their current operations in the UK, we draw conclusions about the potentials of their contribution to a sustained and balanced programme of industrialisation (oriented towards international competitiveness) and on the policy bases most likely to secure the greatest benefits.

NOTES

1. Hymer (1960/1976) demonstrated that the observed directions of international flows of direct investment capital could not be adequately explained by a macro-level theory that saw such capital as inevitably flowing from capital-rich to capital-poor countries in response to differential rates of return that reflected these degrees of capital availability. Building on Hymer's original perceptions, subsequent analysis has sought to generate a micro-level theory of the multinational enterprise that can explain the international extension of firms' value-adding activities (foreign direct investment in a more complete sense) in terms of their broader resource scope, their competitive needs and strategic motivations. For more detailed evaluation of Hymer's contribution, see Yamin (1991), Cantwell (1991a) and Dunning and Rugman (1985).
2. For influential typologies of the motivations for firms' expansion into internationalised value-added activities, see Behrman (1984) and Dunning (1993a). It may be indicative of the developments central to our arguments that whilst Behrman (1984, p.83) could subsume 'technological skills' and the 'science community' among the decision factors relevant to

locating an efficiency-seeking operation in a particular country, it was viable for Dunning, a decade later (1993a, pp.60–61), to discern a separate strategic asset-seeking imperative.

3. In Dunning's eclectic paradigm (1977, 1988, 1993a, 1995), location advantages are those characteristics of countries that lead an enterprise to create or utilise its sources of competitive advantage within their borders. These firm-level sources of distinctive competitiveness are termed ownership advantages.

4. Operating what Porter (1986) would later call a 'multidomestic strategy'.

5. Ideally the firm pursuing inputs to an innovation process will look for knowledge that significantly extends the scope of its existing technology, and for market perceptions that provide a basis for new products that can expand its range in a significant, but logical and cohesive, fashion. To fully define, for an outside consultant overseas, the characteristics of the new knowledge/market trends sought would need the communication of very extensive details of the extant technology and product scope (to which it would be expected to contribute). Usually this would be considered to be neither feasible nor desirable.

6. In a recent survey analysis of the geographical sources of competitiveness in leading MNEs (Dunning, 1996; Dunning and Lundan, 1998), it was found that 'the more multinational a company is, the more likely it is to be more dependent on foreign sources of technology' (Dunning and Lundan, 1998, p.124). Generally, in the terms adopted by the authors, the more multinational a firm becomes the more it tends to seek sources of competitiveness through the linking of domestic and foreign diamonds of competitive advantage (Porter, 1990). In a similar vein, much of the analysis in this book could be articulated in terms of foreign MNEs seeking to benefit from involvement in aspects of the UK diamond.

7. For analysis and documentation of the opening up of national systems of innovation under the pressures of globalisation, see Niosi and Bellon (1996).

8. Vernon (1979) subsequently perceived how changing conditions in the international environment could provide a basis for more globalised approaches to innovation.

9. Kojima (1978) provides a formalised exposition of how, within a process of orderly technology transfer, MNEs can operate as temporary tutors and help initiate and sustain the process of industrialisation in developing countries. This does, however, involve separate waves of investors investing and disinvesting in order to facilitate the subsequent upgrading of the emerging industrial sector. The emerging scope for systematic upgrading of the status of individual subsidiaries could provide a potential for the embodiment of the Kojima scenario within one subsidiary's evolution, that is subsidiaries could be embedded in a sustained industrialisation process to the mutual benefit of the MNE and the host country.

10. In his later work, Hymer (1970, 1972) provided an explicitly bleak view of the relationship of MNEs to the development of the poorer countries. This builds on an interpretation of the MNE as a seemingly immutable global hierarchy, with all high-value-added activity (organisation and creativity) located in a developed metropolis and routine low-value-added production delegated to the underdeveloped hinterland. This provides a psychological reinforcement to the submissive position of hinterland countries, since MNE managers who 'occupy at best a medium position in the corporate structure and are restricted in authority and horizons to a lower level of decision making' are at the same time representatives of many of the largest corporations in the host country so that these 'top executives play an influential role in [its] political social and cultural life' (Hymer, 1972). The MNE manager's submissive branch-plant mentality is argued to thereby reinforce a resigned acceptance of the lowly status of the hinterland in influential host-country decision makers (for example, politicians or planners with whom they associate). This stifles activation of higher-level potentials in that 'in the multinational corporate system the demand for high-level education in low-ranking areas is limited, and a country does not become a world centre simply by having a better education system', and again 'one can hardly expect such a country to bring forth the creative imagination needed to apply science and technology to the problems of degrading poverty'. Our interpretation of the contemporary MNE as a flexible and dynamic heterarchy can be seen to provide local executives with the scope to take a more positive view of host-country potentials and of their own ability to benefit from activating them

within evolving group-level creative programmes. The interface between MNE executives and local decision makers *can* then be one of mutually-supportive resource development rather than one of shared resignation and defeatism.

11. A likely constraint here may be that an uncompromising public exposition of the decline of local industry and the dimensions of its perceived inadequacies may attract hostility as unpatriotic or even subversive. This may deny those with the clearest understanding of the problems (and positive views of potentials for regeneration) access to levels of power from which to actively articulate a course of recovery.

12. The relationship between changing comparative advantage and the timing and motivation of direct investment can also be elaborated from the point of view of MNEs' home countries. Ozawa (1991a, 1991b, 1992a) provides detailed analysis of the Japanese experience, which delineates 'the *close inter-relatedness* between structural upgrading, dynamic comparative advantage and FDI, along the paths of its physical/human-capital-intensive factor endowment and technological progress' (Ozawa, 1992b, p.39).

13. The 812 companies surveyed comprised all the relevant subsidiaries that could be identified from the National Register Publishing Company's *International Directory of Corporate Affiliations*. The questionnaire was addressed, in the first instance, to the Managing Director, although there is evidence that in some cases the responsibility for reply was delegated to senior subordinates. The initial mailout was carried out in late 1993 with a follow-up in the early spring of 1994.

14 . The questionnaire was sent to all R&D units of foreign MNEs that could be distinguished from the *Longman's Directory of European Research Centres*. The first mailout took place in the spring of 1994 with a follow-up in the early summer. The questionnaire was directed to the Director of R&D. In 1995 a number of research directors were interviewed to secure confirmation and/or elaboration of perspectives emerging from the analysis of the survey replies. The questionnaire was sent to 180 laboratories and 48 satisfactory replies were received. Of the responding laboratories 19 were controlled by Japanese MNEs, 13 by US ones, and 16 by MNEs from elsewhere in Europe. By industry, 17 of the laboratories were in pharmaceuticals, 9 in chemicals, 11 in electronics and 11 in other industries.

2. Roles of subsidiaries and MNE evolution

INTRODUCTION

The previous chapter emphasised that the nature of the effects of inward investment on the industrial competitiveness of the UK (and comparable host countries) depends on the strategic aims of the multinational enterprises (MNEs) carrying out the investment, and therefore of the roles played by the resulting subsidiaries' operations. These perceptions build on a very rich body of analysis, substantially emerging over the past decade, which addressed the reformulation of the strategic organisation of MNEs and the differentiated roles thereby played by subsidiaries to secure a widened range of objectives in an increasingly competitive and globalised environment. In this chapter we derive the subsidiary typology chosen to underpin the analysis of the subsequent chapters, placing this within a wider review of the approaches to subsidiary categorisation and MNE strategic orientation.

In the next section we review the 'scope' typology of subsidiaries, which serves as the key building block of our own analytical approach. Thus it is in this section that we provide a detailed scrutiny of the characteristics and strategic origins of the subsidiary forms that we use in the investigations of subsequent chapters. Here we also outline the results of a number of previous studies that have demonstrated the value of applying this typology to MNE operations in the UK.

The status of the knowledge- and technology-related aspects of subsidiaries is another central theme of our investigation, and one very clearly positioned within the scope typology. However, other typologies, reviewed in the third section, have placed the knowledge scope and positioning of subsidiaries at the centre of their conceptualisation in valuable ways that have decisive resonances with our own approach.

A long-standing area of debate in international strategy has related to the apparently contrasting imperatives of integration and responsiveness. In our analysis we argue that increased global competition, related to a freer trade environment, enhanced the need for the production efficiencies that can be secured by linking specialised production subsidiaries in integrated supply networks. But we also pursue strongly the belief that dispersed technology competences, and in some industries continued differences of market needs and trends, provided new dimensions to the pursuit of decentralised responsiveness. The fourth section therefore looks at the typologies that enshrine integration and responsiveness as the key differential characteristics.

Different roles for subsidiaries must mean somewhat differential treatment for them within the broad decision-making processes, and therefore strategic evolution, of MNE groups. How well individual subsidiaries respond to their treatment in this regard is clearly a vital issue in the effectiveness of their contribution to overall group performance. At several places in our analysis, indications of stresses, or of subversively individualised decision making at the subsidiary level, emerge. To help understand this, the fifth section outlines a recently derived typology which adopts the concept of procedural justice, alongside autonomy, in order to usefully clarify the status, and motivational conditioning, of various groups of subsidiaries.

As already observed, the growth of analysis of variegated subsidiary types has paralleled a complementary approach that addresses the reformulation of MNE groups as globally-competing and increasingly differentiated organisational structures. The sixth section scrutinises these, seeing how they relate to, and inform the articulation of, our subsequent analysis.

SCOPE TYPOLOGIES

The first approach to distinguishing between types of subsidiaries derives from the pioneering work of White and Poynter (1984). Here, three characteristics play crucial roles in discriminating between the types in White and Poynter's typology. Firstly, *product scope* which 'is the latitude exercised by a subsidiary's business with regard to product line extensions and new product areas' (1984, p.59). Secondly, *market scope* in terms of 'the range of geographic markets available to the subsidiary'. Lastly, *value-added scope*, which 'refers to the range of ways a subsidiary adds value, whether through development, manufacturing or marketing activities'. For our purposes it is also convenient to equate value-added scope with functional scope, so that, for example, the presence of development is likely to imply a subsidiary's possession of an in-house R&D unit, whilst commitment to marketing requires a dedicated marketing unit (which should also provide inputs to its development process).

From this, White and Poynter (1984, pp.60–61) discern five business strategies for subsidiaries. Firstly, a *marketing satellite* merely markets locally imported goods that are manufactured elsewhere in the group. Clearly this type is defined by a very low market scope (host country only) and, even where its marketing activity is quite sophisticated (for example, including 'extensive distribution, marketing, sales application oriented development and customer support services'), low value-added scope (that is, excluding production and, therefore, product and process development). White and Poynter point out that this strategy is most viable for MNEs when relating to 'a standardised global product serving multiple markets [with] tangible characteristics sufficiently close to [local] preferences, or a price/cost advantage great enough to induce [local] acceptance of a global product'.

The *miniature replica* subsidiary is defined by White and Poynter (1984, p.60) as one that 'produces and markets some of the parent's product lines or related product lines in the local country. Some low volume products may still be imported from the multinational parent, but generally the business is a small scale replica of the parent'. The presence of miniature replicas may be most commonly associated with strong natural or artificial restraints on trade, the existence of distinctive local preferences and low or moderate economies of scale in production. Three variants of miniature replicas are distinguished by White and Poynter: (i) the *adopter* which takes 'products and marketing programmes from the multinational parent and introduces them' locally with minimal changes, (ii) the *adapter* which again takes a parent's product but now 'will change product characteristics and marketing programmes to suit local conditions', whilst (iii) *innovators* develop new products, but usually very closely related to those already existing in the group. All variants of the miniature replica have low market scope, but the move through the adopter, adapter, innovator progression is seen as involving a potential widening of both product and value-added scope.

For White and Poynter (1984, p.61), the *rationalised manufacturer* 'describes the strategy of a business producing a designated set of component parts or products in [the host country] for a multi-country or global market'. Its output is then usually distributed intra-group, either for further processing in other parts of the MNE or for sale through its network of marketing satellites in other countries. Since rationalised manufacturers are not expected to develop the products they supply, they have a narrow value-added scope. The presence of this type of subsidiary in MNEs is usually a response to the benefits of centralised production, where this is encouraged by input-cost factors, scale economies and product standardisation.

White and Poynter's *product specialist* 'develops, produces, and markets a limited product line for global markets'. Although such a subsidiary 'is generally self-sufficient in terms of value added by way of applied R&D, production and marketing' it nevertheless specialises 'within product areas related to the core business of the multinational parent'. It has strategic control over its own products, but it is not seeking to challenge the essential technological or business scope of the group.

The final subsidiary type delineated by White and Poynter is the *strategic independent*. Such subsidiaries 'have the freedom and resources to develop lines of business for either a local, multi-country or a global market', often by pursuing opportunities in product areas that are unrelated to those previously established by the parent company, doing so 'by way of either internal development or acquisition'. Like the product specialist, the strategic independent has a global market scope and extensive value-added scope. However its defining difference, in terms of its independence in key areas of strategic decision making, provides it with relatively unconstrained product scope and especially the freedom to extend that scope beyond that currently existing in the group in ways that are prohibited to the product specialist. White and Poynter consider that the MNE parent 'assumes the role of passive investor' in strategic independents, often operating with only administrative and financial links (1984, p.61).

Also working (as had White and Poynter) from observation of subsidiaries in Canada, D'Cruz (1986) derived a complementary typology. Starting from a position where foreign-produced goods are initially being imported into Canada, either directly or through agents, D'Cruz then distinguishes two forms of subsidiary that may be established to, in essence, increase the effectiveness of this process. Firstly, the *satellite business* imports subassemblies and then assembles the final product locally. This occurs where price becomes a key basis for local competitiveness and where costs can be lowered due to possible savings on transport costs, or because tariffs are lower on components or subassemblies than on completed goods. Secondly, a *local service business* may emerge where non-price competition is more prevalent.Thus 'while remaining dependent on the parent for the product and technology, a local service business unit can establish and manage its own market linkages' (1986, p.83). This can involve a network of local sales or service facilities, providing service support to wholesalers and retailers, or training customer personnel.

Although the local service business and the satellite business involve local value-added activity, neither incorporates full-scale production. In D'Cruz typology this step is taken with the emergence of a *branch plant*. In the Canadian case, D'Cruz discerns the origins of branch plants to lie in tariff protection which stimulated the localised production of goods that would otherwise have been imported. Although such branch plants may have developed a quite strong individualised ability in locally-focused marketing, and a smaller degree of distinctive technology, their profitability continued to be sustained mainly by protection from more efficiently produced, and therefore potentially price-competitive, imports. So once a momentum towards tariff cuts developed in the global economy, branch plants became increasingly vulnerable.

An obvious strategic response to the declining viability of subsidiaries that depend almost uniquely on host-country markets, is to reorientate their market focus towards the global (that is, allow them to become a source of exports). D'Cruz delineates two substantially different variants on this. The first is as a *globally rationalised* business, involving a strong integration within MNE group supply programmes. Thus 'the Canadian subsidiary is structured to supply a limited portion of the product line for the entire world market, and imports the remainder of its requirements from plants in other parts of the world. Each production facility is world-scale and concentrates on becoming the low cost producer of those parts of the line for which it is responsible' (D'Cruz, 1986, p.86). Such operations are most necessary and viable in 'product lines where transportation costs are low relative to selling price and where market requirements have become relatively standardised'.

For our purposes, a significant contribution of D'Cruz's categorisation is the inclusion (as the second export-oriented type) of the *world product mandate* in a wider typology of MNE subsidiaries.[1] Here, rather than inheriting production of an already well-established good, the mandated subsidiary takes an overall responsibility for a product, including its development and worldwide marketing as well as its manufacture. Clearly this role endows the subsidiary with much wider functional (value-added) scope than the others, including higher levels of strategic decision making in management and substantive in-house R&D.

Building on the earlier analysis in the scope-typology tradition we have previously adopted[2] a three-type approach to the operations of manufacturing subsidiaries in MNEs.[3] Firstly a *truncated miniature replica* (TMR) subsidiary 'adopts a classic form of market-seeking behaviour, supplying a substantial part of its MNE group's established product range to its host-country market, usually with the protection of tariffs or other trade barriers' (Pearce and Papanastassiou, 1996a, p.34). Such TMRs therefore take positions in the multidomestic strategies (Porter, 1986) of horizontally-integrated MNEs. With a very narrow market scope (that is, that of the host country), but a product scope that can embrace most of the goods supplied by the MNE parent company (or other leading subsidiaries in the group) this type of subsidiary encompasses both the adapter and adopter variants of White and Poynter's miniature replica. However, we define an explicitly truncated functional scope in a way that excludes the innovator form.

The presence of marketing and (possibly) R&D in TMRs relates to the need to sell established group products as effectively as possible in the host-country market. Thus the maximum creativity expected of marketing is to detect any manifestation of local tastes that may be leading to the rejection of particular characteristics of the existing products, and to help recommend the nature of appropriate adaptation. In some cases the implementation of such changes may lead to the presence of a supporting R&D unit, though this work may often be achieved by skilled members of the subsidiary's engineering unit or through advice from elsewhere in the group. In the traditional TMRs it would be expected that the small and relatively captive local market would preclude the expense and risk of more radically innovative product development at the subsidiary level. The managerial needs of a normally functioning TMR are relatively routine and dependent, though the presence of more entrepreneurial drives have proved crucial in surviving the increased vulnerability of such operations and in determining the type of role to which the subsidiary can accede.

In line with the wider critiques of import substitution as an industrialisation strategy, TMRs possessed a natural tendency towards inefficiency that made them increasingly vulnerable as the post-war global economy evolved. Thus relatively small national markets usually led to a failure to achieve economies of scale in production, whilst the wide product range often went well beyond that which might yield logical economies of scope and began to provoke diseconomies. We can point here to two reasons why, despite such sources of operative inefficiency, TMRs remained competitive contributors to their MNE groups' profitability for 20 to 30 years after the Second World War. Firstly, they were protected from external competition, in the form of imports, by high levels of tariffs and other sources of trade restraint. Secondly, the TMRs derived from a relatively select group of MNEs that themselves mainly emanated from the US and a very small number of European countries, where a strong technology base (sometimes reinforced by the commercial application of new wartime scientific breakthroughs) and relatively high-quality education and management training systems provided the firms with sources of strong knowledge advantage. This advantage, when manifested in distinctive products and processes, provided TMRs with an edge over internal competition (indigenous firms) even when it was applied at less than full efficiency (for the reasons outline above).

Two of the key factors in the increasing intensification of globalised competition can be seen to explicitly undermine the sources of TMRs' ability to sustain profitability, and therefore to retain a position in MNE worldwide operations. Firstly, the persistent lowering of tariff protection through successive rounds of GATT negotiations, backed up by removal of trade restraint within regional integration programmes[4] has increasingly diminished the market isolation of TMRs and opened them to external competition from more efficient production located elsewhere. Although some tariff reduction has been offset by the alternative trade restraint policies of the new protectionism it may be argued (Pearce, 1992) that the *ad hoc,* and often politically contentious, nature of these measures means that they cannot be relied upon as a stable decision-making variable in determining the role taken by an MNE subsidiary. Therefore changes in the international trade environment can be perceived as a factor provoking the need to change the role of TMR-type subsidiaries.

A second factor that may be seen to have increasingly challenged the viability of TMRs is a growing international dispersion of technological and industrial skills. Thus, following successful post-war reconstruction, firms from more and more countries were able to derive commercially competitive technology from national science bases that began to generate world-class knowledge (in at least some key disciplines) and from increasingly effective education and training systems. This generated new competitive pressures on TMRs in two ways. Firstly, in at least some host countries, indigenous firms began to close the technology gap on MNE TMR subsidiaries (that is, enhanced internal competition). Two further factors may then have reinforced the ability of local enterprises to use their enhanced technological competences effectively in competition with the local-market-focused MNE operations. Firstly, they may use their technology more effectively than TMRs in terms of more sympathetic responsiveness to local tastes (products) and local production conditions (processes).[5] Secondly, the indigenous firms may combine their new technological scope with the other change (freer trade) by using export possibilities as part of their market (in a way that may be denied to TMRs by MNE group decision making) and thus benefit from more complete realisation of economies of scale.

The second element in the change to the environment that originally supported TMRs, which also derives substantially from increased international dispersion of knowledge and skills, has been the intensification of global competition due to the emergence of a large number of new multinationals from an extended range of source countries. Thus companies from Japan, additional European countries and the newly industrialised countries, have all used access to new technology, and the organisational skills to apply it effectively, as key elements in their ability to emerge as significant global players with international perspectives on markets and production. These MNEs have also responded, from their initiation, to the other noted change by implementing their global production and marketing programmes in the light of the potentials of freer trade. The efficiencies thus generated through global strategies would again constitute an external threat to the competitiveness of inward-oriented TMRs in traditional MNEs that retain a multidomestic approach to international operations.

We thus suggest that their TMR subsidiaries began to lose strategic viability for traditional MNEs as the technological hegemony of these companies substantially declined, and as new internationally-competitive enterprises sought to use the organisational potentials of freer trade to enhance productive efficiency. In some cases, MNEs were able to simply close TMRs and themselves use trade to continue to supply the relevant market. Often, however, the costs of closure and, in particular, the loss of goodwill in the local market, made this a less than ideal option in MNEs seeking to retain an effective global strategy. The alternative, then, was to reposition these subsidiaries within restructured approaches to globalised operations. Our typology thus embraces two possible subsidiary roles that might replace the mainly market-seeking orientation of TMRs. The first of these would be an efficiency-seeking position within the application of the MNE group's existing technology, with such a subsidiary focusing on the cost-effective supply of a small part of the company's established product range to international markets. This option predominantly seeks to turn the first source of TMRs' problems (freer trade) into a strategic potential.

As technology and product development became even more important to the competitive evolution of international firms a second, knowledge-seeking, option became available to MNEs wishing to provide new roles for outmoded TMRs. Thus in host countries with increasingly original science bases and/or market trends, MNEs can now achieve strategic benefit from tapping into these knowledge sources through the operations of subsidiaries that seek to embody such localised perspectives in the development of distinctive products. Such subsidiaries thus actually contribute to the extension of their MNE's scope, in ways that may sometimes amount to a position in a globalised approach to innovation. This then provides an approach through which, as multidomestic MNEs evolve to truly globalised strategies, they can also turn the second threat (dispersed knowledge capacity) to their advantage.

The first of these two new strategic positions for overseas operations in MNEs may be termed the *rationalised product subsidiary* (RPS). The essence of such a role is to take a specialised position within the MNE group's supply programme for its existing products. This could involve the manufacture of limited parts of the group's current range of final products, supply of component parts for assembly by other group subsidiaries, or performing a particular stage in a vertically-integrated production process. In all these cases, the RPS applies knowledge that is already well established in the parent group and embodied in already commercially proven and effectively produced goods. It may well be that an increased organisational ability to achieve the effective intra-group transfer of such knowledge, and the scope for improved communications to facilitate the efficient coordination of its decentralised use, has contributed to the growth of RPSs as one means through which MNEs respond to other changes in the global environment. If this means that potentially any subsidiary has access to the key competitive advantages of its MNE group, then an important source of the value of the RPS form (alongside an obvious improved ability to realise economies of scale) is that what it does can be closely matched to specific host-country factor availabilities. This makes clear that the decisive aim of the use of RP subsidiaries in MNEs is efficiency seeking (by contrast with the often inefficient market seeking of TMRs), but that fulfilment of this also involves resource seeking (at least with regard to standardised inputs, for example, production labour, energy and raw materials).

The RPSs are distinguished from TMRs by a much wider geographical market scope (export-oriented access to predetermined parts of their MNE's global supply network) and much narrower product scope, but share with them a positioning within predominantly externally-determined knowledge scope (that is, that of the group's established technology and skills). This suggests for RPSs a functional scope that is perhaps more truncated than that of TMRs. Having acquired (more due to host-country location advantages than distinctive subsidiary-level competences) the RP role, the subsidiary is likely to supply its allocated product(s) to its group's internal distribution network, leaving no scope for its own marketing. This is also likely to preclude the need for the subsidiary to make any adaptation of the goods it produces, and if the group has indeed allocated supply responsibility to the most appropriate locations there should also be little need for changes to the production process. This limits the likelihood that an RPS could justify the presence of an R&D unit. The ultimate logic of this is also for a limited scope for management in RPSs. This should involve merely executing effectively an externally determined position, with little discretion over its immediate parameters (what to supply to which markets) and little of the functional scope needed to alter or expand that role.[6] Overall, therefore, the RPS appears to provide the MNE with a positive response to one potential of the new environment (freer trade) but ignores the other (host-country creative and knowledge capacities).

A more complete MNE response to the challenges of the contemporary global competitive environment has been to use both freedom of trade and dispersed creative competences through *world (or regional) product mandate (WPM/RPM) subsidiaries*. Such subsidiaries are considered to take responsibility for the creation of particular products, and for their sustained competitive evolution, as well as for their production and marketing. The crucial defining feature of product mandate units is discerned as being their value-added scope, this being enhanced by a substantial incorporation of truly creative capacity in all key functional areas. Thus complete realisation of the potentials of the WPM/RPM subsidiary form needs the presence of entrepreneurial management, a highly creative and originally perceptive marketing unit and an R&D facility capable of organising the unique technological basis of the product to be developed. Nevertheless, it is an emphasis of our view that ultimately the functional scope of the WPM/RPM should be that which allows it to take *responsibility* for all creative elements of its product(s) rather than, necessarily, to fully achieve all requirements from in-house competences. Although full functional autonomy is a valid limiting case of the WPM/RPM form, such subsidiaries may often provide their optimal contribution to their group's efficiency by securing some inputs to their operations from elsewhere in their group. If this is initiated willingly and of their own volition (that is, as part of their uncompromised responsibility for these functions) then the development of intra-group interdependencies can enhance the manner in which subsidiary-level individualism in WPM/RPM supports group-level objectives.[7]

It should be accepted that the primary driving attribute of management in WPM/RPM subsidiaries is the entrepreneurial desire to create unique positions in group operations around their own products, backed up by their distinctive competences. A willingness to exercise the levels of responsibility earned through these mandated positions by a careful balancing of internalised creative competences and those accessed in a supportive manner elsewhere in the group (or externally in the host economy) is then perceived as a crucial additional attribute of subsidiary management. Creating a group-level environment in which creative subsidiaries are willing to exercise their individualism in an interdependent, rather than autarchic, fashion is then the key challenge of central management in such heterarchical MNEs (which should themselves therefore avoid being autocratic).

A marketing unit also takes a greatly enhanced position within a WPM/RPM subsidiary, since it has the responsibility of acquiring those perspectives on emerging consumer tastes and trends in relevant regional (RPM) or global (WPM) markets that need to be encompassed in the new product(s) being created. Such activity will remain at the core of a successful PM operation since it will seek to sustain the competitiveness of its current mandates over time and also to add new products. As a way of supporting and building on creative marketing at this level, a PM may also build up its own international distribution network, either through owned facilities or through contracts with independent agents. Alternatively, such a subsidiary may also work with a network of the MNE group.[8] However, this may be implemented as a semi-arm's-length contractual agreement, in order to emphasise that the PM retains responsibility for its product and *uses* the group supply network (to their mutual advantage) rather than becoming a dependent part of it. The suggestion that PM subsidiaries would at least be more likely to export their products independently than would RPSs will be investigated in the next chapter.

It is a natural assumption that the vast majority of WPM/RPM subsidiaries will possess an in-house R&D unit. The predominant objective of such a facility will then be to work with marketing, engineering, and so on, in the same subsidiary, in order to initially define the technological needs of the product development process and then to take responsibility for the acquisition of this knowledge. How subsidiary-level R&D units achieve this objective is one of the key areas investigated in the research reported in subsequent chapters. Here we can again suggest that a strong in-house R&D commitment, directly related to the subsidiary's product development aims, may be articulated through interdependencies with other elements of the MNE group's technology programmes and with other institutions in the host-country science base. The R&D unit's work will be a crucial element in individualising the subsidiary's position, but will still do so in ways that retain mutually-valuable coherence in the MNE's scientific work and technological evolution. Thus the subsidiary's own distinctive creative evolution will occur as a significant contribution to a cohesive extension of the group's technological trajectory.

The extensive value-added scope of WPM/RPM subsidiaries can confidently be expected to underpin their implied wide geographic market scope. This export orientation can be expected to be both necessary, in order to generate the income needed to support the costly functional capacities needed to create and revitalise the product(s), and feasible, since the new goods are distinctive and specialised additions to the group's range. The product scope of mandate subsidiaries is theoretically unconstrained, but in practice likely to be relatively narrowly focused. Thus the value of the PM concept to an MNE group is to achieve the most effective evolution of a number of distinctive but complementary strands in its technological scope and product range, through separate operations with strongly specialised competences and individualised motivation. For much of the time (though by no means always or inevitably) individual PM subsidiaries may then recognise that the best way to sustain their position, both in their markets and within the group, is to remain focused on the logical development of those products and capacities that have secured their current competitiveness.

Over the past decade a number of studies carried out by scholars at the University of Strathclyde have contributed greatly to our knowledge of the strategic evolution of MNE subsidiaries in the UK, structuring analysis within variants of the White and Poynter (1984) typology. Thus Hood and Young (1988) applied the typology to data on 140 subsidiaries in the UK collected in the early 1980s. Application of cluster analysis suggested the presence of 63 miniature replicas, 12 rationalised manufacturers, 36 product specialists and 29 strategic independents. Perhaps reflecting the relatively low presence of the last two subsidiary types, Hood and Young noted that nearly three-fifths of this sample lacked R&D at the plant level. It was also observed that within the overall sample the US MNE subsidiaries were more Europe oriented in terms of markets than those from European parents.[9]

A 1986 survey of manufacturing industry subsidiaries in Scotland provided Young, Hood and Dunlop (1988) with 129 replies, which then yielded four distinct groupings in a cluster analysis. A cluster incorporating 45 (mainly US) subsidiaries covered the product specialist/strategic independent area of the typology. These tended to have the widest market area (often spreading beyond Europe) and quite autonomous control over a wide functional scope. The numerically largest group, however, were rationalised manufacturers with 50 (again mainly US) cases. Reflecting their often mainly assembly-type operations, these subsidiaries were usually closely integrated into the wider manufacturing programmes of the MNE, and supplied their output (to quite extensive geographical areas) through group networks.

The Young, Hood and Dunlop study located two groupings, each of 17 members and each with a relatively strong non-US presence, which were categorised as variants on the miniature replica form. The first of these two clusters comprised the smallest subsidiaries and supplied a relatively narrow product range to mainly UK markets. The second miniature replica group had a wider product range and extensive access to the European market, along with some more positive elements of functional scope and a certain degree of managerial autonomy. This could represent attempts at progress towards the high-value-added positioning of the subsidiaries in the first cluster.

In their discussion Young, Hood and Dunlop (1988, pp.489–91) draw attention to a growing presence and complexity of R&D in subsidiaries in Scotland.[10] Analysis of their 1986 sample vindicated this with only 19 of the 129 respondents reporting no R&D. For 32 respondents, their R&D was characterised as 'development of new and improved products for UK/European markets' and for another 31 as 'development of new products and processes for world markets'. This type of work predominates in the product specialist/strategic independent group, but must obviously also occur in some others (again perhaps to set up conditions for access to the more advanced subsidiary status). 'Customer technical services and adaptation of manufacturing technology' was the reported R&D of 42 respondents. The remaining five cases reported probably the most ambitious R & D contribution of all in the form of 'generation of new technology for the corporate parent'.

Interesting evidence on the strategic positioning of Japanese subsidiaries emerges in a study by Hood, Young and Lal (1994) of 16 of the 24 such manufacturing operations in Scotland in 1992. Firstly, nine of these subsidiaries broadly felt that their primary strategic objective was 'the support of the European market which already existed for their parent's products'. Six of these fulfilled this role as rationalised manufacturers and three as miniature replicas. Secondly, six of the 16 respondents seemed to have 'a more aggressive strategy reflecting the parent company's drive for world leadership in their product/technology'. This more ambitious target led to four of these having product specialist status, along with one rationalised manufacturer and one miniature replica. Of the four product specialists two had been set up with that role, but two had evolved into it (one from rationalised manufacturer and one from miniature replica). The last subsidiary was a miniature replica 'that was located in Scotland at the request of a major adjacent Japanese customer which had specialist requirements'. All the product specialists believed the main source of their R&D was in their own Scottish operations, whilst the remainder said it was accessed from Japan, although some 'might have a measure of responsibility for European R&D' (Hood, Young and Lal, 1994, p.108).

Particularly clear and decisive evidence on the patterns of strategic evolution of subsidiaries in the UK derives from an analysis of 68 US-controlled and 63 European-controlled respondents to a survey carried out by Taggart (1997b). Over the five-year period covered, the number of the 131 cases that Taggart's analysis classified as strategic mandates (product specialists plus strategic independents) rose from 34 to 51 (Table 2.1). The compensating decline came from miniature replicas, where the adopter and adapter variants fell from 34 to 24 and the innovator variant from 45 to 37. Finally, the rationalised manufacturers rose marginally from 18 to 19. Further indication of the current commitment to strategic mandates emerges in the fact that 91 per cent of the subsidiaries that took that status originally retained it five years later, whilst the comparable figures were only 64 per cent for the innovator form of miniature replica and 56 per cent for each of the other two subsidiary types.

Further information on the specific content of such evolutionary processes is provided by Taggart's (1996a) study of 123 manufacturing subsidiaries located in Scotland in 1994.[11] This indicates strong evidence of increased complexity in subsidiary scope and deepening of various levels of responsibility over both 1989/94 (observed changes) and 1994/99 (projected developments). In terms of the scope typology, market areas served became more extensive; the product range offered becomes wider; and R&D activities develop to a more advanced stage. In addition the degree of complexity of production technology increases and subsidiary-level autonomy in decision making with respect to new markets and new products grows. In a part of the analysis focusing on complexity of subsidiary-level R&D this was found to be consistently related to the subsidiary's overall strategic positioning and also to the level of its production technology. In particular Taggart (1996a, p.461) notes that 'from 1989 right through to 1999, the typical subsidiary carrying out lower levels of R&D had

Table 2.1 *Roles of foreign MNE subsidiaries in the UK, 1989 and 1994*

Roles 1989	Roles 1994 (number of subsidiaries)				
	Miniature[1] replica(A)	Miniature[2] replica (I)	Rationalised manufacturer	Strategic mandate	Total
Miniature replica (A)[1]	19	6	6	3	34
Miniature replica (I)[2]	5	29	1	10	45
Rationalised manufacturer	0	1	10	7	18
Strategic mandate	0	1	2	31	34
Total	24	37	19	51	131

Notes:
1. Miniature replica – adapter and adopter types.
2. Miniature replica – innovator type.

Source: Taggart 1997b.

a rationalised manufacturer strategy while higher levels of R&D were typically associated with a product specialist subsidiary strategy'.

KNOWLEDGE– AND INNOVATION–RELATED TYPOLOGIES

A differential scope for subsidiary-level contributions to MNE creativity is a crucial element that emerges within a typology derived by Bartlett and Ghoshal (1986) from analysis of the way that leading companies were responding to dispersed market trends and knowledge competences in the global economy. Three attributes were thus discerned as necessary in order to react in a fully competitive way to this emerging environment. Firstly, the capacity 'to sense changes in market needs and industry structure' that occur outside the company's home country. Secondly, 'the resources to analyse data and develop strategic responses to competitive challenges that were emerging worldwide'. Thirdly, the incorporation in overseas subsidiaries of managerial initiative, motivation and capability adequate 'to respond imaginatively to the diverse and fast-changing operating environments' implied by the first two factors.

These perceptions supply the background to the two dimensions which, in turn, provide the basis for the typology within which Bartlett and Ghoshal (1986, p.90) position subsidiaries in the creative activities of MNEs. The first of these dimensions is the strategic importance of the local environment. Thus the 'strategic importance of a specific country unit is strongly influenced by the significance of its national environment to the company's global strategy'. Although the size of the host-country market is clearly of relevance here, its degree of sophistication and the presence of advanced technology is perhaps a more distinctive characteristic in terms of the typology. The home countries of major competitors also take on an obvious strategic importance.

The second dimension defining the Bartlett and Ghoshal typology is the competence of the local organisation, that is, the subsidiary's distinctive scope in terms of technology, production, marketing, management, and so on. The nurturing and successful application to group strategies of such subsidiary-level competences is emphasised by Bartlett and Ghoshal as a key element in the evolution of MNEs. Thus 'relegating the national subsidiaries to the role of local implementers and adopters of global directives......risks grossly under-utilising the company's worldwide assets and organisational capabilities' by depriving country managers of the opportunity to use their skills and creative energy, so that they may 'come to feel demotivated and even disenfranchised' (1986, p.88).

A subsidiary with a high level of competence that is located in a host-country environment with a high strategic importance is termed a *strategic leader*. Such a subsidiary not only seeks to detect signals for change that emerge from its local environment, but involves itself in the generation of an appropriate response by committing its own resources to analysing the threats and opportunities. Thus the strategic leader 'serves as a partner of headquarters in developing and implementing strategy' (1986, p.90), and makes sure it has the in-house competences to sustain a high-value-added status in this strategy.

In the Bartlett and Ghoshal typology, a *contributor* occupies the quadrant of high subsidiary competence in an environment of low strategic importance. Here rather idiosyncratic circumstances[12] may have resulted in a subsidiary having an R&D base and technological competence that exceeds that of units in other countries of similar size or importance. Rather than allowing these capacities to atrophy, or be dissipated in solving strategically-irrelevant local problems, they should be co-opted into contributing specialised inputs to projects of corporate importance. A potential contemporary context for the contributor may exist in the transition economies of Central and Eastern Europe. Here it is argued[13] that sometimes the level of scientific knowledge generated under the research programmes supported by the previous Communist regimes has not been adequately accessed for commercial purposes. If MNE subsidiaries in these countries tap into this local technology stock and research capacity, they could create in-house competences that transcend the current needs of their local market operations, but instead contribute important knowledge to group-level programmes.

Next, the *implementer* has only 'just enough competence' to maintain its operation in a market of low strategic importance. Although this means that implementers do not contribute to the strategic evolution of their group, they are nevertheless seen as vital 'deliverers of the company's value added' if they achieve the efficient supply of existing products. Thus it is the implementers 'that produce the opportunity to capture economies of scale and scope that are crucial to most company's global strategies' (1986, p.91).

Finally, a subsidiary with low competence in a market of high strategic importance is seen as a very problematic *black hole* in an MNE's global operations. This situation means both that a significant market is inadequately supplied in the short term, and that the potential to make medium-term contributions to the group's knowledge development is also lost (that is, a relevant part of the learning environment is neglected). Whilst filling the black hole with a full-scale subsidiary of completely regenerated competences is a long-term proposition, Bartlett and Ghoshal note advocation of 'a sensory outpost' within the environment so as to at least exploit the learning potential. Attempts to do this, however, tended to provide very disappointing results. Purely monitoring activities ('eyes and ears' alone) did not get adequately 'inside the bloodstream of the business', which required 'constant and direct access to distribution channels, component suppliers, and equipment manufacturers' (1986, p.91).

In the Bartlett and Ghoshal typology, strategic leaders and contributors generate knowledge for the MNE group, whilst implementers apply effectively that which already exists. This implies that intra-group knowledge flows are a key element in the contemporary MNE, and that the extent and nature of their involvement in such flows is one factor that discriminates between types of subsidiaries. This is formalised in a typology derived by Gupta and Govindarajan (1994, pp.445–6; 1991, pp.773–5).

Here a *global innovator* subsidiary is responsible for a high outflow of knowledge to the rest of its MNE group, but itself receives a very low inflow from the parent or sister units. Next, the *integrated player* is again responsible for a high gross knowledge outflow, but also receives a comparably large inflow from the rest of its group. Both these types relate to the need of contemporary MNEs to harness distinctive knowledge generating attributes wherever they are available. The global innovator might be perceived as achieving a fully self-supporting product development process and then supplying the relevant knowledge to other production units in the group. The integrated player's activity relates more closely to the type of interdependent exercise of knowledge-related individualism that we advocate at various points here.

Gupta and Govindarajan's *implementer* has a low knowledge outflow, but a high inflow. It thus matches Bartlett and Ghoshal's implementer by taking an externally-determined specialised-production position in a rationalised supply network of its group. Finally, the *local innovator* has both a low outflow and a low inflow of knowledge. Such a subsidiary might actually generate considerable amounts of knowledge, but of such an idiosyncratic nature as to be most effective within a multidomestic strategy (Porter, 1986) or as a part of the local-for-local approach to innovation of Bartlett and Ghoshal (1990).

Gupta and Govindarajan use their knowledge-flow typology to derive a number of premises and propositions relating mainly to management-control procedures in MNEs. Two of their areas of investigation do, however, have valuable resonances with issues of concern to us. Firstly, it is observed (1991, p.780) that because of their substantial provision of knowledge to other parts of the MNE, the global innovators and integrated players have high levels of responsibility towards the rest of the group that implementers and local innovators do not have. Nevertheless, their general managers are still only likely to have direct authority within their own subsidiaries. Therefore responsibility/authority gaps are likely to exist in global innovators and integrated players to a much greater extent than in implementers and local innovators. Thus Gupta and Govindarajan (1991, p.781) point to the need for control mechanisms that motivate subsidiary managers to perceive their responsibilities in either global or local terms, as is appropriate, and in particular to seek to 'mitigate the emergence of frustration in those contexts where the manager's responsibility exceeds his or her authority'. Transposing it to our own perspectives, this perception of Gupta and Govindarajan can be seen to underline the new types of managerial challenge facing heterarchical MNEs that seek to maximise the contribution of creative RPM/WPM subsidiaries to the progress of the group's overall knowledge development.

It is also observed by Gupta and Govindarajan (1991, p.783) that 'the greater the magnitude and scope of knowledge creation expected from a subsidiary, the greater should be the need for exercise of autonomous initiative by the subsidiary'. Thus the need for autonomous initiative would be greatest in global innovators because, in our terms, they not only take responsibility for very ambitious development programmes but seek to implement almost all the work themselves. In integrated players there is an intermediate need for autonomous initiative because although the level of responsibility remains very ambitious, the amount of work implemented in-house is lower, with supporting knowledge acquired from elsewhere in the group (our position of interdependent individualism). Autonomous initiative is also at an inter-mediate level in the local innovator because, although the level of creative ambition is presumed to be lower, it is again implemented through in-house activity. Finally (as with Bartlett and Ghoshal's implementer and our rationalised product subsidiary) autonomous initiative is very low in Gupta and Govindarajan's implementer since it is responsible only for applying effectively knowledge already generated elsewhere in the group.

INTEGRATION/RESPONSIVENESS TYPOLOGIES

A key theme in discussion of organisational and strategic priorities in MNEs during the 1980s related to the need for integration and responsiveness. The growing intensity of global competition, taken with improved freedom of trade and better communications, suggested that MNEs both faced the need to increase the efficiency of their worldwide operations and had available the conditions from which to do so. At the core of this would be a greatly enhanced integration of their international operations, with individual subsidiaries taking specialised positions within carefully coordinated group-level supply networks. In our terms, integration would mainly involve the metamorphosis of subsidiaries from TMRs to RP operations. Amongst the characteristics of subsidiaries taking positions in integrated MNE strategies would be (Taggart, 1997c) a strong subjection to centralised production planning (including the adoption of existing product specifications); a notable tendency to serve intra-group customers and to receive material flows from sister units; and a rather dependent sharing of current group technology.

Another strand of argument suggested that whilst the efficiency-seeking aims of integrated strategies might be necessary, they were not likely to be sufficient to fulfil all the needs of sustained competitiveness in MNEs. At one level it was suggested that the value of integrated strategies was greatest where worldwide tastes were most homogeneous (Levitt, 1983). Where this was not so, MNEs could instead benefit competitively from allowing their subsidiaries to respond to local taste idiosyncrasies through product adaptation or development. Beyond this, as we have already observed within other typologies, more distinctively strategic benefits might accrue to MNEs from allowing subsidiaries to react in a more profoundly proactive way to local heterogeneity in market trends and technological development. Thus a responsive strategy in an MNE provides some subsidiaries with the scope to make substantially autonomous decisions in areas such as the markets to be supplied; the product range; advertising and promotion; the scope of their in-house R&D; production capacity, and the technology used (Taggart, 1997c). The freedom to thereby build distinctive localised creative competences into their operations clearly moves these subsidiaries towards product mandate or strategic leader status. We have already noted that how such individualised subsidiary scope is operationalised for group benefit is a crucial issue, and empirical investigation of the integration(I)/responsiveness(R) typology proved fruitful in elucidating the options.

Initial analysis, articulated in terms of group-level (corporate) strategies, tended to emphasise the trade-off options. Thus Bartlett (1986) distinguished global organisations with a high–I, low–R approach and multinational organisations with low–I and high–R. Similarly, Prahalad and Doz (1987) discerned a global business (high–I, low–R) and a locally responsive business (low-I, high-R). Prahalad and Doz's integration/responsiveness grid was systematically operationalised at the subsidiary level (using a survey of manufacturing MNE operations in Scotland) by Taggart (1996b). Here cluster analysis validated the presence of subsidiaries in the low–R, high–I quadrant (27 cases) and in the high–R, low–I quadrant (24 cases), as well as in an intermediate position on the diagonal between these (28 cases) which matches Prahalad and Doz's prediction of MNEs with a multifocal strategy.[14] In addition, Taggart's cluster analysis located a group of subsidiaries (24 cases) off the Prahalad and Doz 'reverse diagonal' in the high–R, high–I quadrant. The study also suggested in general terms that 'the overall level of responsiveness is rising steadily.....[whilst] integration is falling off somewhat' (Taggart, 1996b, p.537).[15]

The perspectives of the integration/responsiveness framework were applied to an analysis of MNE subsidiaries in Spain by Jarillo and Martinez (1990).[16] This validated the original 'trade-off' possibilities of this approach by locating what they termed 'receptive subsidiaries' in the high–I, low–R quadrant and also 'autonomous subsidiaries' in the low–I, high–R quadrant. Jarillo and Martinez also partly supported Bartlett and Ghoshal's (1989) extension of Bartlett's (1986) strategy options by finding subsidiaries in a quite high–R, high–I position. These subsidiaries were termed 'active' by Jarillo and Martinez and would be positioned in what Bartlett and Ghoshal termed a 'transnational' global strategy. However, Bartlett and Ghoshal's hypothesis of an 'international organisation' embodying low–I and low–R subsidiaries found no supportive cases in the Jarillo and Martinez study.[17]

Taggart (1997c, 1997d) applied the Jarillo and Martinez typology to an analysis of 171 manufacturing subsidiaries in the UK in the expectation, *inter alia*, of finding cases of what he termed 'quiescent subsidiaries' in the low–R, low–I quadrant. The most prevalent case in Taggart's study, however, emerged as the high–R, high–I active. This provided 51 cases in 1995, an increase of eight from 1990. This is certainly compatible with a strategic momentum in the contemporary MNE that seeks to combine the benefits of both responsiveness and integration, seeking to resolve the organisational problems that might have constrained them to one or other of the 'trade-off' options. As we have suggested earlier, once a subsidiary has individualised its competences by responding positively to the problems and potentials of its immediate environment, it can often then benefit the group most thoroughly if it exercises its distinctive scope interdependently (via various modes of integration) with sister units. In line with this, Taggart's results pinpoint as a particular distinctive characteristic of actives the extent to which they 'develop products responsive to the market needs of sister subsidiaries'. Actives also share with the other responsive type (autonomous) the most advanced commitment to in-house R&D.

By contrast with actives, the low integration variant of the responsive type, autonomous subsidiaries, suffered the largest decline in numbers, retreating from the most prevalent in 1990 (56 cases) to third place by 1995 (39 cases). Again this would be compatible with a strong corporate desire to co-opt the distinctive capacities of responsiveness towards group-level aims.[18] Although sharing high R&D commitment with actives, autonomous subsidiaries have the lowest propensity to develop products responsively (that is, to meet the needs of sister subsidiaries). Other aspects of their independence emerge as the lowest export propensity, the smallest degree to which marketing activity is coordinated with the internal group network, and the least participation in the 'extent to which skills and resources are spread around the internal network'.

The high–I, low–R receptive subsidiary was the least prevalent form in both years, although their numbers did achieve a modest increase from 31 to 35. Certain characteristics of receptives discerned by Taggart would tend to support their equation with our RP subsidiaries. Thus they share with actives the highest export propensity, have the lowest complexity of R&D ('typically confining themselves to adaptation of manufacturing technology with perhaps minimal capability in product adaptation'), and appear to accept dependence on access to important skills and resources that are concentrated at corporate headquarters.

Finally Taggart's analysis found 46 cases of the low–R, low–I quiescent in 1995, an increase of five since 1990. In fact, being located outside of the two driving imperatives of MNE strategy (as perceived by the integration/responsiveness approach), the quiescent would appear to be a very vulnerable strategic positioning. Thus Taggart documents (1997c, pp.18–20; 1997d, pp.311–13) a number of cases in the UK to suggest 'that a period during which the affiliate is deintegrated from the internal network and simultaneously denied the resources necessary to be adequately responsive is rapidly followed by run-down or closure' (1997c, p.20). It is also noteworthy that the quiescents of 1995 included ten that had been actives and 19 that had been autonomous five years earlier. If, to some extent, responsive positioning equates to high-value-added operations then the policy message is not just that that status is far from immutable, but that it can also be one quite quick stage from closure (that is, via quiescence). Thus environmental conditions conducive to support of responsiveness should be actively encouraged with, perhaps, note taken that active and autonomous subsidiaries are the most committed to advanced R&D.

AUTONOMY AND PROCEDURAL JUSTICE TYPOLOGY

A recurring theme throughout the analysis in this book, as in much other recent work,[19] is that as MNEs undergo crucial processes of competitive evolution their individual subsidiaries increasingly become aware of the need to actively defend their current status (if perceived as desirable) and/or to be able to articulate convincing claims on a new higher-value-added position. Their approach to building and asserting their intra-group positioning (for example, through open negotiation or surreptitiously subversive behaviour) may then depend on how fairly and equitably they expect to be treated by corporate (parent-company or headquarters: HQ) decision-making processes.[20] Building on the pioneering analysis of Kim and Mauborgne (1991, 1993, a,b), Taggart (1997e) suggests that subsidiary strategy is likely to be conditioned by perceived access to procedural justice[21] and degree of autonomy. Applying cluster analysis to survey replies from 171 MNE manufacturing subsidiaries operating in the UK, Taggart derived a solution validating four distinct subsidiary types differentiated by their level of autonomy and their perception of procedural justice.

In Taggart's typology *partner* subsidiaries operate with high autonomy (high–A) and in a group environment of high procedural justice (high–PJ), and thus may correlate to the condition of interdependent individualism desired by our WPM/RPM subsidiaries. Thus they have the autonomy to take decisions about the development and implementation of their own creative competences in a corporate environment where they feel confident in revealing these scopes and ambitions to group-level decision makers, without undue fear of unfair or biased suppression or of distorted and opportunistic (unrewarded or unacknowledged) spread of their expertise to other parts of the MNE's operations. In fact, they feel confident that they will be treated as proactive partners in the evolution of group operations.[22]

The cluster analysis provided Taggart with 38 cases in the high–A, high–PJ partner quadrant. These also possessed high values of all three dimensions of the scope typology. Thus they recorded 'by far the highest value added scope in the sample' and even included 'five firms that have responsibility for generating new technology for the corporate parent'. In addition, they developed or adapted locally more than half their product lines and over half of them had a market scope that extended beyond Europe (Taggart, 1997e, p.66). Although subject to low integration pressures (little control exercised by HQ), partner subsidiaries were involved in high levels of coordination, particularly regarding technology links with sister subsidiaries. This may suggest the exercise of an interdependent positioning of these partner units in ways that might mitigate some of Taggart's concern that a perceived special relationship with HQ might be resented by other subsidiaries in the group.

The 54 *collaborator* (low–A, high–PJ) subsidiaries detected by Taggart's cluster analysis may correlate to effective and smoothly functioning RPSs, which are induced to feel satisfied with a dependent and networked supply situation. Thus a collaborator 'has little real bargaining power with HQ, but retains its place in the network through flexibility, co-operation, and delivering acceptable performance as part of a tightly inter-linked group of affiliates' (1997e, p.68). They possess the highest market scope in the sample, but fairly narrow product scope and considerably restricted value-added scope (often limited 'to adaptation of manufacturing technology'). Technological dependence seems a key characteristic of collaborator subsidiaries with their generally high levels of coordination particularly manifest in intra-network transfer (mainly receipt) of technology and production knowhow, as a result of R&D activities being mainly located at HQ and technology development also being centralised (at least for the goods they are asked to supply).

The cluster analysis provides Taggart with 50 subsidiaries in the *militant* (high–A, low–PJ) quadrant. Reflecting the highest level of responsiveness, the militants appear to be characterised by a considerable degree of localised individuality. This embodies high-value-added scope (37 develop or adapt products for European and world markets), the highest product scope (three-quarters of the product line developed or adapted locally) but a relatively low market scope (usually limited to Europe, with a few venturing beyond). Although their levels of all three aspects of scope considerably transcend those we would expect to be present in traditional TMRs it is still tempting to see militants as ambitious examples of such subsidiaries, which have put into place the capacity to make the creative transition to higher-value-added roles. The source of their militancy may then stem from lack of comparable foresight at the corporate level, so that strategic and organisational perspectives are not yet ready to accommodate dispersed creative scope and misunderstandings thus arise (provoking perceptions of low–PJ).[23] It is central to the view of contemporary MNEs enshrined in this book that they seek to harness dispersed knowledge, technology, skills and market developments to enrich group competitiveness through subsidiaries' locally-responsive perceptions. We could then argue that a key to this scenario is improvement of the corporate environment in terms of PJ, so that the militant 'problem child' becomes a mature partner contributing to the cohesive growth of the MNE family.

Finally Taggart's cluster analysis provides 29 *vassal* subsidiaries in the low–A, low–PJ quadrant. These, perhaps rather dysfunctional subsidiaries, are most notably characterised by the lowest value-added scope, the lowest market scope (confined to Europe) and most restricted product scope. A possible explanation for vassal status, within our scenario, would be that they are poorly functioning RPS-type operations that do not willingly accept their dependent and networked supply situation. This condition may have emerged when poor central management had failed to convince (thereby imparting a sense of low–PJ) TMRs with low value-added scope (unlike those that become militants) of the need to subside into the compliant collaborator role, as the group restructures to the needs of the new global competitive environment. This situation 'characterised by dissent, mistrust, and a master/servant relationship' (Taggart, 1997e, p.58) provides no positive or stable input into a modern MNE's global strategy. Moreover, the low–PJ condition is likely to preclude any subsidiary-initiated move towards a more credible contribution. Harnessing such potentials as their local environment may impart to such subsidiaries needs 'major changes at HQ in terms of leadership, strategy and operational proficiency'.

SUBSIDIARY EVOLUTION AND ORGANISATIONAL CHANGE IN MNES

The points made earlier concerning the evolution of subsidiary roles within the scope typology underline recent perceptions of new global organisation structures for MNEs. This reflects two factors.

Firstly, there is now a much wider spectrum of roles that subsidiaries can play. At extremes these can be either dependent roles applying existing group technology within externally-organised supply programmes or creative operations whose aim is to extend the MNE's product range, and perhaps in the process also have deeper effects on extending its technology and knowledge scope.

Secondly, the latter type of subsidiary sets up new challenges for the MNE. Its value is its *individualism*, in the form of distinctive new subsidiary-level knowledge and the managerial drive to take initiatives based around it. But this has to contribute to coherent group progress and not go off in independent directions that the subsidiary ultimately will not have the in-house scope to fully develop. A degree of *interdependence* has to be retained that then supports the subsidiary and/or provides benefits to the group, but does not in the process stifle the subsidiary's capacity to exercise its creative scope.

These perspectives define the move from hierarchy to heterarchy (Hedlund 1986, 1993) and outline the organisational problems of benefiting from heterarchy. In a hierarchy there are a very limited number of decision-making centres, with perhaps only the home-country parent having any real strategic influence over long-term development programmes. The vast majority of overseas subsidiaries occupy positions that are predominantly dependent on decisions that the centre takes (their position is *allocated*) and have very little scope to create individualised knowledge or skills in the process of playing that role.[24]

In heterarchy (responding to the types of technological and market heterogeneity we have emphasised) some subsidiaries *earn* or *claim* the more powerful product development roles. But they do this by demonstrating original abilities and the scope to do distinctive things in distinctive ways, that is, they manifest a unique source of competitiveness within the group. This individualism is what makes them valuable to the group but, of course, it removes them from the dependence and control of subsidiaries in hierarchies. Their role is not defined within a centrally-driven 'master plan' but becomes a proactive component in an overall programme that includes other subsidiaries that are also seeking to exercise their own individualised competences.[25] As previously emphasised, this should benefit the group because it provides perhaps the best way of accessing the two types of heterogeneity and operationalising them to achieve group-level aims. But this then makes clear the problem of organising for heterogeneity; it needs to access these sources of knowledge, taste trends, and so on, through individually motivated subsidiaries but still ultimately harness this to full support of group objectives (global competitiveness).

The heterarchy must be a *coalition* of separate creative operations. However, this cannot be either too loose a coalition (individualised subsidiaries may not have the resources to develop all their scope autonomously; knowledge generated at the subsidiary level must be available to other parts of the group where it can also be used constructively) or too tight (excessive supervision may suffocate the creative independence that provides the potential value). Thus the HQ responsibility is to support the emergence of individualised scope within subsidiaries, but in a group climate that recognises the benefits of interdependencies. The subsidiary's abilities must evolve within (but not be too constrained by) mutually understood (and influenced) broad group parameters. Ultimately, very original creative attributes that emerge in subsidiaries *can* change the group parameters themselves, but in the normal course of progress there must be a degree of coherence and cohesion in what the subsidiaries are doing (without too much of this being *imposed* from above in a hierarchical way).

As will be investigated as a key theme of Chapter 4, technology creation and application are usually central to the potentials and problems of heterarchy. The individualised scope of creative subsidiaries does not usually come from technological autarchy, but more often derives from building unique areas of knowledge scope from positions in two separate networks. These are the science and research community of the host country and the technological scope and programmes of the MNE group. Where subsidiaries effectively access and combine relevant aspects of the scope and competences of these two distinct knowledge communities, they should then build distinctive technology perspectives of their own. These should certainly enrich the overall technological basis for competitiveness of the group within its currently broadly understood knowledge and commercial parameters and, in more exceptional cases, may open up more radical potentials that clearly challenge the limits of these parameters. It should be accepted as beneficial to have occasions where subsidiaries can bring forth perspectives that challenge the prevailing technological norms, but when it happens it needs to be subject to negotiation with central planning (at one extreme it should not be condemned outright or, at the other, be allowed to proceed unevaluated and unsupervised). A certain level of technological *autonomy* is desirable for subsidiaries in heterarchies, but this cannot be allowed to collapse into *anarchy* for the group. These aspects of organising and controlling technology in heterarchical MNEs will be discussed further in Chapter 4.

The concept of heterarchy has been formally defined (Hedlund and Rolander, 1990, p.15) as entailing 'a geographical diffusion of core strategic activities and coordinating roles, a break with the notion of one uniform hierarchy of decisions as well as organisation positions, and an increased focus on normative control mechanisms'.[26] From Hedlund and Rolander's (1990, pp.25–6) full delineation of the characteristics of heterarchy, six are particularly germane to the concerns of our investigation as outlined earlier.

Firstly, there are 'many centres, of different kinds', with traditional HQ functions increasingly 'geographically diffused, and no dimension (product, country, function) uniformly superordinate'. Such dispersion of key scope needs a 'structure that is flexible over time' so that 'the heterarchical firm does not worry too much about logical inconsistency, but instead focuses on practical coherence'. This leads to the second characteristic of 'a strategic role for foreign subsidiaries', which operates 'for the corporation as a whole [so that] corporate level strategy has to be both formulated and implemented in a geographically scattered network'.

Thirdly, the heterarchical MNE uses 'a wide range of governance modes between pure market and hierarchy', with joint ventures serving in one area, externalised transactions and in-house business organised on an arm's-length basis in another,[27] whilst internalisation and 'governance by management fiat' works best in a third context. Fourthly, heterarchical MNEs encourage 'coalitions with other firms and with other types of actors....in order to utilise potentials for synergy in the global environment'. Our analysis of coll-aborations with local scientific institutions (Chapter 7) and suppliers (Chapter 8) exemplifies this characteristic.

Next, the heterarchical MNE encourages 'radical problem orientation, rather than starting from existing resources, or from competitive positions in narrow fields of business' which may, finally, lead to 'action programmes for seeking and generating new firm-specific advantages through global spread'. This, of course, provides a central theme of our broad investigation, which is in line with Hedlund and Rolander's view (1990, p.26) that 'exploitation of given, home country based advantages is emphasised in the theory of the MNC, but this should not entrap the MNC in its action'.

The key contrasts of heterarchy with hierarchy have been summarised by Birkinshaw (1994, p.134). Thus the dimensions of hierarchy are (i) coordination by vertical referral, (ii) centralised resources and decisions, and (iii) formal control. The comparable dimensions of heterarchy are then, (i) lateral coordination, (ii) dispersed resources and decisions, and (iii) informal control and socialisation. It should also be observed, however, that given the range of roles now available to MNE subsidiaries, the emergence of heterarchy does not so much replace hierarchy as subsume it within heterogeneous structures and control procedures. Thus (Birkinshaw and Morrison, 1995, p.737) 'a heterarchical MNC could easily have certain subsidiaries that were controlled in a 'hierarchical' (i.e. bureaucratic) manner'. In our subsidiary typology it would be expected that RP subsidiaries would be most subject to hierarchical control[28] and WPM/RPMs most amenable to socialisation/normalisation processes.

Another valuable conceptualisation of the emerging organisation of MNEs is the *transnational* of Bartlett and Ghoshal (1989, 1987a,b). Here it is suggested that these internationally-competing enterprises need to simultaneously address three imperatives, 'global efficiency, national responsiveness, and the ability to develop and exploit knowledge on a world-wide basis' (1989, p.58). The detailed analysis of the competitive strengths and weaknesses of nine leading MNEs led the authors to suggest that three more traditional modes had been based *separately* around each of the three competitive priorities. Thus Bartlett and Ghoshal's work ultimately provides a four-part typology of MNEs based around their driving competitive imperatives.

In what Bartlett and Ghoshal (1989, p.15) called the *multinational* corporation, the main strategic posture was that of 'building strong local presence through sensitivity and responsiveness to national differences'. Thus these companies often comprised, in effect, no more than a portfolio of multiple national entities. Through decentralised decision making and dispersed resources, the individual subsidiaries in such multinational corporations delivered the group's defining competitive strength in the form of a distinctive ability to respond to local needs. However, this fragmentation of activity carried almost inevitable penalties in terms of inefficiency. In addition, and of increasing significance, learning suffered as the group's knowledge was not adequately consolidated, with flows between the parts often blocked by the separate interests of individual subsidiaries. Thus, whilst subsidiaries often possessed the scope to be separately innovative this often represented little more than the attempts of their management to protect their autonomy and resource exclusivity, with the persistent danger of 'reinventing the wheel' within the group (Bartlett and Ghoshal, 1989, p.59).

By contrast, Bartlett and Ghoshal's *global* corporation places the priority on building cost advantages, which it seeks 'through centralised global-scale operation' (1989, p.15). In their defining pursuit of such efficiency, the configuration of these companies is based on a centralisation of assets, resources and responsibilities, so that their overseas operations are used merely to reach foreign markets in order to build global scale. Thus the role of dispersed subsidiaries may be limited to sales and service and, at least in a pure global corporation, would be certainly unlikely to exceed assembly. Hence 'the dominant management perspective was that the world could, and should, be treated as a single integrated market in which similarities were more important than differences. The entire globe was the prime unit of analysis' (1989, p.52). This posture logically precludes any product development (or even adaptation) in the highly cost-conscious subsidiaries, and by a like token makes it unlikely that the (otherwise presumably very effective) centralised innovation process could be influenced by product ideas or taste trends emanating in overseas environments.

Bartlett and Ghoshal (1989, p.15) define the *international* corporation, their third traditional organisation form, as 'exploiting parent company knowledge and capabilities through world-wide diffusion and adaptation'. Whilst overseas subsidiaries in international corporations shared some characteristics of those in multinationals, in that they were often expected to adapt centrally-derived knowledge so as to be responsive to their specific local conditions, the fact that they were thus dependent on the parent company for new products, processes or ideas then meant they were also more subject to HQ coordination and control. On the other hand, the HQ control in international corporations seeks to leverage their own knowledge capabilities worldwide through supporting creative work in dispersed subsidiaries, rather than making these overseas operations primarily cost-efficiency motivated (and functionally limited) as they would be in global corporations.

Summing up the traditional options, Bartlett and Ghoshal (1989, p.61) note that

> in the global organisation the cost and quality advantages of global efficiency are expected to provide sufficient value that customers will eschew idiosyncratic differences in preferences and accept standard products. In the multinational organisation, it is assumed that tailoring products and strategies to individual national markets will offset the higher costs that may result. The international organisation settles on a middle path, allowing local operations to choose from a menu of products and processes, perhaps modifying them in minor ways to suit local conditions.

However, they further observe (1989, p.16), 'by the mid-1980s the forces of global integration, local differentiation, and world-wide innovation had all become strong and compelling, and none could be ignored. To compete effectively, a company had to develop global competitiveness, multinational flexibility, and world-wide learning capability *simultaneously*'. From this imperative, they suggest, the *transnational* organisation is emerging.

In Bartlett and Ghoshal's conceptualisation (1989, p.67), the transnational thus seeks to address *all* of three priorities now faced by companies' seeking to compete worldwide. Firstly, *global competitiveness* is pursued through 'dispersed and interdependent assets and resources'. A key organisational innovation emerges decisively here. Whilst all three of the traditional forms 'make a common assumption: the subsidiary's role is local, limited to activities within its own environment', now efficiency-motivated subsidiaries can develop export-oriented links within globalised supply perspectives. Thus the transnational pioneers the configuration of worldwide resources as an *integrated network*.[29]

However, the content of transnationals' networks can vary, including not only components, products and resources, but also people, knowledge and information. This then relates to the second problem addressed in this organisational form, namely the need for *multinational flexibility*, which is secured through differentiated and specialised subsidiary roles. Some subsidiaries are still defined primarily by the multinational role of supplying local markets in a responsive manner. Others play a more contemporary form of global-efficiency role by exporting standardised products to their group's worldwide supply networks. This activates one host-country attribute (cost-effective production inputs) to support global competitiveness. Increasingly, though, a third subsidiary role may operationalise another local attribute, knowledge and technology, for corporate-level use.

The emergence of this third subsidiary role points to the last of the contemporary imperatives addressed by Bartlett and Ghoshal's transnationals. Thus they increasingly pursue *worldwide learning* through the joint development and groupwide sharing of knowledge. This can take the form of subsidiaries that make use of leading-edge technology that is locally available in order to develop products that may be applied elsewhere in the group. Here (in the manner of our product mandates) responsibility for a product is still centralised, but no longer in the home country. Thus headquarters relinquishes (as a part of a policy of 'flexible centralisation') some of its lead role to subsidiaries, 'a key attribute of the transnational that contrasts sharply with the uniformity of organisational roles in more traditional companies' (1989, p.62). The new approaches to innovation available to transnationals are spelt out very clearly by Bartlett and Ghoshal and will be discussed further in Chapter 4.[30]

In a survey analysis of senior executives of 131 leading companies, Leong and Tan (1993) found that 23 considered themselves to be transnationals, 51 took the multinational form, 26 were global organisations and 31 rated themselves as international corporations. Since Bartlett and Ghoshal had only considered the transnational to be an idealised format in current practice (none of their nine enterprises were considered to have fully adopted it) the relatively low number in Leong and Tan's sample is probably not surprising. The fact that the reported transnationals did not conform as closely, in terms of their detailed characteristics, to the prescribed form as did some of the other types may also be related to their evolutionary status. However, in terms of our wider concerns it is interesting to note that Leong and Tan suggest that in general the surveyed corporations seemed to be trying to 'think global' and 'act local', with a 'strong level of agreement towards the expanded and proactive role of overseas units coupled with world-wide integration of activities and free transfer of knowledge to all locations' supporting that viewpoint.

SUMMARY

The review of recent conceptual and empirical analysis carried out in this chapter provides an underpinning to key themes in our own investigation of MNE activity in the UK. From recent thinking on the organisational nature of the contemporary MNE we find notable endorsement for our emphasis on heterogeneity as a driving imperative in the global strategies of these companies. This we perceive to have two dimensions. Firstly, there is a *need* to respond to elements of globalised heterogeneity. This may still occur in some industries, and in some regions and countries, in terms of different tastes for goods and in the conditions relating to production processes. Also, and of equal relevance to our analysis, such heterogeneity is increasingly visible in geographically dispersed sources of specialised knowledge and skills. Secondly, the *means* to respond fully to these new forces and conditions also involves heterogeneity in the organisational structures of globally-competing enterprises. For our purposes this manifests itself very decisively in the emergence of a range of different roles that MNEs' subsidiaries can play, with these having very distinctive implications for the ways in which their operations activate and interact with host-country sources of comparative advantage.

The second section of this chapter incorporated a detailed discussion of the typology of subsidiaries that we use in our investigations. This is seen as deriving from a valuable tradition that differentiates subsidiaries according to various dimensions of their scope. The subsequent sections reviewed other typologies of MNE subsidiaries, demonstrating that these elaborate usefully on other perspectives that inform the issues we seek to address and that frequently have resonances that usefully complement our own typology.

The first of our subsidiary types, the truncated miniature replica (TMR), supplies an extensive part of its MNE group's existing product range to its host-country market. In our exposition we place emphasis on this occurring as a means of avoiding trade restraints and, therefore, as potentially generating the inefficiency of import-substitution strategies. However, we also allow TMRs scope for adaptation to local conditions. Such close attention to local needs and conditions plays a more significant role in typologies that emphasise responsiveness (R) and integration (I) as MNE imperatives, with a close equivalent to our TMRs emerging in the form of 'autonomous' subsidiaries that combine low–I with high–R (Jarillo and Martinez, Taggart).

Our discussion noted that TMRs have become increasingly vulnerable as effective parts of an MNE group's overall strategy, as the forces of globalised competition have intensified. We have therefore observed two alternative types of strategic positioning into which subsidiaries may evolve (rationalised

product subsidiaries and product mandates). Once such evolutionary processes
become crucial to the continued competitiveness of MNE global operations,
however, it is necessary for them to secure the willingness of subsidiaries to
make the metamorphosis into the role that maximises their continued
contribution. Where subsidiaries feel fairly treated (that is, have access to
adequate procedural justice) they should willingly accede to the most
appropriate of the new roles. Where these transition processes are badly
handled, however, subsidiaries may continue to occupy unhappy positions
with persistent elements of outmoded TMR status. Thus Taggart noted the
presence of 'militant' subsidiaries which have high autonomy (based on
notable levels of in-house competence) which they feel unable to exercise
properly in the MNE (poor access to procedural justice), so they have the
potential to become disruptive forces compromising overall group-level
progress. Alternatively, 'vassal' subsidiaries have low autonomy (limited
subsidiary-level competences) and low access to procedural justice so that
they have not secured their logical move into group supply programmes as
rationalised product subsidiaries. The considerable presence of vassals and
militants in Taggart's study emphasises the care with which MNEs need to
handle the processes of strategic evolution at the subsidiary level in order to
fully address the problems and potentials of the environment of globalised
competition.

The first of the evolutionary options, in terms of new subsidiary roles in our
typology, is the rationalised product subsidiary (RPS). An RPS specialises in
the supply of a much narrower range of established products to a much more
extensive (that is, export-oriented) market area. As this logically precludes any
responsiveness to local-market needs the factors attracting RPSs to a particular
location tend to be the standardised inputs into the cost-effective production of
already successfully marketed goods, rather than any higher-value-added
creative resources that could individualise a subsidiary's status. This
positioning has an obvious equivalent in the integration/responsiveness
framework in the form of the high–I, low–R 'receptive'.

Bartlett and Ghoshal's 'implementer' also may well play the RPS role, with
just enough competence to fulfil a position that does not contribute to their
group's strategic evolution but helps to deliver its routine standardised sources
of value-added. Although, in line with Bartlett and Ghoshal's definition of the
implementer, our RPSs are most likely to exist in host countries of low
strategic importance they may also coexist, with more ambitious subsidiary
roles, in more competitively significant locations.[31]

Finally, world or regional product mandate (WPM/RPM) subsidiaries are
most decisively distinguished, for the purposes of our articulation, by a high-
value-added degree of functional competence that allows them to develop new

products that significantly extend the scope of their MNE group's range. The need of these subsidiaries to operate with the high level of creative fixed costs implied by their PM status is assumed to normally imply access to wide (that is, export) market scope. We also discern here a deeper degree of local responsiveness, in that the subsidiary is seeking to activate, on behalf of its MNE group, distinctive knowledge and creative inputs into development processes that enrich the enterprise's overall competitive capability. We thus emphasise that despite a strong degree of individualised competence (that is, potential for exercise of autonomy) these subsidiaries are most effective when working interdependently with other group operations. Thus our WPM/RPM subsidiaries may often be positioned in a manner that resembles the high–I, high–R 'active' of Jarillo and Martinez, and Taggart.[32]

An ability of MNEs to respond to distinctive host-country attributes and developments (for example, technological progress, market trends) through subsidiaries which acquire and operationalise localised competences is a key element in the Bartlett and Ghoshal typology. Thus our WPM/RPM subsidiaries may correlate to both the strategic leader (which operates in a host country of considerable strategic relevance) and the contributor (which also possesses notable in-house competence but in a less strategically significant host-country environment). Whereas strategic leaders have an obvious relevance to sustaining the dynamic global competitiveness of MNEs, the contributor form is also a case with notable resonances for the broader concerns of our analysis. Thus it relates to the way in which PM-type subsidiaries may *lead* the industrialisation of a host country which has not yet been able to assert itself strategically, by operationalising (in a creative transition) underrealised local knowledge potentials into globally-competitive parts of an MNE group's scope.

The ideal organisational positioning of our PM subsidiaries, we emphasise, is one that encourages them to generate a degree of individualised functional scope that provides a high-motivating sense of autonomy, which they are nevertheless still prepared to exercise interdependently within a group environment where they perceive themselves as being treated fairly. In this high autonomy, high procedural justice situation (Taggart), they feel themselves to be fully-fledged 'partners' for all other elements of the group (including the home-country parent) and activate their potentials in an enthusiastic and mutually-supportive manner.

NOTES

1. Important early analysis of the world product mandate form, from mainly Canadian evidence, includes Rugman (1983), Rugman and Bennett (1982), Poynter and Rugman (1982), Rugman and Douglas (1986), and Crookell and Morrison (1990). Pioneering attempts at formalised analysis of product mandates can be found in Roth and Morrison (1992), and Birkinshaw and Morrison (1995).
2. Pearce (1989, 1992), Papanastassiou (1995), Papanastassiou and Pearce (1994a), and Pearce and Papanastassiou (1996a).
3. On the basis of a thorough and careful empirical investigation of subsidiaries in Scotland, Taggart (1997a, p.636) suggests that 'perhaps, White and Poynter's typology could be reduced to three types (without subdivision):   the strategic mandate (combination of strategic independent and product specialist), the rationalised manufacturer (as in the original model), and the miniature replica (combination of adapter, adopter and innovator types)'.
4. For analysis of the effects of regional integration on MNE strategic evolution, in terms of the scope typology, see Tavares and Pearce (1998), Pearce and Tavares (1998).
5. Although long-standing TMRs could also have assimilated and responded to these local conditions, failure to do so adequately may sometimes have been an element of their X-inefficiency during their period of substantial competitive edge.
6. This, of course, characterises RPSs that play by the definitional rules of the form. As we shall see later, many of them possess more entrepreneurial management and, backing this, retain (from TMR status), or subversively create, other functional scope (for example, R&D) that transcends their logical needs. This then serves as a basis to move to a position from which they can seek to justify a move to a more creative (product mandate) role.
7. Thus the degree of autonomy allowed to White and Poynter's 'strategic independent' is only an extreme case of the WPM/RPM form.
8. Crookell (1990, p.106) observes that in product mandate subsidiaries 'product renewal is unmanageable if the subsidiary is not also responsible for international marketing; successful R&D must be shaped by a thorough knowledge of consumer needs. The fact that subsidiaries must be responsible for international marketing does not imply that they are independent of the corporation's international sales force, however.   On the contrary, there must be an ongoing, dynamic interchange between the two'.
9. Taggart's (1997b) study some ten years later confirmed that US subsidiaries remained decisively more export oriented than European ones.
10. For earlier evidence on MNE R&D in Scotland, see Forsythe (1972), Hood and Young (1976, 1980), Haug, Hood and Young (1983).
11. Taggart (1996a, Table 5) classifies 121 of these subsidiaries as 20 miniature replicas, 26 rationalised manufacturers, 48 product specialists and 27 strategic independents.
12. Bartlett and Ghoshal document the factors that generated the possibility for the Australian subsidiary of L.M. Ericsson to play a crucial role in the development of its successful AXE telecommunications switch.
13. See, for example, Manea and Pearce (1997a,b).
14. In Prahalad and Doz's original specification, multi-focal is a compromise on the diagonal between global business and local-responsive business, and therefore has moderate levels of both responsiveness and integration.   It thus differs from the subsequently-derived active subsidiary of Jarillo and Martinez (1990) which has high values of both.
15. Using information at the corporate (rather than subsidiary) level, the Prahalad and Doz grid was tested for a multi-industry sample by Roth and Morrison (1990) and for a group of US construction industry companies by Johnson (1995). Both studies provided strong support for three clusters of firms along essentially the lines predicted by Prahalad and Doz. However, Johnson noted that his multi-focal firms 'evidence high concern for both integration and responsiveness, rather than mid-level concerns for each pressure' (1995, p.631). Similarly Roth

and Morrison (1990, p.557) observe a pattern of activities in their multi-focal cases that have similarities to the high-responsive high-integration aims of the 'transnational' organisation of Bartlett and Ghoshal (1989).

16. Jarillo and Martinez use the term 'localisation' to essentially the same effect as 'responsiveness'. Elsewhere (Martinez and Jarillo, 1991) they also equate 'differentiation' to 'responsiveness'.

17. Jarillo and Martinez (1990) also showed that over the period 1983 to 1991 (projected) there was a big rise in integration and substantial fall in localisation. This seems likely to be a response to increased freedom of trade within Europe, with subsidiaries taking on an increased efficiency-seeking (rather than market-seeking) role within emergent group-coordinated regional supply networks.

18. Although the overall fall in responsives (99 to 90) would not be.

19. For example, Taggart (1993); Forsgren, Holm and Johanson (1992, pp.247-50); Bartlett and Ghoshal (1989, pp.10-12).

20. In the words of Taggart (1997e, pp.56-7) 'the basic proposition is that subsidiary managers will react positively even to a decision that goes against them providing they perceive that the process leading to the decision was similar across all subsidiaries in the network and was fairly implemented at all stages. [Thus] procedural justice enhances compliance of subsidiary managers with corporate strategic decisions [and the] exercise of procedural justice by corporate managers improves both the formulation and implementation of strategy'.

21. In line with Kim and Mauborgne's work, Taggart operationalises procedural justice in terms of five variables, the extent to which effective two-way communication exists between HQ and subsidiary; the extent to which the subsidiary can challenge HQ's strategic views during the strategy formulation process; the degree to which HQ is knowledgeable about the subsidiary's local situation; the extent to which HQ provides the subsidiary with a rational account of strategic decisions; and the uniformity of HQ's decision-making process across all subsidiaries.

22. Thus Taggart (1997e, p.70) suggests HQ may see the presence of partner subsidiaries 'more as a particular form of strategic alliance'. In a similar vein we have argued (Papanastassiou and Pearce, 1997a) that our WPM/RPM subsidiaries are the most ostentatious intra-group manifestation of a move towards MNEs competing worldwide as networks of internal and external collaborative agreements.

23. Specific dimensions of failure in PJ are discerned (Taggart, 1997e, p.66) as poor HQ knowledge of local circumstances, inadequate propensity of HQ to account for its strategic decisions and overall inconsistency of HQ decisions across the network. These may be considered compatible with parent-company operations that have not yet adequately acknowledged the need to respond to global heterogeneity in strategic behaviour.

24. In some cases such hierarchical subsidiaries have, in a perhaps rather subversive way, sought to create or sustain such abilities (in excess of the needs of their current role) and in the process of seeking to use them more proactively have generated some of the forces towards heterarchical evolution.

25. As Birkinshaw (1994, p.115) puts it 'there is no need for a grand design strategy in which each part is assigned a role understood only by the executive. Once the guiding premises of the organisation are internalised each decision maker can act independently yet in accord with the others'.

26. The horizontal organisation of White and Poynter (1990) has similar characteristics, encompassing lateral decision processes, horizontal networks and shared decision premises.

27. This recalls our emphasis that although WPM/RPM subsidiaries take responsibility for the technology and marketing relating to their goods, they may operationalise this through arm's-length arrangements with other elements of their MNE group.

28. Although positioned in supply networks that invoke substantial lateral transactions of goods, their participation is likely to be organised downward from a central node in the network.

29. Kobrin (1991) analysed integration in the form of flows of resources within MNEs, including not only those between the parent and subsidiaries but also those between subsidiaries (as implied by the full development of supply networking).

30. It can be noted here that whilst Bartlett and Ghoshal's international corporation's clearly centralised approach to innovation conforms to the description of the first stage of Vernon's original (1966) product cycle, the transnational's scope for innovation to arise anywhere in the organisation has resonances with the potential of Vernon's (1979) ('hypothetical') 'global scanner'. Here, when MNEs have global networks 'information, once received, is digested at little or no cost [so that] ... markets, wherever located, have an equal opportunity to stimulate the firm to innovation and production' (Vernon, 1979, p.261).
31. If an RPS exists in a high-strategic-importance host without complementary elements of product mandate activity, it faces the danger of slumping into 'black hole' (Bartlett and Ghoshal) status. Thus our discussion presumes a dynamic tendency in RPSs to add financial scope to pursue upgrading to high-value-added status.
32. Empirically, from the studies reviewed in this chapter, the actives share with their PM equivalents in the scope typology analyses, a propensity to grow in numbers over time (usually at the expense of autonomous subsidiaries or their TMR equivalents).

3. Roles and markets of subsidiaries in the UK

INTRODUCTION

The ability of an MNE subsidiary to contribute to the industrial competitiveness and technological development of its host country depends on the scope provided by its role. Improved efficiency in production, and more effective application of a country's standardised sources of static comparative advantage, are likely to result if a subsidiary can refocus its activity towards the supply (through exporting) of wider market areas. The activation of a country's knowledge-related sources of dynamic comparative advantage may also be secured through the operations of the modern MNE, where subsidiaries can acquire a mandate to create products as well as to supply them.

The background to the strategic positioning of MNE subsidiaries in the UK, described in the two main sections of this chapter, reflects quite clearly on these most influential elements of competitive scope. In the next section we look at the relative prevalence of four subsidiary roles, seeking in particular to discern the presence of those that co-opt localised creative capacities into product development processes, in ways that can then impart enhanced dynamism to the UK's industrial sector. After that we investigate the extent and nature of export orientation in the subsidiaries, checking on its relation to their source of strategic motivation. Other characteristics of the subsidiaries (their age, size, and means of establishment) conclude this initial investigation, which serves as a vital prelude to the detailed analysis of their technological scope and positioning.

ROLES OF SUBSIDIARIES

In order to analyse the strategic positioning of manufacturing multinationals' operations in the UK the respondents to the survey were asked to evaluate the degree of presence in their activity of *each* of four possible roles. Whilst each of the roles conforms in a clearcut way to one of the alternative positions delineated by the scope typology the approach here recognises that in practice, and especially in the processes of evolution that result from MNE response to changing global competitive environments, any given subsidiary may well embody elements of more than one of these strategic motivations.[1]

The first subsidiary role was defined as 'to produce for the UK market products that are already established in our MNE group's product range' (ESTPROD/UK). In our articulation of the scope typology (described in detail in the previous chapter) this is the traditional import-substituting truncated miniature replica (TMR) role. Thus a probably quite extensive product range derives from that which is already well established in the MNE group's wider operations, but is applied to the narrow competitive environment of the subsidiary's local (national) market. Although some degree of creative scope (technological and/or marketing) is likely to emerge in these subsidiaries, this is normally only to pursue the adaptation of existing products and processes to local conditions, and still leaves their functional (value-added) capabilities severely truncated by comparison with the parent or other, more strategic, subsidiaries elsewhere.

Of the 185 subsidiaries that evaluated their operations in terms of the ESTPROD/UK role, 15 (8.1 per cent) considered that it was their only one, 69 (37.3 per cent) felt that it took a predominant position, 50 (27.0 per cent) rated it a secondary role and 51 (27.6 per cent) did not include it. Once these replies are summarised in terms of average responses (ARs), Table 3.1 reveals that this, presumably now highly vulnerable, status (see Chapter 2) is still, very marginally, the most pervasive of the four roles. It is, again very marginally, the relatively most prevalent role (when evaluated in terms of ARs) in the operations of European MNE subsidiaries in the UK (most decisively so in electronics), and takes the equal leading role for the US. Food is the industry in which the ESTPROD/UK role is most prevalent (notably due to the commitment of US companies). It is least prominent overall in mechanical engineering and metal manufacture and products, where a frequent need to customise items for individual customers may often mitigate against a routine supply of existing standardised products (even after allowing for scope for local adaptation).

The second type of subsidiary positioning offered for evaluation was 'to play a role in the MNE group's European supply network by specialising in the production and export of part of the established product range' (ESTPROD/EUR). This is the first of two variants of what we earlier termed the rationalised product subsidiary (RPS) role. The most clearly decisive difference from the ESTPROD/UK role is that here the subsidiary uses the potentials of freer trade (especially within Europe) to supply a much more extensive market area through the embodiment of a strong export orientation. This allows it to access economies of scale (usually denied to ESTPROD/UK subsidiaries by a limited national market) as a source of competitiveness, replacing the often compromising pursuit of economies of scope in the TMR.

Thus it can be assumed that the ESTPROD/EUR subsidiary will focus on a specialised expertise in the supply of a narrower (rationalised) product range than ESTPROD/UK. It also seems very likely that this role would need even more limited functional scope than the first. Thus a fully-networked RPS will supply an already completely-formulated product to an externally-coordinated MNE network, thereby eliminating scope for marketing or technological creativity and reducing its management role to the dependent implementation of a position in a wider strategy that it is unlikely to be able to influence.

Of the 185 subsidiaries that evaluated ESTPROD/EUR, only six (3.2 per cent) said it was their only role, but 86 (46.5 per cent) rated it a predominant one, 40 (21.6 per cent) felt it took a secondary position whilst 53 (28.6 per cent) believed it was absent. The AR (Table 3.1) shows that this virtually rates it alongside ESTPROD/UK as the currently most prevalent subsidiary status amongst MNE operations in the UK. In terms of home country, this role has emerged most decisively in the subsidiaries of Japanese MNEs.

ESTPROD/EUR activity is most prevalent in two industries, pharmaceuticals and electronics and electrical appliances, where it might have been expected to encounter some notable constraints. In the case of pharmaceuticals, the frequently observed importance of host-country regulations, and of distinctive elements in consumer tastes, might have been expected to have fragmented the European market in such a manner that the need to adjust products to meet particular national needs would severely curtail the scope for one supply location to meet the wider regional demand for a good. In fact the UK subsidiaries of European and US MNEs both defy this proposition. A possible element in this may be that the reasons for product adaptation may be easy to both discern and communicate in the pharmaceutical industry. Thus specific regulatory requirements (in any case increasingly homogenised, within the European Union, EU, at least) should be set out in a clearly documented form which can be easily communicated, as perhaps may be some relevant aspects of consumer tastes (for example, for medications in tablet, capsule or liquid form). In this way it may be open to a UK pharmaceutical subsidiary to produce a particular product in a number of variants to meet the needs of a range of separate national markets, without this involving the close association with consumers in each of them that is often considered necessary to achieve an effective adaptation process.

In electronics it could have been anticipated that unique European standards (for example, TV transmission systems and electricity supply characteristics) might have meant that US and Japanese companies would need to develop distinctive new versions of their products for the European market, with these embodying many characteristics that go well beyond the mere adaptation of those that originated in the home country. In fact, Japanese and US electronics

MNEs were both able to use their UK subsidiaries very extensively as bases from which to supply established goods to the wider European market. By contrast European electronics MNE UK subsidiaries were very strongly committed to the ESTPROD/UK role, but revealed relatively little involvement in supply to the continental European markets (ESTPROD/EUR). This may mean that European electronics companies are interested mainly in niche markets that are of limited concern to US and Japanese MNEs, and have a noted propensity to adapt goods to national (at least UK) market requirements in pursuit of this objective.

A second type of RPS positioning was designated as 'to play a role in the MNE group's European supply network by producing and exporting component parts for assembly elsewhere' (COMPART). Here again, the emergence of this role in an MNE's European supply network would aim to optimise the more static dimension of efficiency by achieving economies of scale, or by allowing the manufacture of particular components in locations that are especially favourable in terms of costs of relevant inputs. This role proved to be by far the least prevalent of the four, with 127 (70.2 per cent) of the 181 subsidiaries that evaluated it saying it played no part in their operations, whilst only 11 (6.1 per cent) rated it a predominant role and two (1.1 per cent) focused on it uniquely. This could mean that MNEs tend not to make extensive use of such dispersed component-supply networks in their European strategies,[2] and/or that the UK is not often considered a particularly relevant location for COMPART subsidiaries. Table 3.1 shows that the COMPART role is somewhat more prevalent in US subsidiaries than those of Japanese and European MNEs, especially through a strong participation in industries with relatively strong orientation to the role (automobiles, chemicals, pharmaceuticals).

The final role analysed was defined as 'to develop, produce and market for the UK and/or European (or wider) markets, new products additional to the MNE group's existing range' (DEVELPROD). This, therefore, covers the WPM/RPM subsidiary of our tripartite scope typology. As described in detail in the previous chapter, the defining characteristic of the PM role is the widening of the functional scope of the subsidiary in order to allow it to move beyond the dependent supply of established products through the derivation of its own distinctive contribution to its group's capabilities. As in the ESTPROD/EUR and COMPART roles, the DEVELPROD subsidiary's status is again predicated on specialisation. However, here this is not secured by a static ability to apply homogeneous inputs to a part of its group's standardised technology in a cost-effective manner, but rather through a dynamic ability to move the group's knowledge itself forward in the form of new applications in distinctive additional products. The PM subsidiaries' ability to win higher-value-added positions based around their distinctive competences automatically enhances the value of their own human capital by enabling management, engineering, scientific and other personnel to realise their potential more fully. The alleviation of the sense of frustration that is likely to have beset such personnel when their scope was constrained to the dependent implementation of standardised technologies within externally-determined group-level supply programmes is thus likely to be a substantial benefit of a DEVELPROD subsidiary's accession to a more autonomous and creative situation.[3] The host-country location characteristics relevant to securing the DEVELPROD role are thus less likely to be the cost and availability of standard production inputs, but instead the scope and quality of creative assets in the form of managerial, marketing and scientific personnel and the wider local knowledge community (its technological heritage and current research capabilities).

Although our definition of the DEVELPROD subsidiary is agnostic with regard to market scope, we suggested in Chapter 2 that the distinctive character of its products, and the need to cover the extensive fixed costs of creating them, are likely to earn and require substantial export orientation. For such subsidiaries in the UK, Europe (at least) is a presumed target market area. Whilst always seeking to extend the product range that can logically be derived from their particular competences, the PM subsidiaries are also likely to be aware of the dangers of dissipating these genuine strengths in pursuit of more tenuous expansion plans (which could also impinge on the territory of other parts of their group and thereby compromise the benefits of supportive interdependencies). Thus the subsidiaries are most likely to specialise in a limited product range.

Of the 184 respondents who evaluated the DEVELPROD role, 16 (8.7 per cent) said it was their only one, 50 (27.2 per cent) that it took a predominant position, 63 (34.2 per cent) that it was only a secondary commitment and 55 (29.9 per cent) felt it played no part in their operations. In terms of ARs (Table 3.1) the DEVELPROD role currently matches ESTPROD/UK and ESTPROD/EUR in US and European subsidiaries, but falls well behind them in Japanese. This is likely to reflect different states in evolutionary processes. For the Japanese MNEs it seems plausible that they are currently building an initial base in Europe around familiar goods with well-established market positions (the lead position of ESTPROD/EUR), but also likely that once they have achieved greater experience with the host environment they may seek to encompass the more localised creative scope of the DEVELPROD role. The longer-established US subsidiaries may already be substantially committed to processes of restructuring, with ESTPROD/UK operations undergoing a metamorphosis to ESTPROD/EUR and then often further towards DEVEL-

Table 3.1 Roles of subsidiaries in the UK, by home country (average response)[1]

Industry	ESTPROD/UK				ESTPROD/EUR			
	USA	Japan	Europe	Total	USA	Japan	Europe	Total
Food	2.80		2.00	2.56	2.80		2.00	2.33
Automobiles	2.00	2.43	2.50	2.24	2.33	2.14	3.00	2.33
Aerospace	2.20			2.33	1.60			2.17
Electronics and electrical appliances	2.00	2.39	2.71	2.33	2.33	2.77	1.86	2.53
Mechanical engineering	2.25	2.22	1.78	2.08	2.38	2.00	2.44	2.27
Instruments	2.40	2.33	2.00	2.33	2.17	2.33	1.00	2.10
Industrial and agricultural chemicals	2.50	2.00	1.75	2.14	2.08	2.00	2.00	2.03
Pharmaceuticals and consumer chemicals	2.40	2.00	2.20	2.27	2.40	2.00	2.80	2.55
Metal manufacture and products	2.50	1.25		2.09	2.25	2.00		1.90
Other manufacturing	1.00	2.67	2.33	2.44	1.00	2.22	1.00	1.73
Total	2.28	2.31	2.13	2.26^2	2.24	2.41	2.07	2.24^2

	COMPART					DEVELPROD		
Food	1.00		1.50	1.11	2.80		2.50	2.67
Automobiles	1.88	1.29	2.00	1.65	2.50	2.43	1.50	2.35
Aerospace	1.20			1.33	2.00			2.17
Electronics and electrical appliances	1.42	1.45	1.14	1.41	1.83	1.97	2.14	1.96
Mechanical engineering	1.86	1.11	1.13	1.33	2.71	2.22	2.22	2.36
Instruments	1.20	1.67	1.00	1.33	2.43	2.00	3.00	2.36
Industrial and agricultural chemicals	1.75	1.00	1.42	1.48	2.33	2.00	2.08	2.17
Pharmaceuticals and consumer chemicals	1.60	1.00	1.40	1.45	2.00	3.00	1.60	1.91
Metal manufacture and products	1.25	1.00		1.22	2.25	2.00		2.20
Other manufacturing	1.00	1.33	1.00	1.20	1.00	1.67	2.20	1.80
Total	1.52	1.32	1.29	1.38^2	2.27	2.03	2.09	2.15^2

Roles of subsidiaries:
ESTPROD/UK: To produce for the UK market products that are already established in our MNE group's product range.
ESTPROD/EUR: To play a role in the MNE group's European supply network by specialising in the production and export of part of the established product range.
COMPART: To play a role in the MNE group's European supply network by producing and exporting component parts for assembly elsewhere.
DEVELPROD: To develop, produce and market for the UK and/or European (or wider) markets, new products additional to the MNE group's existing range.

Notes:
1. Respondents were asked to evaluate each role as (i) our only role, (ii) a predominant role, (iii) a secondary role, (iv) not a part of our role. The average response is calculated by allocating a value of 4 to 'our only role', 3 to 'a predominant' role, 2 to 'a secondary role' and 1 to 'not a part of our role'.
2. Includes subsidiaries of MNEs from Australia and Canada.
Source: Survey of producing subsidiaries.

PROD status. We can also speculate that for European MNEs' UK subsidiaries the prospects for future DEVELPROD operations may be more vulnerable. Thus as these continental groups develop more pan-European perspectives on product development (as a response to regional integration), they may tend to base such creative scope mainly in their parent (home-country) operations.

Food industry subsidiaries are the most strongly committed to the DEVELPROD role, notably through the involvement of US operations. Since this parallels their strong evaluation of ESTPROD/UK, it may be that these US food subsidiaries initially needed to adapt their established goods quite extensively to meet UK tastes and conditions, and in the process generated types of in-house competences that then encouraged complementary commitment to more extensive product creation. The pervasive strength of DEVELPROD in mechanical engineering reflects the need to supply customised capital goods to meet the specifications of individual firms. The result for instruments predominantly reflects that of US firms, and may indicate the need for these MNEs to apply their existing technology more competitively in Europe through the creation of products that fully meet the distinctive needs of particular scientists, health services, companies, and so on. The strength of product development in automobiles derives from the behaviour of US and Japanese subsidiaries. Thus for European MNEs, their UK subsidiaries operate only as a supply base for cars and components that are already designed to fully meet the needs of the regional market, but US and Japanese companies need to provide their UK facilities with a much more extensive responsibility to contribute to the creation of specifically European parts of their product range.

Pharmaceuticals and electronics are the two industries where DEVELPROD is least prevalent in UK subsidiaries. Taken with its prevalence in food and mechanical engineering, we can comment (Papanastassiou and Pearce, 1997b) that it seems that participation in a technologically dynamic industry is neither necessary nor sufficient to generate subsidiary-level product development operations. Thus 'implementation of such operations is clearly more likely to reflect a wide range of subsidiary and host-country endowments and motivations, rather than predominantly respond to the degree of technological opportunity endemic in the industry' (1997b, p.12). In industries where leading current technology paradigms (biotechnology; microelectronics and information technology) are very influential, the need for a major MNE to maximise the benefits from systematic involvement with relevant scientific progress may lead to greater centralised control over the firm's own technological trajectory, with relatively limited scope for creative initiatives to be dispersed into production subsidiaries.

Thus it seems that in pharmaceuticals most product development is centralised (or at least carried out in laboratories with no direct association with a particular production operation) and can be relatively easily and effectively communicated to specialised production subsidiaries. These, as suggested earlier, may then supply the product to a range of markets using their own in-house capacity to differentiate it as necessary. In electronics, too, it seems that factors that might have provoked the need for US or Japanese MNEs to develop specific European product variants can also take mainly clearly documented or codified forms (regulations or technical specification), rather than involving the types of diffused and evolving taste-related characteristics that need subsidiary-level marketing expertise to detect and, therefore, in-house technological competence to respond to with adequate sensitivity. Thus where the relevant specifications or characteristics are defined sufficiently precisely, the development of a European product can again be carried out away from the specialised production facility, either in the MNE's home country or in a dedicated R&D unit serving all European operations.

To gain some broad indication of the process of evolution amongst subsidiaries, respondents to the questionnaire were asked if their predominant (or only) role had changed in recent years, and if so what their previous main role had been. Although the results reported in Table 3.2 indicate a relatively low perception of such changes in role, some relevant perspectives are still quite clearly indicated. The declining position of TMRs is suggested firstly by the fact that only 13 per cent of current ESTPROD/UK subsidiaries had previously had another role, compared with 17 per cent of DEVELPROD (WPM/RPMs), 21 per cent of ESTPROD/EUR and 29 per cent of COMPART (the two variants of RPSs). Also, over half the subsidiaries that took on the RPS roles had previously been TMRs (ESTPROD/UK). The new DEVEL-PROD subsidiaries were rather more likely to have emerged from ESTPROD/EUR operations, which at least hints that the evolutionary process from TMRs may so far have tended to involve firstly the acquisition of the new wider market focus (RPS) and subsequently the further addition of creative scope (WPM/RPM).

A complementary question asked respondents if they expected a change in their predominant (or only) role in the near future, and if so what they believed their new main role would be. Once again, despite quite low overall propensity to predict such changes, clear perspectives are nevertheless suggested.

As Table 3.3 shows, 17 per cent of ESTPROD/UK respondents anticipated a change in their role, over half directly to DEVELPROD status. This suggests that, with increased understanding of the strategic possibilities for subsidiary

Table 3.2 Previous roles of MNE subsidiaries in the UK, by current role[1]

Previous role	Current predominant (or only) role[2] (per cent)			
	ESTPROD/ UK	ESTPROD/ EUR	COMPART	DEVELPROD
No change in role	86.9	79.3	71.4	82.8
Previous role ESTPROD/UK	–	10.9	21.4	3.1
Previous role ESTPROD/EUR	3.6	–	0	6.3
Previous role COMPART	0	0	–	1.6
Previous role DEVELPROD	4.8	4.3	7.1	–
Total	100.0	100.0	100.0	100.0

Notes:
1. Respondents were asked if their predominant role had changed in recent (e.g. past 10) years, and if so to specify which had been their earlier predominant role.
2. For definitions of subsidiary roles see table 3.1.

Source: Survey of producing subsidiaries.

evolution in MNEs, an intermediate RPS stage may be less often necessary. Nevertheless, the final-product type of RPS role (ESTPROD/EUR) does seem currently to be the most stable, with only 13 per cent anticipating a change of role. The addition of creative scope to become WPM/RPM operations (DEVELPROD) is clearly the most strongly expected change for these RP subsidiaries. By contrast, 29 per cent of COMPART subsidiaries anticipated a broadening of their role, sometimes into the supply of established products (ESTPROD/EUR) but mostly all the way to product development operations. Although the DEVELPROD role is clearly the one that is most decisively gaining ground, 18 per cent of subsidiaries that are currently playing that role also anticipate a change. The most prevalent new role for these subsidiaries is ESTPROD/EUR. Thus it appears that some WPM/RPM subsidiaries expect their long-term operations to crystallise around the supply of the new products they have already taken responsibility for successfully putting into place, with a consequent downgrading of the creative element in their activity.

Table 3.3 Likely future roles of MNE subsidiaries in the UK, by current role[1]

	Current predominant (or only) role[2] (per cent)			
Previous role	ESTPROD/ UK	ESTPROD/ EUR	COMPART	DEVELPROD
No change in role	82.9	86.7	71.4	82.1
Future role ESTPROD/UK	–	1.1	0	3.0
Future role ESTPROD/EUR	3.7	–	7.1	10.4
Future role COMPART	2.4	2.2	–	1.5
Future role DEVELPROD	9.8	8.9	21.4	–
Unspecified future role	1.2			
Total	100.0	100.0	100.0	100.0

Notes:

1. Respondents were asked if they considered that there would be a change in their predominant role in the future, and if so to specify the most likely new predominant role.
2. For definitions of subsidiary roles, see Table 3.1.

Source: Survey of producing subsidiaries.

MARKET ORIENTATION OF SUBSIDIARIES

The likely emergence of a strong degree of export orientation, as a key element in the strategic repositioning of MNE subsidiaries, has already played a central role in our earlier analysis. Aspects of this were investigated in the survey of subsidiaries in the UK through two groups of questions. The first sought evidence on the overall position of exports in the production of subsidiaries, and the proportion of any such exports that are accounted for by intra-group trade and intermediate goods. The second asked respondents to evaluate the status in their operations of four market areas (UK, EU, non-EU Europe, non-Europe).

Table 3.4 presents a frequency distribution of subsidiaries' replies to the question that asked them the proportion of their total production that was exported. The determinants of this export ratio (EXPRAT) were tested in a regression equation (reported in Table 3.5) which included industry dummy variables (with the 'other manufacturing' sector serving as the omitted

Table 3.4 Proportion of production that is exported by MNE subsidiaries in the UK

	Exports as a share of production (percentage of cases)					
	0	0.1 to 30.0	10.1 to 30.0	30.1 to 60.0	Over 60.0	Total
By industry						
Food		44.4	22.2	22.2	11.1	100.0
Automobiles	5.6	16.7	16.7	44.4	16.7	100.0
Aerospace	33.3	16.7		33.3	16.7	100.0
Electronics and electrical appliances	12.0	10.0	10.0	26.0	42.0	100.0
Mechanical engineering		12.5	20.8	33.3	33.3	100.0
Instruments	9.1	18.2	9.1	9.1	54.5	100.0
Industrial and agricultural chemicals	11.1	25.9	7.4	25.9	29.6	100.0
Pharmaceuticals and consumer chemicals	25.0	8.3	8.3	33.3	25.0	100.0
Metal manufacture and products	9.1	18.2	18.2	18.2	36.4	100.0
Other manufacturing	26.7		26.7	33.3	13.3	100.0
Total	11.5	15.3	13.7	28.4	31.1	100.0
By home country						
USA	12.1	12.1	12.1	22.7	40.9	100.0
Japan	9.0	10.4	19.4	31.3	29.9	100.0
Europe	16.3	23.3	7.0	30.2	23.3	100.0
Total[1]	11.5	15.3	13.7	28.4	31.1	100.0

Note:
1. Includes subsidiaries of MNEs from Australia and Canada.

Source: Survey of producing subsidiaries.

dummy), home-country dummies (with the continental European group of companies serving as the omitted group) and the four subsidiary roles introduced in the previous section.

The UK-based subsidiaries emerge with a quite substantial overall commitment to exporting. Thus 31.1 per cent exported over 60 per cent of

Table 3.5 Regression tests of export characteristics of MNE subsidiaries in the UK

	EXPRAT	INTRAEXP	INTEREXP
	Dependent variable		
Intercept	33.3086‡	7.0830	6.0237
	(2.70)	(0.42)	(0.34)
Food	−4.1919*	2.3068	−1.0347
	(−1.70)	(0.66)	(−0.29)
Automobiles	-4.2836	−0.4696	−0.2621
	(−0.42)	(−0.03)	(−0.02)
Aerospace	5.9793	−2.6491	5.5728
	(−0.87)	(−0.28)	(0.57)
Electronics	1.1130	2.7274	2.1872
	(0.53)	(0.93)	(0.70)
Mechanical engineering	0.1208	0.2708	0.5438
	(0.09)	(0.15)	(0.28)
Instruments	2.4197	4.5787*	4.9081*
	(1.24)	(1.70)	(1.74)
Industrial chemicals	−0.5486	0.0858	7.7016*
	(−0.17)	(0.02)	(1.67)
Pharmaceuticals	0.6942	3.0197	1.2945
	(0.49)	(1.56)	(0.66)
Metals	0.5197	−1.6092	5.1298†
	(0.37)	(−0.82)	(2.51)
USA	0.9085	0.1017	−0.8121
	(1.59)	(0.13)	(−1.01)
Japan	0.4134	−0.5125	−0.6539
	(0.77)	(−0.69)	(−0.86)
Sales	0.0004	0.0106	−0.0057
	(0.08)	(1.33)	(−0.69)
ESTPROD/UK[1]	−11.3730‡	−0.1151	−6.2904*
	(−4.60)	(−0.03)	(−1.72)
ESTPROD/EUR	16.4517‡	10.9914‡	5.4433
	(6.20)	(3.04)	(1.43)
COMPART	−5.8205*	1.1874	14.2394‡
	(−1.78)	(0.26)	(3.09)
DEVELPROD	1.7854	−3.2260	−2.6824
	(0.70)	(−0.95)	(−0.76)
R^2	0.3331	0.1903	0.1843
F	4.71‡	2.17‡	2.08†
n	168	165	164

Dependent variables:
EXPRAT: Percentage of subsidiary production that is exported.
INTRAEXP: Percentage of subsidiary exports that go to other parts of MNE group.
INTEREXP: Percentage of subsidiary exports that are intermediate goods.
n number of observations; ‡ significant at 1%; † significant at 5%; * significant at 10%.

Note:
1. For description of subsidiary roles, see Table 3.1.

their output, and a further 28.4 per cent between 30 and 60 per cent, whilst only 26.8 per cent exported less than 10 per cent. Export orientation is strongest amongst US (where 63.6 per cent exported over 30 per cent of output) and Japanese (61.2 per cent) subsidiaries. The relatively lower degree of export orientation in European MNE subsidiaries is not only reflected in the rather small 53.2 per cent that exported over 30 per cent of production, but quite decisively in the 39.3 per cent that exported less than 10 per cent (compared to only 24.2 per cent of US and 19.4 per cent of Japanese). The regression for EXPRAT in Table 3.5 tends to support these perspectives. Thus even with the inclusion of the subsidiary role variables which sometimes incorporate different market commitments, the US and Japanese dummies are both positively signed (and approaching significance in the case of the US).[4]

It has been suggested (Papanastassiou and Pearce, 1996; Pearce and Papanastassiou, 1997) that both demand-side and supply-side influences may have led to these different degrees of export orientation. In terms of response to demand it may be that subsidiaries of European MNEs are better able than those from the US or Japan to perceive, and/or are more willing to respond to, distinctive tastes and needs of the UK market. Where such a response leads to extensive adaptation or development of products in order to meet particular local conditions this will, at the same time, somewhat reduce their acceptability in other European markets, thereby lowering their exportability (relative to the more standardised output of US or Japanese subsidiaries). That their relatively low overall export orientation is not reflected in a substantial difference in the prevalence of the ESTPROD/UK and ESTPROD/EUR types in European MNE subsidiaries (Table 3.1) may suggest an unusually strong UK-market focus of their DEVELPROD activity. This will emerge as compatible with other results in subsequent chapters.

On the supply side, when US and Japanese MNEs wish to centralise the production of a good for the European market, they have the freedom to make an optimal choice of factory location (in response to costs, availability of suitable labour skills and other significant inputs). However, if a European company plans for the centralised production of a good for the wider regional market, it may still do so through a more bounded rationality view of the location decision in which the home country is automatically favoured until very strong evidence emerges to point to a preferred site elsewhere. If such a perspective does prevail, then it would mean that relatively few of the UK (and other) operations of European MNEs outside their home country would have a strong export capability.[5]

Electronics emerges in the frequency distributions (Table 3.4) as a notably export-oriented industry, especially through the operations of Japanese and US subsidiaries (with 73.3 per cent and 53.3 per cent of respondents, respectively, exporting over 30 per cent of their output). Instruments and mechanical engineering also reveal quite strong export propensities, whilst food and aerospace focus most clearly on the UK market. Pharmaceuticals and, to some degree, chemicals, reveal a rather dichotomous performance, with close-to-average shares of respondents exporting over 30 per cent, but also notably high proportions in the low export ranges.

When the influence of subsidiaries' roles on export performance is investigated in the regression equations, ESTPROD/UK and ESTPROD/EUR produce (significantly at the 1 per cent level in both cases) the negative and positive relationships with EXPRAT indicated by their definitions. Although DEVELPROD does provide a positive sign (as our earlier discussion of the role led us to predict), this falls well short of significance. Despite its definition, COMPART is found to be significantly negatively related to EXPRAT, indicating that the more a subsidiary plays this role the more likely it is to supply companies in the UK. Later, we shall develop the suggestion that COMPART subsidiaries in the UK are often involved in product-creation processes, deriving new input goods in a collaborative manner to support a new product that is being created by a customer. Effective implementation of such involvement in an innovation process would benefit greatly from the ease of communication that results from co-location in the UK.

Our approach to subsidiary positioning in contemporary MNEs clearly indicates that export orientation is likely to reflect the possession by their UK operations of some form of specialised status within (mainly) European supply programmes. The extent to which this then implies involvement in intra-group trade was investigated through a question that asked subsidiaries to report the proportion of their exports that were supplied to another part of the same MNE. Table 3.6 reports frequency distributions of the replies to this question, whilst Table 3.5 includes a regression test of this variable (INTRAEXP) against the same independent variables as for EXPRAT.

It can be suggested from Table 3.6 that subsidiaries tend to focus quite strongly on *either* intra-group or extra-group modes of export marketing. Thus, whereas 25.7 per cent reported that over 60 per cent of their exports went through intra-group channels, 56.6 per cent said that less than 10 per cent were traded in this way. Although a notably high proportion of Japanese subsidiaries reported no intra-group exports, the regression tests confirm the overall impression of the frequency distributions that there is no systematic difference in use of intra-group trade between subsidiaries from different home-country MNEs. In terms of industries, intra-group trade appears strongest in pharmaceuticals, food, electronics and instruments and is least prominent in automobiles, aerospace and metals.

Table 3.5 shows that in the regression tests of INTRAEXP the most decisive result for subsidiary roles is a highly significant positive relationship with ESTPROD/EUR. This confirms an intuitive expectation that, where the subsidiary produces an existing good for which European markets are already likely to be well established, the supply is most likely to be organised through a group-marketing network rather than being its own autonomous responsibility. Although the negative sign on DEVELPROD falls well short of significance, its contrast with the strong positive one for ESTPROD/EUR may still be considered to provide support for our suggestion (Chapter 2) that, as subsidiaries make the transition to the more autonomously creative product development role, their responsibility for their own good is often likely to include its marketing independently of group networks.[6]

The insignificant result for COMPART again somewhat confounds its definition. This may then be compatible with a suggestion that component supply subsidiaries are in fact often involved in collaborative creative interaction with independent customers, so that where they do export it is as likely to be outside as inside their MNE group. Finally, the insignificance of ESTPROD/UK indicates that where residual exports do occur in mainly UK-market-focused subsidiaries, they have no tendency to be either intra- or extra-group.

Respondents were also asked to report the percentage of their exports that are intermediate goods (for example, component parts, goods requiring further processing). The positioning of such exports could range from the cost-efficient supply of standardised inputs to group networks to the provision of newly developed components to independent customers. Supply of such goods does not in fact emerge as being of major importance in subsidiary exports (Table 3.7) with 57.7 per cent of subsidiaries not undertaking any and only 22.9 per cent indicating that over 60 per cent of exports were of this type.

Overall systematic differences in this type of export orientation do not emerge between home-country origins of subsidiaries. Amongst industries, though, intermediate products do emerge as a notable part of exports in subsidiaries in metals, instruments, pharmaceuticals and industrial chemicals. Of these, pharmaceuticals and instruments also have above-average

Table 3.6 Proportion of exports of MNE subsidiaries in the UK that are intra-group trade[1]

| | Intra-group exports as a percentage of total exports (percentage of cases) | | | | |
	0	0.1 to 10.0	10.1 to 60.0	Over 60.0	Total
By industry					
Food	12.5	25.0	25.0	37.5	100.0
Automobiles	47.1	17.6	17.6	17.6	100.0
Aerospace	50.0	33.1		16.7	100.0
Electronics and electrical appliances	30.6	14.3	20.4	34.7	100.0
Mechanical engineering	26.9	26.9	26.9	19.2	100.0
Instruments	10.0	40.0	10.0	40.0	100.0
Industrial and agricultural chemicals	26.9	34.6	23.1	15.4	100.0
Pharmaceuticals and consumer chemicals		37.5		62.5	100.0
Metal manufacture and products	63.6	27.3		9.1	100.0
Other manufacturing	42.9	28.6	14.3	14.3	100.0
Total	31.4	25.1	17.7	25.7	100.0
By home country					
USA	24.6	27.9	19.7	27.9	100.0
Japan	41.8	17.9	14.9	25.4	100.0
Europe	22.5	35.0	20.0	22.5	100.0
Total[2]	31.4	25.1	17.7	25.7	100.0

Notes:
1. Respondents were asked what percentage of their exports go to other parts of the MNE group.
2. Includes subsidiaries of MNEs from Australia and Canada.

Source: Survey of producing subsidiaries.

orientation to intra-group exports, perhaps indicating integrated supply networking, whilst metals and, to some extent, industrial chemicals are below average in this respect, supplying intermediates more often to independent customers.

In the regression tests (Table 3.5) this dependent variable (INTEREXP) is most decisively positively related to COMPART, in line with the definition of the latter (and despite its relative UK market orientation discussed earlier).

Table 3.7 *Proportion of exports of MNE subsidiaries in the UK that are intermediate products[1]*

| | Intermediate products as a percentage of total exports (percentage of cases) | | | |
	0	0.1 to 60.0	Over 60.0	Total
By industry				
Food	88.9	11.1		100.0
Automobiles	64.7	23.5	11.8	100.0
Aerospace	50.0	33.3	16.7	100.0
Electronics and electrical appliances	58.7	23.9	17.4	100.0
Mechanical engineering	65.4	19.2	15.4	100.0
Instruments	50.0	10.0	40.0	100.0
Industrial and agricultural chemicals	42.9	14.3	42.9	100.0
Pharmaceuticals and consumer chemicals	22.2	55.6	22.2	100.0
Metal manufacture and products	45.5		54.5	100.0
Other manufacturing	84.6	7.7	7.7	100.0
Total	57.7	19.4	22.9	100.0
By home country				
USA	50.0	29.0	21.0	100.0
Japan	66.2	15.4	18.5	100.0
Europe	58.5	12.2	29.3	100.0
Total[2]	57.7	19.4	22.9	100.0

Notes:
1. Respondents were asked what percentage of their exports were intermediate goods (e.g. component parts; goods requiring further processing).
2. Includes subsidiaries of MNEs from Australia and Canada.

Source: Survey of producing subsidiaries.

ESTPROD/EUR also nears positive significance, indicating that the more important is a systematic, and probably quite dependently networked, supply position to the operations of a subsidiary, the more likely are its exports to include some intermediate goods. If this means of intermediate product supply embodies the cost-efficiency motive most strongly, the more independent and creative type of input supply may be mostly subsumed (in line with earlier suggestions) into COMPART. The insignificance of DEVELPROD is then compatible with that possibility. Finally, the significant negative relationship between ESTPROD/UK and INTEREXP indicates that residual exports from this type of subsidiary are mainly final products, perhaps supplying rather *ad hoc* external niche markets for goods primarily aimed at UK tastes and conditions.

To secure a more disaggregated perspective on the market orientation of MNE subsidiaries in the UK, respondents to the survey were asked to evaluate the degree of importance in their supply profiles of four market areas. Table 3.8 provides frequency distribution results from these replies and Table 3.9 reports regression tests comparable to those in Table 3.5.

The first market investigated was that of the host country. Of course, as a major segment of the European market, the UK would be expected to be a significant supply area for these subsidiaries, even in the absence of any form of traditional (TMR-type) local-market orientation. Even so, the UK market emerges as of quite distinctive prevalence in the subsidiaries' activity, being rated their only market by 12.7 per cent and a major one by 63.5 per cent, whilst only 22.2 per cent felt it was reduced to merely a secondary position and 1.6 per cent excluded it. The strongest local market focus emerges for European MNE subsidiaries (confirming the impression of Table 3.4), and in food (no respondents rating it as less than a main market) and (to a less pronounced degree) automobiles, aerospace, metals, industrial chemicals and pharmaceuticals.

Of the three external market areas investigated, the rest of the EU emerges as the most relevant to the responding subsidiaries' supply profiles. Thus 2.1 per cent rated it their only market, 43.4 per cent considered it to be a main market and the same proportion a secondary one, whilst 11.1 per cent did not supply it. Whilst, in line with earlier results, European MNEs' subsidiaries were clearly least oriented to EU markets, a further difference emerged here in terms of home country. Thus Japanese subsidiaries seem to target EU markets more decisively than those of US companies, an impression that is also indicated in the regression results (Table 3.9) after controlling for industry composition and subsidiary roles. This suggests that the relatively recent wave of Japanese investments is more precisely motivated by the growth potential and/or protection fears that they associate with current developments in the EU, whilst US MNEs may be restructuring their rather older European operations from a more broadly based perspective on the wider region's potential. Electronics and instruments are the industries with the most clearly defined orientation to EU markets, and food and pharmaceuticals least so.

Although playing some role in the markets of over three-quarters of the subsidiaries, other European countries are still notably of less importance than those of the EU. Here 23.0 per cent of subsidiaries did not supply these other

Table 3.8 Relative importance of markets supplied by MNE subsidiaries in the UK

	Importance of market (percentage of cases)									
	UK market					Other EU markets				
	A	B	C	D	Total	A	B	C	D	Total
By industry										
Food		100.0			100.0		22.2	77.8		100.0
Automobiles	5.6	83.3	11.1		100.0	5.6	38.9	50.0	5.6	100.0
Aerospace	20.0	60.0	20.0		100.0	16.7	16.7	50.0	16.7	100.0
Electronics and electrical appliances	11.8	56.9	27.5	3.9	100.0	2.0	62.7	25.5	9.8	100.0
Mechanical engineering	3.8	57.7	38.5		100.0		46.2	46.2	7.7	100.0
Instruments	8.3	50.0	41.7		100.0		58.3	25.0	16.7	100.0
Industrial and agricultural chemicals	20.7	58.6	17.2	3.4	100.0		42.9	42.9	14.3	100.0
Pharmaceuticals and consumer chemicals	25.0	58.3	16.7		100.0		16.7	58.3	25.0	100.0
Metal manufacture and products		81.8	18.2		100.0	9.1	27.3	63.6		100.0
Other manufacturing	31.3	62.5	6.3		100.0		25.0	56.3	18.8	100.0
Total	12.7	63.5	22.2	1.6	100.0	2.1	43.4	43.4	11.1	100.0
By home country										
USA	11.6	60.9	26.1	1.4	100.0		42.9	45.7	11.4	100.0
Japan	10.3	61.8	25.0	2.9	100.0	4.4	55.9	33.8	5.9	100.0
Europe	20.0	64.4	15.6		100.0		31.8	47.7	20.5	100.0
Total[1]	12.7	63.5	22.2	1.6	100.0	2.1	43.4	43.4	11.1	100.0

	Other European markets					Markets outside Europe				
	A	B	C	D	Total	A	B	C	D	Total
By industry										
Food		11.1	66.7	22.2	100.0		55.6	44.4		100.0
Automobiles		11.8	76.5	11.8	100.0	11.8	64.7	23.5		100.0
Aerospace			66.7	33.3	100.0		60.0	40.0		100.0
Electronics and electrical appliances		23.5	58.8	17.6	100.0	5.9	58.8	35.3		100.0
Mechanical engineering	4.0	12.0	68.0	16.0	100.0	16.0	56.0	28.0		100.0
Instruments		16.7	58.3	25.0	100.0	41.7	41.7	16.7		100.0
Industrial and agricultural chemicals		21.4	50.0	28.6	100.0	17.9	50.0	28.6	3.6	100.0
Pharmaceuticals and consumer chemicals		16.7	50.0	33.3	100.0	8.3	66.7	25.0		100.0
Metal manufacture and products		9.1	63.6	27.3	100.0	18.2	45.5	36.4		100.0
Other manufacturing		6.3	56.3	37.5	100.0		50.0	50.0		100.0
Total	0.5	16.0	60.4	23.0	100.0	11.8	55.4	32.3	0.5	100.0
By home country										
USA	1.4	17.1	65.7	15.7	100.0	21.7	50.7	26.1	1.4	100.0
Japan		18.2	63.6	18.2	100.0	1.5	59.1	39.4		100.0
Europe		13.6	45.5	40.9	100.0	11.4	56.8	31.8		100.0
Total	0.5	16.0	60.4	23.0	100.0	11.8	55.4	32.3	0.5	100.0

Importance of markets.
A Our only market; B Main market; C A secondary part of our market; D Not a part of our market.

Note:
1. Includes subsidiaries of MNEs from Australia and Canada.
Source: Survey of producing subsidiaries.

European countries, 60.4 per cent rated them as merely a secondary market, and only 16.5 per cent a main (or only) market. Once again European MNEs emerge as least likely to use their UK subsidiaries to supply this part of the regional market, whilst the regressions suggest that US subsidiaries are most likely to target these countries which, relative to Japanese subsidiaries' orientation, precisely reverses the position for EU markets. This again indicates that longer experience of operations in Europe provides US subsidiaries with perspectives that can easily enable them to encompass markets outside the EU in their decision making, whilst for the Japanese the initial preoccupation is more decisively with the current members of the Union.

Although clearly the least important of the areas investigated, markets outside Europe were nevertheless of some relevance to a majority of responding subsidiaries. Thus while only 12.3 per cent rated these countries as constituting a major (or only) part of their market, 55.4 per cent believed them to represent a secondary one, whilst 32.3 per cent did not supply them. By home country of MNE, the extent of access to non-European markets differs somewhat by comparison with their patterns of European-market supply. Most notably it is the Japanese subsidiaries that are least inclined to supply markets outside Europe. This emerges as a significant negative result in the regression tests (Table 3.9), clearly contrasting with the significant positive result for supply of the EU. This is again indicative of the very precise targeting of the EU as the dominant strategic priority of these subsidiaries, and is also likely to reflect a continued ability of Japanese MNEs to supply leading markets outside Europe from well-established cost-effective production sources (for example, in Japan and Southeast Asia). Overall, the results for Japanese MNE subsidiaries suggest that whilst there has, in practice, been a very *positive* use of sourcing patterns within Europe (most particularly towards the EU), the initial entry decision may, nevertheless, have had strong elements of a *negative* import-substitution motivation which perceived the region as an important but potentially isolated segment of the global economy.

Reflecting the more cosmopolitan market scope of US subsidiaries (notably reflected in their relatively strong accessing of non-EU European markets), these emerge as modestly the most likely to supply goods outside Europe. A relatively distinctive commitment to these wider global markets by European subsidiaries (greater than that of Japanese and their own orientation to non-EU markets in Europe) may also be discerned. In line with our earlier observation (and points to be elaborated subsequently), this may reflect a desire of these European MNE UK subsidiaries to retain a high-value-added DEVELPROD scope that they feel discouraged from exercising towards European markets. One outlet for this (alongside an unusually strong focus on the local market)

Table 3.9 Regression tests of markets supplied by MNE subsidiaries in the UK

		Dependent variable (market)		
	UK markets	Other EU markets	Other European markets	Markets outside Europe
Intercept	3.2685‡	1.1294‡	1.3657‡	1.4307‡
	(13.61)	(4.51)	(5.50)	(5.73)
Food	0.0031	−0.0226	−0.0116	−0.0811
	(0.06)	(−0.52)	(−0.22)	(−1.54)
Automobiles	−0.0608	−0.0201	−0.0421	0.0125
	(−0.29)	(−0.09)	(−0.19)	(0.06)
Aerospace	−0.0691	0.1053	−0.1203	−0.1060
	(−0.46)	(0.71)	(−0.82)	(−0.68)
Electronics	−0.0524	0.0254	0.0139	−0.0017
	(−1.22)	(0.57)	(0.31)	(−0.04)
Mechanical engineering	−0.0509*	0.0014	0.0056	0.0037
	(−1.87)	(0.05)	(0.20)	(0.13)
Instruments	−0.1026†	0.0334	−0.0237	0.0792*
	(−2.54)	(0.79)	(−0.57)	(1.89)
Industrial chemicals	−0.0426	0.0150	0.0098	0.0486
	(−0.68)	(0.23)	(0.15)	(0.75)
Pharmaceuticals	0.0018	−0.0390	−0.0098	0.0037
	(0.07)	(−1.44)	(−0.37)	(0.14)
Metals	−0.0251	0.0309	−0.0026	0.0167
	(−0.86)	(1.01)	(−0.09)	(0.55)
USA	−0.0212*	0.0032	0.0274†	0.0110
	(−1.94)	(0.28)	(2.36)	(0.95)
Japan	−0.0197	0.0220†	0.0136	−0.0242†
	(−1.02)	(1.99)	(1.23)	(−2.19)
ESTPROD/UK[1]	0.1628‡	-0.0665	−0.1472‡	−0.1159†
	(3.27)	(-1.27)	(−2.83)	(−2.21)
ESTPROD/EUR	−0.2681‡	0.3603‡	0.2557‡	0.1887‡
	(−5.13)	(6.67)	(4.69)	(3.43)
COMPART	0.1577†	0.0480	0.0429	−0.0460
	(2.33)	(0.67)	(0.60)	(−0.64)
DEVELPROD	−0.0486	0.1832‡	0.0602	0.1411‡
	(−1.01)	(3.62)	(1.19)	(2.77)
R^2	0.2607	0.3441	0.2168	0.2319
F	3.88‡	5.77‡	3.01‡	3.26‡
n	181	181	179	178

Notes:
1. For description of subsidiary roles, see Table 3.1.
n Number of observations; ‡ significant at 1%; † significant at 5%; * significant at 10%.

may be in markets outside Europe. This would suggest that European MNEs' DEVELPROD subsidiaries in the UK would be much more likely to have WPMs than US or Japanese ones, where RPMs clearly predominate.

In the regression tests of Table 3.9, the ESTPROD/UK role fully conforms with its definition, being significantly positively related to supply of the UK market and significantly negatively to all three export-market areas. That its negative relationship with exports is least strong for EU countries may suggest that where residual exports do emerge from ESTPROD/UK subsidiaries they are most likely to find niche markets in this area, perhaps reflecting geographical proximity, higher levels of cultural familiarity, and easier communications. ESTPROD/EUR also conforms to definition, being significantly negatively related to supply of the UK market and positively related to all three export markets. The export relationship is strongest for the EU and weakest for markets outside Europe. If cost efficiency is an important determinant of ESTPROD/EUR motivation, then this pattern of responsiveness may well reflect an element of transport costs.

DEVELPROD is insignificantly negatively related to supply of the UK market and positively to all three export markets, although this is strongest (and significant) for the EU and non-European areas. This suggests that subsidiaries with RPMs tend to focus most decisively on EU tastes and needs, with such products then often finding quite substantial supplementary markets elsewhere in Europe. DEVELPROD's strong relationship with markets outside Europe may reflect the longer established global-marketing perspectives of US MNEs, but in particular could be associated with the pursuit of WPM positioning by subsidiaries of European MNEs that we have hypothesised. COMPART is significantly positively related to supply of the UK market, in a way that parallels its negative relationship with EXPRAT in Table 3.5. COMPART is positively signed for its relationship with both European market areas, and negatively so with that outside Europe, but always so weakly so that these results can provide only token indication that such component-supply subsidiaries tend to support production inside, rather than outside, Europe.

OTHER SUBSIDIARY CHARACTERISTICS

Age

In the survey of subsidiaries, 188 replied to a question that asked them to give the year of the operation's establishment in the UK. Overall, 34 had been set up before 1950 and 28 more in the years up to 1965. The period 1966 to 1979 saw the creation of 39 more of the subsidiaries, followed by a concentrated growth of numbers in the 1980s with 66, the remaining 21 being set up in 1990 or subsequently.

Table 3.10 confirms the particularly recent growth of Japanese MNE operations, with 83.4 per cent of their UK subsidiaries set up since 1980. By contrast, 54.5 per cent of US and 44.5 per cent of European subsidiaries were in place before 1966. Food, automobiles, industrial chemicals and pharmaceuticals MNEs were most likely to have established their UK subsidiaries in the earlier periods, whilst aerospace and electronics have emerged rather more strongly in recent years. Apart from a concentration of COMPART subsidiaries in the 1980s, there seems to be little relationship between the current leading role reported by subsidiaries and their year of establishment in the UK.

Size

As Table 3.11 shows, 53.4 per cent of the 183 subsidiaries that reported their size (sales or turnover) said it was less than £20 million, though 18.3 per cent were of over £100 million. US subsidiaries are most prevalent amongst those in the largest size group, although Europeans are of well-above-average prominence in the range from £40 to £100 million. The relatively small size of Japanese subsidiaries seems most likely to reflect their more recent origins, allowing scope for strong expansion. The DEVELPROD subsidiaries seem somewhat the least likely to be present in the largest size groups, perhaps indicating a preference in their creative imperatives for flexibility rather than sheer size.

Although only 155 subsidiaries were able to supply information on their size (sales) as a proportion of their MNE group's global operations, this still provides some relevant information (Table 3.12). Overall, 63.9 per cent of subsidiaries felt they accounted for less than 5 per cent of their group's sales (36.8 per cent less than 1 per cent), although 20.0 per cent considered their operations were more than one-tenth of those of the group. US subsidiaries were most likely to claim the more quantitatively significant position in their group's activity (almost one-third in the over 10 per cent group), whilst those of European MNEs tended to see themselves as relatively small. ESTPROD/UK subsidiaries have a greater tendency to be concentrated in the smallest relative size group (less than 1 per cent) than ESTPROD/EUR, while the position is reversed in the largest group (over 10 per cent). This is indicative of a rationalisation process where smaller numbers of efficiency-seeking RPSs replace the plethora of relatively small market-seeking TMRs implied by the earlier multidomestic strategy.

Table 3.10 Dates of establishment of UK subsidiaries

	Dates of establishment (per cent of cases)					
	Before 1950	1951–1965	1966–1979	1980–1989	1990 and later	Total
By industry						
Food	44.4	33.3		11.1	11.1	100.0
Automobiles	33.3	11.1	5.6	33.3	16.7	100.0
Aerospace		16.7	16.7	33.3	33.3	100.0
Electronics and electrical applicances	2.0	17.6	15.7	39.2	15.7	100.0
Mechanical engineering	24.0	16.0	28.0	20.0	12.0	100.0
Instruments	25.0	8.3	16.7	50.0		100.0
Industrial and agricultural chemicals	21.4	17.9	25.0	28.6	7.1	100.0
Pharmaceuticals	41.7	16.7	25.0	16.7		100.0
Metal manufacture and products	18.2	9.1	45.5	18.2	9.1	100.0
Other manufacturing	6.3		31.3	56.3	6.3	100.0
Total	18.1	14.9	20.7	35.1	11.2	100.0
By home country						
USA	26.5	27.9	22.1	22.1	1.5	100.0
Japan	1.5	1.5	14.7	57.4	25.0	100.0
Europe	28.9	15.6	26.7	24.4	4.4	100.0
Total[1]	18.1	14.9	20.7	35.1	11.2	100.0

By subsidiary type[2]

ESTPROD/UK	20.7	9.8	17.1	40.2	12.2	100.0
ESTPROD/EUR	21.7	15.2	15.2	35.9	12.0	100.0
COMPART	7.7	15.4	15.4	61.5		100.0
DEVELPROD	20.3	18.8	15.6	29.7	15.6	100.0

Notes:

1. Includes subsidiaries of MNEs from Australia and Canada.
2. Covers subsidiaries that described themselves as 'only' or 'predominantly' each type. For definitions see table 3.1.

Source: Survey of producing subsidiaries.

81

Table 3.11 Size of subsidiaries in the UK

| | Size range[1] – £m (per cent of cases) | | | | | |
	less than 10.0	10.0 to 19.9	20.0 to 39.9	40.0 to 99.9	100.0 and over	Total
By industry						
Food	11.1		11.1	11.1	66.7	100.0
Automobiles	16.7	16.7	44.4	11.1	11.1	100.0
Aerospace	50.0	16.7	16.7		16.7	100.0
Electronics and electrical applicances	16.3	24.5	14.3	26.5	18.4	100.0
Mechanical engineering	34.6	15.4	15.4	26.9	7.7	100.0
Instruments	45.5	18.2	9.1	9.1	18.2	100.0
Industrial and agricultural chemicals	16.0	32.0	20.0	16.0	16.0	100.0
Pharmaceuticals	8.3	16.7	16.7	16.7	41.7	100.0
Metal manufacture and products	63.6	18.2	9.1	9.1		100.0
Other manufacturing	56.3	6.3	18.8	12.5	6.3	100.0
Total	27.3	19.1	18.0	18.0	17.5	100.0
By home country						
USA	28.4	11.9	19.4	14.9	25.4	100.0
Japan	31.3	23.9	19.4	16.4	8.9	100.0
Europe	19.0	21.4	14.3	28.6	16.7	100.0
Total[2]	27.3	19.1	18.0	18.0	17.5	100.0

By subsidiary type[3]

ESTPROD/UK	28.0	18.3	8.5	17.1	28.0	100.0
ESTPROD/EUR	16.7	18.9	13.3	20.0	31.1	100.0
COMPART	7.7	30.8	23.1	15.4	23.1	100.0
DEVELPROD	26.7	26.7	16.7	11.7	18.3	100.0

Notes:
1. Sales or turnover.
2. Includes subsidiaries of MNEs from Australia and Canada.
3. Covers subsidiaries that described themselves as 'only' or 'predominantly' each type. For definitions see table 3.1.

Source: Survey of producing subsidiaries.

83

Table 3.12 Share of subsidiaries in the UK of the global sales of their MNE group

| | Share of group sales [1] (per cent of cases) | | | | |
	Up to 1.0%	1.1% to 5.0%	5.1% to 10.0%	over 10%	Total
By industry					
Food	22.2	22.2	11.1	44.4	100.0
Automobiles	21.4	42.9	14.3	21.4	100.0
Aerospace	66.7	16.7		16.7	100.0
Electronics and electrical applicances	35.1	21.6	16.2	27.0	100.0
Mechanical engineering	21.7	39.1	21.7	17.4	100.0
Instruments	22.2	33.3	33.3	11.1	100.0
Industrial and agricultural chemicals	48.0	12.0	20.0	20.0	100.0
Pharmaceuticals	44.4	44.4	11.1		100.0
Metal manufacture and products	40.0	30.0	10.0	20.0	100.0
Other manufacturing	61.5	23.1	7.7	7.7	100.0
Total	36.8	27.1	16.1	20.0	100.0
By home country					
USA	18.8	31.3	17.2	32.8	100.0
Japan	38.3	29.8	21.3	10.6	100.0
Europe	62.2	21.6	10.8	5.4	100.0
Total[2]	36.8	27.1	16.1	20.0	100.0
By subsidiary type[3]					
ESTPROD/UK	41.3	25.4	15.9	17.5	100.0
ESTPROD/EUR	31.0	28.2	15.5	25.4	100.0
COMPART	30.0	10.0	20.0	40.0	100.0
DEVELPROD	43.9	21.1	14.0	21.1	100.0

Notes:
1. Respondents were asked to report the proportion of the total global sales of their MNE group that they accounted for.
2. Includes subsidiaries of MNEs from Australia and Canada.
3. Covers subsidiaries that described themselves as 'only' or 'predominantly' each type. For definitions, see Table 3.1.

Source: Survey of producing subsidiaries

84

Means of establishment of subsidiaries

Exactly one-third of responding subsidiaries said that they had originally been set up 'by the creation of a new company with its own production facilities' (Table 3.13). Such greenfield investments were somewhat most prevalent for US subsidiaries and least so for European, as well as being notably strong in the pharmaceuticals and instruments industries. Establishment 'by the takeover of an existing UK company' accounted for 21.4 per cent of respondents, being of notable prevalence in European MNE subsidiaries and in industrial chemicals and aerospace. Only 11.9 per cent of subsidiaries said they had been created 'as a joint venture with an existing UK company'. The joint-venture route was relatively strong amongst Japanese operations (contrasting with a notably below average use of takeovers) and in automobiles. Apart from a distinctive prevalence of takeovers in COMPART operations there seems little sign of variation in mode of establishment in terms of subsidiaries' current strategic roles.

CONCLUSIONS

The survey evidence presented in this chapter supports the presence of two crucial elements in MNE subsidiaries' operations in the UK that need to be understood, supported and carefully nurtured. Firstly, the competitiveness of these subsidiaries increasingly targets European (and even wider) markets, rather than continuing an introverted focus on the national market. Although significant amounts of the subsidiaries' output is still sold in the UK, this is now usually more as an important segment of the European market than as a reflection of a defining strategic motivation. Thus the evolutionary processes in MNE subsidiaries indicate that it is the local-market-focused TMR role that is most clearly vulnerable as these companies restructure their operations to fulfil positions in integrated and cohesive globalised approaches to competitiveness. The apparent willingness of US MNEs to restructure and refocus their UK subsidiaries as significant elements in their European supply strategies, and of Japanese companies to choose the UK as a major entry point for their approach to supply within the region, is likely to be sustained only if it can be articulated with the decisive support of a public policy stance that sees the competitive future for British industry as inevitably defined by a positioning in such wider market environments.

Secondly, it is also clear from the survey results that MNE subsidiaries in the UK pursue their reoriented competitiveness through the presence of two strategic imperatives. Not only do they have a commitment to the cost-

Table 3.13 Means of establishment of subsidiaries in the UK

	Means of establishment (per cent)			
	A	B	C	Total
By industry				
Food	22.2	77.8		100.0
Automobiles	16.7	61.1	22.2	100.0
Aerospace	33.3	66.7		100.0
Electronics and electrical applicances	13.5	67.3	19.2	100.0
Mechanical engineering	19.2	69.2	11.6	100.0
Instruments	16.7	75.0	8.3	100.0
Industrial and agricultural chemicals	40.0	53.3	6.7	100.0
Pharmaceuticals	8.3	91.7		100.0
Metal manufacture and products	18.2	72.7	9.1	100.0
Other manufacturing	31.3	56.3	12.4	100.0
Total	21.4	66.7	11.9	100.0
By home country				
USA	20.0	71.4	8.6	100.0
Japan	13.0	66.7	20.3	100.0
Europe	34.8	58.7	6.6	100.0
Total[1]	21.4	66.7	11.9	100.0
By subsidiary type[2]				
ESTPROD/UK	22.6	66.5	11.9	100.0
ESTPROD/EUR	18.5	73.9	7.6	100.0
COMPART	38.5	53.8	7.7	100.0
DEVELPROD	25.8	63.6	12.3	100.0

Means of establishment:
A By the takeover of an existing UK company.
B By the creation of a new company with its own production facilities.
C As a joint venture with an existing UK company.

Notes:
1. Includes subsidiaries of MNEs from Australia and Canada.
1. Covers subsidiaries that described themselves as 'only' or 'predominantly' each type. For definitions, see Table 3.1.

Source: Survey of producing subsidiaries.

effective production of already successfully innovated goods but also, to an increasing degree, to the knowledge-related processes of new product creation. At present it seems that UK-based subsidiaries are not only claiming positions within their MNE groups' European supply programmes, but are often capable of doing so in ways that assert their status as distinctive and individualised high points in these networks.

In the ever-evolving competitive environment *within* the contemporary heterarchical MNE, possession and defence of the high-value-added and strategically-influential product development role is crucial. From such a position a subsidiary can activate, and achieve the further development of, the full range of its host-country's sources of comparative advantage. The emerging status of product mandate subsidiaries in the UK is clearly encouraging, suggesting an ability of these facilities to operationalise powerful sources of local competitiveness for wider (regional or global) market areas in ways that are indicative of the possession of competences that are distinctive and influential within the group. To be able to continue this high-value-added status is vital and by no means easy, as other subsidiaries in other countries seek to build comparable sources of individualised competitiveness. Subsequent chapters seek to provide further evidence on the technological bases for these subsidiaries' intra-group positioning, and thus to see how they can be supported as a means of operationalising (and ensuring the further evolution of) the UK's scientific and tacit knowledge capacities.

NOTES

1. Overall, 39 respondents indicated that they focused on a unique role, whilst there were 216 evaluations of particular roles as being predominant ones (Papanastassiou and Pearce, 1997b). This reflects the reluctance of some respondents to separate two roles in terms of the lead (predominant) position in their subsidiary's overall operations. The subsidiaries of European MNEs were somewhat the most able to discern distinct lead roles and/or to delineate clearly the hierarchy of roles in their operations. Thus 'whilst the proportion of European subsidiaries that discerned a particular role as being their only one was very close to the average for all res–pondents, an above average proportion reported certain roles as absent from their operations and a below average proportion considered roles to be their predominant one' (Papanastassiou and Pearce, 1997b, p.7). This provides an explanation of why European subsidiaries record average responses of below the full-sample average (albeit by varying degrees) for all four roles in Table 3.1.
2. See Chapter 8 for analysis of the input sourcing behaviour of subsidiaries in the UK.
3. On this basis, the DEVELPROD subsidiaries are likely to equate to Taggart's (1997e) *partner* in that they exercise a high-level of creative autonomy in a group context where they perceive themselves to benefit from high procedural justice.
4. Hood and Young (1988) also found, in an analysis of US and continental MNE subsidiaries in the UK, that 'American MNEs were more European-oriented in their markets than their European counterparts'. Young (1992) subsequently observed 'the European multinationals, being insiders by definition and historically even more country-centred, face an even greater challenge to reorganise, rationalise and Europeanize'. In an analysis of investments in the UK by smaller European firms, Buckley, Berkova and Newbould (1983, pp.173–9) also found evidence of a strong local-market focus. Thus by far the most prevalent types of 'primary' motive for their operations related to supply of the UK market, whilst using the UK as a base for

international market servicing was never more than a 'secondary' motive, and then in only four of 35 respondents. In the case of operations in Belgium, Sleuwaegen (1988) observed that for European companies the local Belgian market was more important compared with very high export intensities of American MNE subsidiaries.

5. Awareness of such a mode of HQ thinking might deter subsidiary managers from lobbying for a network supply position and thereby reinforce an introverted focus on their national market.

6. We have elaborated elsewhere (Pearce and Papanastassiou, 1997, p. 248) on the parallel with Almor and Hirsch's (1995) distinction between Heckscher and Ohlin goods (that is, 'mature products characterised by publicly available technologies') which are likely to be traded through arm's-length markets (intra-group networks in our analogy) and Schumpeter goods (that is, 'technology-intensive products characterised by firm-specific [subsidiary–specific for us], technical, marketing, and managerial knowledge') which are more likely to be distributed through controlled channels (that is, marketed by the subsidiary itself rather than left to a group network).

4. Technology in subsidiaries

INTRODUCTION

The previous two chapters' discussion and documentation of the various roles played by subsidiaries in MNE strategies for global competitiveness points decisively to technology as a key differentiating factor. Some subsidiaries are strongly dependent on existing group technologies which they use to produce already commercially established goods, whilst others generate in-house knowledge competences as a basis for a product development scope that individualises their position in group supply programmes. This perception parallels views of the positioning of technology implied by recent conceptualisation of the strategic nature of the modern MNE (see Chapter 2). Earlier thinking suggested that the approach to technology in the dispersed parts of MNE groups was limited mostly to the application of centrally-generated technology through the production of goods whose original creation derived from home-country innovation processes. The recent evolution of the MNE is now seen as greatly expanding the scope of decentralised operations in terms of technology, with producing subsidiaries increasingly involved in the innovation of new goods for their group and overseas R&D laboratories contributing to the expansion of core technologies in order to underpin its longer-term competitiveness. MNEs now need global perspectives on not only the application of technology but also its generation. This chapter discusses and documents these dimensions of technology positioning in MNEs.

In the next section we set out in more detail both the benefits and challenges that emerge once MNEs acknowledge the need to see technology as a dynamic element *throughout* their group-wide operations. A particular aspect of this provides the subject of the third section, in the form of a discussion of recent perceptions of decentralised approaches to innovation as an increasingly relevant aspect of globalised competition strategies. The following section then provides the empirical core of the chapter, in the form of a review of the relative status of seven different sources of technology in the operations of MNE UK-based subsidiaries. The fifth and sixth sections can be seen as investigating respectively modern and traditional modes of technological activity in subsidiaries. Thus the first of these reviews evidence on the presence of two different approaches to subsidiary-level product innovation, one involving substantial subsidiary independence and one operating more interdependently as part of a global innovation strategy. The more traditional technology positioning then emerges in the form of product and process adaptation, investigated in the second of these two sections.

DECENTRALISED TECHNOLOGY IN MNES

As already emphasised, increasingly decentralised approaches to the creation and application of technology are at the core of both the development potentials and organisational problems of the contemporary globally-competing enterprise.[1] The accessing and creative use of technology in a decentralised fashion should enrich both the knowledge available to a group and the effectiveness with which it is used commercially. In a global environment that is increasingly characterised by technological and market heterogeneity, creative subsidiaries with product mandates may be the best way of effectively monitoring such knowledge on behalf of the MNE group. Allowing them to develop their own individualised scope around these localised perceptions, then, provides the strongest motivation for them to do this monitoring job well. They should then benefit the group in two ways. Firstly, by themselves becoming innovative (product development) operations in ways that directly increase the competitive scope of the group. Secondly, by making their original perceptions on market trends and technological progress available to the wider group, so as to influence its overall progress.

By looking at the technological dimensions of product mandate subsidiaries in this way, we are again emphasising that they should be individualising their knowledge scope in ways that remain valuably interdependent with the group's overall technological progress. Usually this will mean enriching the group's core technology in evolutionary ways. Occasionally, though, it could challenge the scope and limits of this core technology in a more radical and revolutionary manner. When this happens it becomes a key responsibility of HQ technology planners to decide whether it should be attempted to decisively assimilate these radical new perspectives into mainstream group progress, to suppress them outright, or allow them to be further investigated as a tentative and provisional independent strand. Crucially, such radical possibilities should not be allowed to proceed on a more or less autonomous basis that may, nevertheless, still have potential to divert key resources, disrupt other parts of technology programmes, reduce the cohesion and coherence of progress and, at an extreme, lead to collapse into anarchy in creative scope.[2]

A relevant way of looking at these issues is to recall that usually the manner in which creative subsidiaries individualise their technology capacity is by deriving distinctive perspectives from a position in two knowledge communities, that of the MNE group and that of the host-country research institutions and science base. Where the first of these prevails, the local element may then serve to strengthen the subsidiary's scope in ways that remain securely anchored by the mainstream technology of the group. Valuably enhanced use of core knowledge thereby emerges, but with limited contributions to longer-term technological progress alongside little danger of challenge to the coherence and balance of group operations. Where the second (that is, local) knowledge community prevails the subsidiary's individualised competence has the potential to be much more radical and much less firmly grounded in current group technology. Here there may be a bigger potential (significant reinforcement of the longer-term technological development of the group) but also a greater danger in terms of loss of control over important areas of knowledge generation.

In pursuing the sustained evolution of its technology, an MNE probably needs to be prepared to support both of the above possibilities, but may feel considerable concern over appropriate control of the latter. This again points to the emerging challenges for MNE central scientists and technology managers. They will no longer be the dominant source of new technology, nor will they define all the knowledge creation aims of the group. The technology trajectory of the group will no longer be a unique 'master plan' of central management. Nevertheless, responsibility for supervising and organising the cohesive and coherent progress of the technological trajectory will still remain an ultimately centralised function.

Therefore HQ technology planning now has to monitor, evaluate and balance all the decentralised initiatives that may emerge through those overseas subsidiaries that are allowed degrees of independent scope to explore and develop localised knowledge. If central planners change from all-seeing 'generals' to 'jugglers' of separate initiatives, they still remain the ultimate custodians of the technological trajectory of their group. HQ now has to set the broad parameters of the group's scope and evolution, and then to scrutinise decentralised technological initiatives in the light of these parameters in order to get a balanced but progressive programme. At extremes it certainly should be open to allowing the more radical dispersed initiatives to actively challenge the expected limits of these knowledge parameters and thus, in exceptional cases, to permit them to thereby alter the direction of technological evolution of the group.

HQ management thus emerges as the custodian of a technological trajectory which seeks to provide the knowledge-based parameters for a balanced and logical progress in the MNE group's scope. It has to understand the characteristics of the technological trajectory and be continually open to re-evaluation of its progress as the group's knowledge environment evolves and widens. The technological trajectory can thus be perceived to have two components.

Firstly, a clear and precise understanding of the MNE's current core technologies and the ways in which they underpin the existing levels and patterns of competitiveness (that is, the ways they are combined in different parts of the product range).[3]

Secondly, a by no means dogmatic or immutable, but nevertheless clearly formulated, view of the way the group's technological scope will evolve over time. This may derive from synthesising market developments (which can be perceived as mainly exogenous and independent of the firm's technological progress) and new potentials that do derive from new knowledge (either generated in the firm or accessible to it).

Whereas traditional views of overseas operations in MNEs would have expected them to be involved in the competitive implementation of the first element of the technological trajectory, we are now arguing that decentralised inputs increasingly influence the formulation and/or revision of the second. Where ideas from such dispersed sources are sufficiently promising or radical, headquarters may need to impose changes on other elements of the group in order to accommodate and support the new direction and retain coherence (that is, ultimately to change the direction of the technological trajectory, whilst retaining its balanced cohesion as a strong way forward).

INNOVATION IN MULTINATIONALS

The emergence of product mandate subsidiaries (and their kindred forms in other typologies) is, in effect, the manifestation of decentralised approaches to innovation in MNEs. This can be seen to reflect both an enhanced prioritisation of innovation *per se* as an essential competitive weapon and growing perception of the value of co-opting globalised perspectives (technological and market) in its implementation.

The significance of technology-related competitive pressures, and thus of a renewed drive towards innovation in leading enterprises, is well documented in a study by Granstrand and Sjolander (1992) of technology executives in 42 companies.[4] On a scale from 0 (unimportant) to 3 (of major importance), 12 technology issues averaged 2.31 for US firms, 2.33 for Japanese and 1.60 for Swedish, compared with 1.74, 1.76 and 1.59, respectively, for 16 non-technology issues. Here 'demand for higher quality' and 'keeping pace with new product technologies' rate well above the average for all technology issues for all three countries, reflecting the continued relevance of sensing and responding to market needs and technological developments in existing product areas. However, issues relating to the need for more dynamic and radical approaches to product evolution are discerned in very strong responses (especially for US and Japanese companies) to 'shorter market lifetime of products', 'pressure for more frequent introduction of new generations of products' and 'pressure for shorter innovation lead times'. Japanese companies provide a particularly strong response to 'increased complexity (fusion) of technology' (also of above-average significance to US and Swedish respondents) and 'increased fusion between science and technologies' (relatively unimportant to the other two groups). This may suggest that the Japanese enterprises are either leading, or particularly concerned by, the trend towards a widening technological base in the progress of several leading industries. Although the Japanese companies (along with US and Swedish ones) did not react particularly strongly to 'pressure to acquire technology from abroad', many of the aspects of the strategic dispersal of R&D and other knowledge-related activities should be considered as a logical part of the response to the reported need for technological diversity in their creative activity.

In a trend analysis of managerial perceptions between the two time-periods 1983/87 and 1988/92, Granstrand and Sjolander (1992, pp.186–7) detected clear expectations for an overall more challenging environment globally. Most notably, the issues that emerged as being significantly more important in the second period than in the first were all technology, and often innovation, related; namely, shorter innovation lead times and shorter market lifetimes of products, increased external acquisition (sourcing) of technology, technological protectionism, increased fusion of technologies and of science with technology, and increased demand for higher quality.

Bearing in mind the competitive priorities implied by the Granstrand and Sjolander evidence, and perceptions derived from aspects of our own results (reported in subsequent chapters), we have formulated an idealised approach to a global innovation strategy available to contemporary MNEs (Pearce and Papanastassiou, 1996a, pp.38–40). Such a global innovation strategy is perceived to have three aims. Firstly, it needs to articulate the effective performance of the full range of basic scientific research necessary to cover all the disciplines that are likely to contribute to the underlying progress of a technological base that can support commercial evolution in any plausibly relevant direction. Although costs are not irrelevant here, it would still be expected that the concerns of this precompetitive objective are predominantly related to scope and quality of inputs.[5] The greatest worry would be missing out crucially significant disciplines or accessing only second-class inputs in vital ones.

The second objective of a global innovation strategy is to get any significant new products into all key segments of the global marketplace with the greatest possible alacrity. Innovation-related market leadership is likely to be very transitory and therefore monopoly rents need to be maximised through the fullest possible geographical spread during that phase. Such speed, however, still needs to be not only quick but also responsive. In many industries an ability to differentiate products in response to local taste differences is still a crucially relevant competitive priority. The third aim of the global innovation strategy, therefore, suggests that the product creation process itself should embody this type of dispersed responsiveness.

The objectives of a global innovation strategy, then, can be seen to imply a two-phase approach. The initial phase targets the first objective described above, and thus seeks to assemble a programme of precompetitive (basic and applied) research that enriches group scope in logical directions. In the case of a specific innovation, this phase ends with the definition of a new product concept. This product concept will extend the industry's scope in quite radical ways, and the completion of the first phase will have secured the full definition of its characteristics, in terms of what it does and how it does it, and provided all the technology needed to allow its commercial development. However, at this point, the precise details of the form in which the product will be offered to consumers, or how it will be produced, are not specified. The implementation of the first phase of the global innovation strategy is perceived as likely to involve a centrally-coordinated, but internationally-dispersed, network of precompetitive research-oriented laboratories, which seek to access all the appropriate areas of specialised inputs. This represents part of an MNE's response to technological heterogeneity as described earlier. From such research programmes the central (parent company) facilities are expected to pull together the relevant results that ultimately provide for the formulation of the product concept.

The second phase of the global innovation strategy then seeks to complete the process by addressing the second and third objectives. Here a more development-oriented set of laboratories, operating within RPM subsidiaries, pick up the technology of the new product concept and work with associated engineering and marketing groups in order to define the precise characteristics, and most effective production process, that optimise its competitive performance in the relevant environment. Thus 'the new product reaches global markets through a series of more-or-less simultaneous differentiated innovations that result in a set of product variants, each of which meets the detailed needs and conditions of a separate national or regional market' (Pearce and Papanastassiou, 1996a, p.40). This constitutes a response to market heterogeneity.[6]

Working from similar perceptions of the needs of contemporary competition,[7] Bartlett and Ghoshal (1990) derive a four-part typology of approaches to innovation in a global context, whilst emphasising that the organisational challenge is to articulate the appropriate balance of any of the four modes rather than choose the uniquely suitable variant. Two of the innovation approaches are deemed to be traditional whilst two are associated more clearly with the needs of the emerging transnational corporation.

The first of the traditional forms is designated as a *centre-for-global* approach to innovation. Here a new opportunity is sensed in the home country, with the centralised resources of the parent company then used to create a new product or process that can, subsequently, be exploited worldwide. It is an approach that would have been most likely to achieve its apotheosis in Bartlett and Ghoshal's global corporation, for which it could 'create new products and processes at relatively low cost and high speed' (1989, p.58). The virtues of the centre-for-global approach are very similar to those traditionally considered to be benefits of centralising R&D in MNEs (see Chapter 5). Thus certain capabilities of the MNE are retained at the headquarters because of a perceived administrative need to protect its core competences and to achieve economies of specialisation and scale in R&D. Especially when operating within a pure global corporation, this approach to innovation embodies obvious limitations in that it is likely to lead to products that are insensitive to market needs outside the home country and provides no mechanism for effectively tapping into dispersed learning environments. Attempts to improve the responsiveness of the centre-for-global approach may merely reduce its accepted benefits for limited gains. Thus 'even when diverse local needs are understood, the central response can be inappropriate because of either over-specification that tries to satisfy all the demands, or a grand compromise that satisfies none' (Bartlett and Ghoshal, 1989, pp. 58–9).

The second traditional innovation process discerned by Bartlett and Ghoshal would have been more likely to occur in their multinational corporation. Thus *local-for-local* innovation occurs through 'national subsidiaries of MNCs using their own resources and capabilities to create innovations that respond to the needs of their own environments' (1990, p.217). Against the obvious benefits of local responsiveness gained through this decentralised approach costs, in terms of lack of integration or coordination, would also be likely to occur. On occasion the national subsidiaries might commit themselves to innovation programmes, and to the generation of creative resources (for example, in-house R&D, an ambitious marketing unit), which greatly exceed the genuine differential needs of their local operations. This could be done more to assert a distinctive identity and autonomy *within the group* than to optimise their competitiveness and efficiency in the local environment. Even in the absence of unnecessarily inflated localised competences, the lack of any centralised overview can lead to a duplication of efforts and extensive redundancy of resources that lead in effect to diminished returns to creative inputs group-wide. Finally, with fragmented innovation efforts articulated through subsidiaries with mainly local-market-related objectives and limited budgets, the local-for-local approach provides no obvious position for the sorts of precompetitive research that the centralised operations in a centre-for-global situation might perceive positively and fund adequately. In terms of our discussions of strategic competitiveness (Chapter 5), local-for-local is very effective in achieving short-term objectives, but is likely to leave a vacuum where long-term needs are concerned.[8]

The two transnational approaches described by Bartlett and Ghoshal seek to harness proactively to group-level competitiveness those differences in international environments (diversity of consumer needs, market trends, technological breakthroughs and government demands) that tended to prove so problematical to traditional modes of innovation. The *locally-leveraged* innovation process utilises the resources of a national subsidiary to create innovations that not only respond to its local market but can be effectively exploited on a worldwide basis. The *globally-linked* approach, however, pools the resources and capabilities of many different components of the group (the parent company and multiple subsidiaries, along with decentralised laboratories) to jointly create and implement an innovation. Both processes pursue the scope economies available to globally-dispersed enterprises through the benefits of worldwide learning (a key attribute of the transnational– see Chapter 2). Thus they 'are based on the ability to leverage existing innovative resources and capabilities by capturing synergies in their combined application or gaining scale and scope economies through broader exploitation of innovation' (1990, p.248).

TYPES OF TECHNOLOGY USED BY SUBSIDIARIES IN THE UK

The nature of subsidiaries' involvement with the technological evolution and innovation capabilities of their MNE groups is clearly decisively related to the sources of knowledge and expertise that they use. Broadly we can argue (Papanastassiou and Pearce, 1997a, p.273) that their technological positioning should change quite radically as they go through the process of creative transition that moves them from an allocated role (in a hierarchical MNE) to one that they are able to claim for themselves (in a more differentiated heterarchical environment). Thus the technological basis of a subsidiary is likely to be substantially defined by its role in the former case, whilst in the latter the knowledge and skill competences it has acquired in-house increasingly have the potential to help define its role.

At its extreme, the argument indicates a reversal in direction of causation, from one in which the technological profile of a subsidiary is entirely determined by the strategic role it is expected to play to one where it is the distinctive elements of its own creative knowledge capacity that determines its particular status in the group's competitive programmes. Thus traditionally the role played by overseas subsidiaries was usually perceived as being determined by the need to apply already standardised sources of group-level competitiveness in ways that responded to market needs and the availability and cost of physical inputs into the production process. Once these conventional influences had determined the role that is to be played by the subsidiary, it would be expected that its technological needs would thereby have been clearly defined within the scope of the group's established knowledge capacity. Therefore it can be suggested (Papanastassiou and Pearce, 1997b, p.13) that in these traditional circumstances the upper limit to the technological scope required within a subsidiary would be the ability to assimilate relevant knowledge that it is expected to acquire from elsewhere in the MNE, and the capacity to detect the need for, and implement effectively, any product or process adaptation necessary to optimise the efficiency of such standard group technology in its particular market and production environment.

The previously reviewed perceptions of the contemporary MNE now envisage greatly expanded scope for some subsidiaries, at least, to generate their own creative competences, in ways that are likely to reflect aspects of the wider scientific and educational background of their host country. Although these creative subsidiaries are likely to still operate in ways that retain strong interdependencies with (rather than dependence on) the mainstream of group technology, they are also likely to broaden their range of knowledge sources through greatly augmented in-house scope (notably an R&D unit) and the implementation of collaborative arrangements with other elements of the host-country scientific community.

These aspects of the strategic positioning of MNE operations in the UK were investigated in the survey of the producing subsidiaries through a question which asked them to evaluate each of seven sources of technology as being either their 'only source', a 'major source', a 'secondary source' or 'not a source'. The first two of these sources represent ways in which subsidiaries can address and operationalise for their own competitive environment, core commercial technology of their group either as already embodied in existing products (ESTPRODTECH) or in a disembodied form (for example, a new outline product concept) awaiting effective innovation (GROUPTECH). We would expect a strong presence of these sources of technology to confirm that, even whilst individualising their in-house competences and competitive scope, subsidiaries are still likely to operate substantially within a pervasive technological trajectory that is a key element in defining the MNE group of which they are a part. However, the remaining five technology sources do reflect ways in which the subsidiaries can seek to build their own quite distinctive competitive basis within the group's evolving knowledge scope and on occasion, as we have noted, to derive more revolutionary perspectives that may challenge the limits of the existing technology trajectory. These five sources can then involve in-house scope (an R&D unit, OWNLAB, or talented engineering personnel, ENGUNIT), a more discretionary accessing of R&D capacity elsewhere in the group (GROUPLAB) or collaborations with host-country scientific institutions (LOCALINST) or other firms (OTHERFIRM).

Technology of established products

The first source of technology that producing subsidiaries were asked to evaluate was 'existing technology embodied in established products we produce' (ESTPRODTECH). Overall, 7.7 per cent of the respondents that evaluated this source rated it their only one, 74.6 per cent considered it a major source and 13.3 per cent more a secondary one. As Table 4.1 shows, when these results are summarised in the form of average responses (ARs) this source of technology emerges as the most prevalent in all industries and for all home countries.

ESTPRODTECH also emerges as the strongest source of technology in all four subsidiary types. Although in the first three types there is clear expectation of a strong positioning within the current commercial embodiment of the group's technological trajectory, as mediated most decisively by the presence of this source of technology, the outcome is more surprising for DEVELPROD subsidiaries. An explanation can be suggested[9] that relates to both the evolutionary processes we have discerned in subsidiaries and in the evolutionary interpretation of technological progress.[10] This result can support a view that the essence of much subsidiary-level product development emerges from a synergistic interaction between the facility's established knowledge and skills (already individualised to a significant degree by a product heritage that embodies significant localised elements) and access

Table 4.1 Relative importance of sources of technology in MNE subsidiaries in the UK

	Importance of technology source[1] (average response[2])						
	A	B	C	D	E	F	G
By industry							
Food	2.89	2.22	2.50	1.78	1.56	1.67	2.00
Automobiles	2.72	2.18	1.83	2.65	1.71	1.39	2.00
Aerospace	2.60	2.50	1.50	1.83	1.17	1.33	2.17
Electronics and electrical appliances	2.79	2.35	1.98	2.33	1.43	1.32	2.13
Mechanical engineering	2.85	2.46	1.85	2.00	1.42	1.62	2.19
Instruments	2.82	2.00	2.27	2.18	1.45	1.73	2.50
Industrial and agricultural chemicals	3.24	2.21	2.31	2.31	1.62	1.52	1.79
Pharmaceutical and consumer chemicals	3.00	2.40	2.30	2.40	1.70	1.60	1.70
Metal manufacture and products	2.91	2.09	1.91	1.82	1.27	1.36	2.09
Other manufacturing	3.13	2.47	1.71	2.14	1.29	1.50	1.64
Total	2.86	2.30	2.02	2.22	1.48	1.48	2.02
By home country							
USA	2.78	2.25	2.15	2.18	1.57	1.62	2.06
Japan	2.88	2.35	1.78	2.23	1.31	1.27	2.02
Europe	2.91	2.30	2.12	2.25	1.57	1.55	1.88
Total[3]	2.86	2.30	2.02	2.22	1.48	1.48	2.02
By subsidiary type[4]							
ESTPROD/UK	2.88	2.27	1.85	2.29	1.41	1.39	2.01
ESTPROD/EUR	2.92	2.36	2.08	2.27	1.52	1.41	2.11
COMPART	2.83	2.62	2.17	2.08	1.67	1.58	2.17
DEVELPROD	2.86	2.33	2.52	2.05	1.55	1.62	2.13

Sources of technology:

A Existing technology embodied in established products we produce (ESTPRODTECH).

B Technology of our MNE group from which we introduce new products for the UK/European market, that differ from other variants introduced in other markets (GROUPTECH).

C R&D carried out by our own laboratory (OWNLAB).

D R&D carried out for us by another R&D laboratory of our MNE group (GROUPLAB).

E R&D carried out in collaboration with another firm (OTHERFIRM).

F R&D carried out for us by local scientific institutions (e.g. Universities; independent labs; industry labs) (LOCALINST).

Table 4.1 continued

G Development and adaptation carried out less formally by members of our engineering unit and production personnel (ENGUNIT).

Notes:
1. Respondents were asked to grade each source of technology for their operations as (i) our only source, (ii) a major source, (iii) a secondary source, (iv) not a source.
2. The average response was calculated by allocating 'only source' the value of 4, 'major source' the value of 3, 'secondary source' the value of 2, 'not a source' the value of 1.
3. Includes subsidiaries of MNEs from Australia and Canada.
4. Covers subsidiaries that described themselves as 'only' or 'predominantly' each type. For definitions, see Table 3.1.

Source: Survey of producing subsidiaries.

(either locally or from other group sources) to more distinctive new technology and/or market perceptions that will provide the basis for its creation of substantially original goods. The ability of a subsidiary to evolve to a status that becomes predominantly motivated by a product development commitment is likely to be most decisively embodied in its human capital, in the form of entrepreneurial managers along with talented and creative technologists and marketing executives. However, not only will the general high degree of dynamism and competence of such personnel underpin the subsidiary's transition to a more creative role, but more explicit elements of their tacit knowledge and experience are likely to then condition the detail of the product development programmes they feel motivated to articulate (or participate in) and capable of implementing. The predominant source of these key motivating elements of tacit knowledge is likely to lie in the products previously, and perhaps still, supplied by the subsidiary. Therefore the DEVELPROD status of a subsidiary may often be built on a foundation of in-house attributes which still derive quite substantially from the ESTPRODTECH that defined traditional (or now defunct) parts of its product range.

When ESTPRODTECH is tested in a multiple regression test that controls for industry and home-country effects through dummy variables (Table 4.2), the ESTPROD/EUR subsidiary role emerges as a significant positive determinant. In fact tests of home-country sub-samples (that is, for the US, Japan and European subsidiaries) show (Papanastassiou and Pearce, 1997a) that the significance of this result derives from the Japanese sample, although ESTPROD/EUR is positively signed in all three groups (as is DEVELPROD). This suggests a very clearcut perception in these relatively new Japanese subsidiaries that a key part of their initial positioning is the application of their group's established sources of competitiveness to the European market context.

New group technology

The second technology source was defined as 'technology of our MNE group from which we introduce new products for the UK/European market, that differ from other variants introduced in other markets' (GROUPTECH). By comparison with the first type of technology this source moves the subsidiary's position from one of feeding off established group knowledge in a mainly dependent fashion to that of being involved, in a much more interdependent way, in its evolution and implementation. Very explicitly it relates to a context within a global innovation strategy in that it envisages a UK subsidiary accessing the technology of a major new product concept in order to develop its precise European variant (paralleling alternative development processes in other subsidiaries aimed at other leading market areas). Of respondents who evaluated GROUPTECH, 4.4 per cent thought it was their only source, 44.2 per cent a major one and 28.8 per cent a secondary one. That this indicates that only 22.6 per cent of subsidiaries did not access this technology source shows a growing relevance of this type of knowledge interdependency, but the average responses of Table 4.1 nevertheless show that its current intensity rates are well below that of ESTPRODTECH.

The only weakly positive relationship between GROUPTECH and DEVELPROD in Table 4.2 in fact reflects a significant positive relationship in the Japanese sub-sample and a significantly negative one for European subsidiaries (the US is insignificantly positive). For the Japanese subsidiaries this positive relationship may complement that between ESTPRODTECH and ESTPROD/EUR. Thus the latter result, as previously suggested, represents one level of the companies' confidence in their current technology, in that they feel able to build a competitive bridgehead in Europe around existing products. The relationship between GROUPTECH and DEVELPROD, then, indicates a growing willingness to emerge from that bridgehead by involving European subsidiaries (here in the UK) in a product creation process, albeit one that still derives from centrally-generated technology (in the manner of the second phase of a global innovation strategy, which also helps induce a degree of creative transition in the subsidiaries). These perspectives broadly indicate an increasing interdependence in the technology strategies of Japanese MNEs, with a sustained centralised competence in generating the basis of new product concepts being augmented by decentralised innovation procedures targeting specific market areas.

In the case of European MNEs it is plausible that new GROUPTECH is most likely to emerge in the continental home-country operations of these companies, and that the derivation of the European-market variants of the product to be based on it will then, most logically, also be carried out there. It seems that this exclusion from the centrally-legitimised development process may have two possible implications in the UK subsidiaries of these European MNEs. Firstly, that they implement much more self-contained, perhaps even subversive, product development operations of their own based around especially strong generation of in-house attributes (an R&D laboratory and localised tacit knowledge) to sustain, in particular, their relatively strong local-market focus. Secondly, that although denied its use in full-scale product development, these subsidiaries have some access to GROUPTECH (Table 4.1) to sharpen the characteristics of the goods they already produce for their parent companies' European supply networks by combining it with other local creative capacities (ESTPROD/EUR is positively, though not significantly, related to GROUPTECH and significantly positively related to the use of an in-house laboratory for these European MNE subsidiaries).[11]

The strong position of GROUPTECH in component part supplying subsidiaries is indicative of a systematic involvement of some of these facilities in creative programmes (rather than a routine and dependent supply of mature inputs to standardised final goods). Thus where a COMPART facility supplies a DEVELPROD subsidiary that is developing new products on the basis of GROUPTECH, then the component manufacturer may be expected to create a new input by itself accessing the same element of new knowledge.

In-house R&D

Many of the key themes of our previous discussion have already indicated circumstances in which an in-house R&D unit would be a key attribute of MNE overseas subsidiaries. Subsidiaries themselves are likely to see the implementation of an R&D laboratory as a vital element in their desire to individualise their competences and stake a claim to a higher value-added status in group operations. Although it may, on occasion, then represent the pursuit of excessive subsidiary-level autonomy, or lead their technology in radical directions that may be ultimately disruptive to logical group-level progress, our later discussion (Chapters 5 and 6) will elaborate many circumstances where such decentralised R&D supports positive inter-dependencies in MNE creative programmes. The ways in which laboratories help their subsidiaries to respond to distinctive elements in their *local* technological and market environments can also be seen as part of the mechanism through which MNEs access and activate these crucial heterogeneities in support of *global* competitiveness. Also, these laboratories may be a vital agent in their subsidiaries' successful application of the types of MNE technology already reviewed in this section, by sharpening the competitiveness of established products (ESTPRODTECH) or by mediating in a localised product development process based on new group-level knowledge (GROUPTECH).

Of the subsidiaries that evaluated 'R&D carried out by our own laboratory' (OWNLAB) as a source of technology, 3.4 per cent said it was their only one, 35.8 per cent rated it a major source and 20.1 per cent a secondary one. Although this implies that 40.7 per cent of subsidiaries did not have an in-house source of R&D, it also seems that where a laboratory was present it usually provided a strong input to its subsidiary's knowledge scope. Thus of the subsidiaries with laboratories, 66.0 per cent rated OWNLAB as a major (or only) source of technology. The evidence on the positioning of in-house R & D will be discussed in much more detail in the next two chapters and we need only note here the predicted strong presence in DEVELPROD subsidiaries (Table 4.1), with this relationship strongly confirmed in the regression (Table 4.2) where ESTPROD/EUR is also significantly positive (perhaps complementing the use of GROUPTECH to sharpen the competitiveness of these subsidiaries' established products, as suggested earlier).

Other sources of R&D in the MNE

As a source of technology accessed by MNE subsidiaries in the UK 'R&D carried out for us by another R&D laboratory of our MNE group' (GROUPLAB) was rated the only source by 5.0 per cent, a major one by 38.1 per cent and a secondary one by 30.4 per cent. That this provides an overall greater AR than OWNLAB (2.22 compared to 2.02 in Table 4.1) reflects its use by more subsidiaries (absent from only 26.5 per cent against 40.7 per cent) rather than intensity of contribution when applied.

The relative positioning of the two sources of R&D from within the group are quite distinctive. Thus Table 4.1 shows that in the two ESTPROD types of subsidiaries, GROUPLAB is clearly more relevant than OWNLAB. This suggests that here the predominant need for R&D support still relates to the effective local application of the standard group technology already embodied in successful products, and that advice from laboratories elsewhere (perhaps those already familiar with the goods in question) is often sufficient. In DEVELPROD subsidiaries (and to a lesser degree COMPART − again indicating closer similarity to product development than to established product

Table 4.2 Regressions with subsidiaries' sources of technology as dependent variable

	ESTPROD TECH	GROUP TECH	OWNLAB	GROUP LAB	OTHER FIRM	LOCAL INST	ENG UNIT
Intercept	2.8738‡	2.1902‡	0.9336‡	2.4279‡	1.3004‡	1.8209‡	1.1469‡
	(10.85)	(5.68)	(2.61)	(6.27)	(4.81)	(7.30)	(3.94)
Food	−0.0560	−0.0569	0.0313	−0.0669	0.0209	−0.0008	0.0407
	(−1.02)	(−0.72)	(0.41)	(−0.83)	(0.37)	(−0.01)	(0.65)
Automobiles	−0.4316*	−0.4362	−0.2593	0.6105*	0.2532	−0.2065	0.1946
	(−1.89)	(−1.34)	(0.85)	(1.82)	(1.09)	(−0.96)	(0.78)
Aerospace	−0.2087	0.0181	−0.2760	−0.1330	−0.1484	−0.1849	0.2157
	(−1.28)	(0.08)	(−1.34)	(−0.59)	(−0.95)	(−1.28)	(1.29)
Electronics	−0.0960†	−0.0602	0.0246	0.0609	0.0133	−0.0410	0.0938*
	(−2.00)	(−0.89)	(0.36)	(0.86)	(0.27)	(−0.91)	(1.79)
Mechanical engineering	−0.0466	−0.0275	−0.0246	−0.0033	−0.0001	0.0081	0.0588*
	(−1.52)	(−0.65)	(−0.61)	(−0.07)	(−0.00)	(0.29)	(1.80)
Instruments	−0.0514	−0.0657	0.0276	0.0041	0.0087	0.0129	0.1201†
	(−1.17)	(−1.03)	(0.47)	(0.06)	(0.19)	(0.31)	(2.50)
Chemicals	−0.0662	−0.1134	0.0861	0.0722	0.0436	−0.0419	0.0046
	(−0.96)	(−1.16)	(0.93)	(0.72)	(0.62)	(−0.65)	(0.06)
Pharmaceuticals	−0.0190	−0.0314	0.0359	0.0167	0.0108	0.0090	−0.0121
	(−0.65)	(−0.75)	(0.91)	(0.39)	(0.36)	(0.33)	(−0.38)
Metals	−0.0402	−0.0649	−0.0236	−0.0230	−0.0088	−0.0246	0.0634*
	(−1.26)	(−1.41)	(−0.55)	(−0.49)	(−0.27)	(−0.82)	(1.82)
USA	−0.0067	−0.0031	−0.0025	−0.0085	−0.0034	0.0073	−0.0086
	(−0.56)	(−0.18)	(−0.15)	(−0.47)	(−0.28)	(0.63)	(−0.64)

Japan	0.0012	0.0050	-0.0311†	-0.0130	-0.0232†	-0.0244†	-0.0098
	(0.10)	(0.30)	(-2.02)	(-0.77)	(-1.99)	(-2.27)	(-0.78)
ESTPROD/UK^2	-0.0444	-0.0991	-0.0509	0.0465	-0.0724	-0.0685	0.0195
	(-0.81)	(-1.25)	(-0.69)	(0.58)	(-1.30)	(-1.34)	(0.32)
ESTPRODEUR	0.1398†	0.1087	0.1626†	0.0282	0.0354	-0.0185	0.0510
	(2.44)	(1.32)	(2.12)	(0.34)	(0.61)	(-0.35)	(0.82)
COMPART	-0.0557	0.1405	-0.0596	-0.1163	0.1732†	-0.0159	0.1560*
	(-0.75)	(1.32)	(-0.59)	(-1.07)	(2.28)	(-0.23)	(1.90)
DEVELPROD	0.0681	0.0666	0.4799‡	-0.1213	0.0298	0.0170	0.1444†
	(1.27)	(0.86)	(6.70)	(-1.56)	(0.55)	(0.34)	(2.45)
R^2	0.0802	0.0604	0.3279	0.0946	0.1253	0.1322	0.1564
F	0.92	0.69	5.14‡	1.12	1.53	1.62*	1.95†
n	175	178	174	177	176	174	174

Notes:
1. For full description of technology sources (dependent variable), see Table 4.1.
2. For definitions of the independent variables, see Table 3.1.

n number of observations; ‡ significant at 1%; † significant at 5%; * significant at 10%.

positioning), it is OWNLAB that prevails. Thus here the defining commitment to a creative objective requires the presence of an in-house R&D capability, although this then often augments its scope by securing supporting inputs from other group laboratories.

From this we can suggest (Pearce and Papanastassiou, 1996b) that changing modes of accessing R&D closely reflect the evolutionary processes of subsidiaries. Thus the limited technological ambition of the pure ESTPROD roles causes subsidiaries to settle for GROUPLAB as an adequate source of R&D support. Nevertheless this might be already perceived as substituting for the input of an absent in-house unit, which could perhaps have performed the work more effectively from a position of closer association with the subsidiary's capacities and needs. Therefore, as subsidiaries begin to increase their degree of creative ambition, this perception of the limitations of GROUPLAB as the unique source of R&D support may reach a threshold level which then precipitates the implementation of their own laboratory. This, though, does not preclude the continued accessing of inputs from other group laboratories. The function of the in-house laboratory is now to define the technological needs of its subsidiary and to fulfil as many of them as it feels to be appropriate (OWNLAB as a source), but also to articulate collaborative arrangements with other group facilities in order to secure supplementary inputs to complete its programme in the most effective way. Here, then, access to the specialised abilities of these other laboratories enables the subsidiary to position GROUPLAB as a complement to its own unit's work (OWNLAB) rather than as substituting for it (as in the case of many ESTPROD operations). Thus 'the strong development of distinctive subsidiary-level technology competences built around their own R&D unit does not seem to preclude the pursuit of complementary synergies within the network of decentralised laboratories in a MNE group' (Pearce and Papanastassiou, 1996b, p.319).

Collaborative R & D with another firm

The first of two sources of technology that derive from a collaborative arrangement outside the group was 'R&D carried out in collaboration with another firm' (OTHERFIRM). This clearly played a very limited role in the operations of responding subsidiaries, with 58.9 per cent saying it made no contribution to their technological scope and a further 35.0 per cent believing it to be no more than a secondary source. Although there has been substantial recent analysis[12] of inter-firm technological collaboration, it therefore seems that when these arrangements involve the performance of joint R&D[13] this provides a sufficiently strategic (perhaps predominantly precompetitive) context for their organisation to be articulated through central-group planners rather than at the subsidiary level.

These inter-firm collaborations by UK subsidiaries are somewhat strongest for component part supplying units. In line with other suggestions of creative ambitions within such COMPART subsidiaries, this may suggest an aim of widening and individualising their markets by supplying components to firms outside their own group by entering into technological collaboration agreements with such independent companies to develop new inputs for their goods. Japanese subsidiaries are least likely to use OTHERFIRM as a technology source, perhaps indicating that in the industries where they have invested most strongly they see limited scope for UK firms to provide creative inputs that can complement and enhance their own existing scope.

Collaboration with UK scientific institutions

The use of local UK scientific institutions as a second possible source of collaborative R&D accessed outside the firm was also reported as relatively limited. Thus 'R&D carried out for us by local scientific institutions (for example, Universities, independent laboratories, industry laboratories)' (LOCALINST) was not perceived as relevant by 56.5 per cent of responding subsidiaries and rated as no more than a secondary source by 40.3 per cent more.

There may be two reasons why these results somewhat understate the relevance of such local scientific collaborations in the technological activity of MNEs. Firstly, the producing subsidiaries responding to this question may often evaluate quite highly the inputs to their operations of their own laboratories (OWNLAB), but be less clearly aware of any contribution to that that might have been made by associations with local research institutions. This suggestion that MNE collaborations with UK scientific institutions are most likely to be articulated through their subsidiaries' in-house units leads to the second reason why such arrangements may be understated here. Thus it may well be that the content of such shared research programmes is relatively strongly oriented to the types of precompetitive work that are often the focus of stand-alone MNE laboratories, which operate independently of local producing subsidiaries.[14] These laboratories' arrangements would not have been detected in the replies of the manufacturing subsidiaries reported here. In fact the direct survey of laboratories (that is, including stand-alone units) did suggest a stronger role for such collaborations, and their role and content is investigated in detail in Chapter 7.

Even in the results reported here, the association of LOCALINST with more ambitious scientific work, and therefore with subsidiaries' in-house laboratories, is clearly suggested by the fact that four of the five industries with the strongest use of LOCALINST[15] are the ones that also provide distinctly the strongest role for OWNLAB (Table 4.1). The use of this source of technology is least well developed in Japanese subsidiaries (significantly negative dummy in Table 4.2). This may be mainly the result of the relative newness of these companies' UK operations, as there is some perception that in several industries (even those where the current status of their technology is clearly competitive) there are some doubts about the ability of the home-country science-base to sustain their commercial evolution. It may be, therefore, that once the Japanese companies have used the strength of their current commercial technology to build a secure basis for their European operations, an enhanced experience of local conditions may provide the confidence to extend their activity into greater levels of creativity, including collaborative research programmes to reinforce the longer-term knowledge scope.

Work of engineers and production personnel

A potential in-house source of distinctive technology, which nevertheless falls short of formal R&D, was defined as 'development and adaptation carried out less formally by members of our engineering unit and production personnel'. With 0.6 per cent of respondents considering this their only source, 23.0 per cent rating it a major source, 54.5 per cent a secondary source and only 21.9 per cent believing it played no role, this provides (Table 4.1) an identical overall AR to OWNLAB, the other (more formal) in-house technology source. The essence of this source is the tacit knowledge embodied in such personnel, which is likely to reflect a variable mix of the mainstream characteristics of the group's technological trajectory and distinctive elements of the subsidiary's own knowledge heritage. As would be expected, inputs to the subsidiary's activity that arise from these tacit competences emerge (Table 4.1) as clearly relevant to the use of established technology (in the first two subsidiary roles), which is likely to emanate from the same part of the group's knowledge background. Thus these personnel are well equipped to mediate in applying such mainstream technology to the particular circumstances with which they are familiar. For the first three subsidiary roles, therefore, ENGUNIT at least matches OWNLAB as an in-house knowledge source.

In the case of DEVELPROD subsidiaries, ENGUNIT clearly takes a secondary position to OWNLAB as a source of technology, but its presence nevertheless still matches that in the other three roles. Thus, even where the work of an in-house laboratory leads in a substantive product development process, the tacit skills of other personnel help to ensure that the evolutionary benefits of a coherent grounding in existing localised engineering and marketing competences (themselves incorporating a substantial basis in the group's technological heritage) are secured. In fact when industry and home country are controlled for in multiple regressions (Table 4.2) the positive relationship between ENGUNIT and DEVELPROD emerges as significant. Although this relationship only just misses significance in the US sub-sample (Papanastassiou and Pearce, 1997a) it is in the Japanese sample that it emerges decisively. This may complement the similarly decisive positive relationship between DEVELPROD and GROUPTECH noted earlier. Thus in the relatively young Japanese subsidiaries the tacit knowledge embodied in ENGUNIT may be more strongly reflective of the home-country tradition, and so far less locally conditioned than in comparable US or European subsidiaries, which then provides them with a distinctive ability to access and apply new central technology. This could also be interpreted as a relative lack of the not-invented-here syndrome in such new subsidiaries, perhaps still strongly influenced by expatriate personnel and home-country training carried out to facilitate the initial setup of the operation.

PRODUCT DEVELOPMENT IN SUBSIDIARIES

The most proactive involvement of subsidiaries in the evolution of MNE technology is seen to come through their participation in product development processes. Our earlier discussion, however, can be seen to imply two quite distinct mechanisms through which such involvement may be activated. To investigate this the survey of production subsidiaries asked all those who, to any degree, played the DEVELPROD role to evaluate the relevance to their product creation activity of two alternate approaches.

The first of these approaches was defined as 'using our own R & D results to meet a new need that we detect in our market'. This implies the application of an integrated set of creative competences that can be activated by the subsidiary (including technology and managerial and marketing expertise), in a manner that allows it to achieve a substantial degree of independent control over its creative efforts. The discussion of the previous sections indicates both the desirability and likelihood of product development activity of this type still being implemented within the broad confines of the group's technological trajectory, being often strongly conditioned by the subsidiary's past production of established goods. Nevertheless, its original perceptions are still likely to allow a subsidiary operating in this way to achieve very distinctive extensions of the product range available within the scope of the evolving technological trajectory. The implication is thus that the products generated in this way will often be quite idiosyncratic in the group's global range, so that they may gain quite strong entry into markets beyond the local or regional (here UK or European), endowing successful subsidiaries with WPM status. Of 129 subsidiaries that evaluated this approach to product development 57.4 per cent rated it their main one, 27.1 per cent said they partly used it, and 15.5 per cent did not use it at all.

The second approach to product development by subsidiaries was defined as 'applying new original scientific results created in our MNE group to derive a new product suitable for our market, using our technology and marketing resources'. Whereas intuitive forces were seen as usually likely to retain the first approach within the evolution of the group's technological trajectory, this one is much more systematically interdependent with group-level knowledge generation and commercial development. It is likely to be carried out by RPMs that are securing the effective local implementation of a new product concept in the second phase of a global innovation strategy. Although only 20.3 per cent of 128 respondents who evaluated this product development approach considered that it was their main one, 53.1 per cent applied it partly, with 26.6 per cent not using it. Thus the majority of respondents felt that this approach did contribute to their product development operations, but relatively few considered that it took a primary position in the way they articulated such efforts. Therefore, as Table 4.3 shows, when the responses are summarised as ARs it is the first approach that emerges as clearly the most prevalent in underpinning the current product creation activity at the subsidiary level. Japanese subsidiaries provided the least strong evaluation of both of the designated approaches. This may parallel the relatively low prevalence of product development itself in Japanese subsidiaries (Table 3.1), suggesting that a distinctive technological competence is not perceived as yet being well developed in their operations, so that other more *ad hoc* factors are more likely to support and motivate this role where it does emerge. Within this overall position, however, the second of the approaches is *relatively* most prevalent in Japanese subsidiaries (in the sense of a smaller gap in AR between it and the first approach than for US or European units). This may reflect a lack of confidence in the ability of subsidiary-level competences to currently support more autonomous creativity, which encourages reluctant acceptance of the more interdependent second approach. Alternatively it may well be that Japanese MNE groups as a whole are already relatively keener on the systematic adoption of a globalised approach to innovation and its implied role for subsidiaries.

Table 4.3 Approaches to product development in subsidiaries

	Approach (average response)[1]	
	A	B
By industry		
Food	2.78	2.22
Automobiles	2.21	1.79
Aerospace	2.00	1.75
Electronics and electrical appliances	2.33	1.83
Mechanical engineering	2.36	2.05
Instruments	2.71	2.14
Industrial and agricultural chemicals	2.55	2.00
Pharmaceuticals and consumer chemicals	2.50	2.00
Metal manufacture and products	2.25	1.63
Other manufacturing	2.57	2.00
Total	2.42	1.94
By home country		
USA	2.40	1.98
Japan	2.17	1.86
Europe	2.75	2.00
Total[2]	2.42	1.94

Approaches to product development by subsidiaries:
A Using our own R&D results to meet a new need we detect in our market.
B Applying new original scientific results created in our MNE group to derive a new product suitable for our market, using our technology and marketing resources.

Notes:
1. The question was addressed to subsidiaries that develop, produce and market an original product, and asked if they used the innovation approaches, (i) mainly, (ii) partly, (iii) not at all. The average response was calculated by allocating 'mainly' a value of 3, 'partly' a value of 2 and 'not at all' a value of 1.
2. Includes subsidiaries of MNEs from Australia and Canada.

Source: Survey of producing subsidiaries.

The leading position of the first approach is clearly most decisive in the UK subsidiaries of continental European MNEs. The long-established position of many of them may have led to the possession of strong creative competences in such facilities, along with the confidence to pursue their relatively autonomous use in WPM operations. Increasingly, it may also be that these subsidiaries feel a need to act in this way to sustain their status against a tendency for their European parent MNEs to retain much of their European-market-oriented product creation in home-country operations.

Both of these approaches make relatively strong contributions to product development in subsidiaries in food, instruments, industrial and agricultural chemicals and pharmaceuticals, reflecting a particularly strong position for in-house R&D (OWNLAB) in all these cases (Table 4.1). Two quite technologically-advanced industries where both of the approaches are of somewhat below-average relevance to creation in UK subsidiaries are automobiles and electronics. In these cases it may be that the UK subsidiaries often have product development responsibilities within a Europe-wide strategy that is articulated from European headquarters and supported technologically from a very strong centralised R&D laboratory, which then substantially substitutes for subsidiary-level work.

ADAPTATION OF TECHNOLOGY IN SUBSIDIARIES

In an era when manufacturing MNEs operated through a portfolio of local-market-focused TMRs, these subsidiaries were perceived as possessing a quite clear, albeit strategically limited, technological imperative in the form of the frequent need to *adapt* to local needs and conditions the (mainly centrally-generated) product characteristics and production processes relating to the goods that they inherited as the core of their capacity to play this role. The changes in subsidiary roles that we discern as central to the recent strategic evolution of MNEs clearly indicate a decline in the relative status of adaptation in the technological positioning of these units. In a pure PM subsidiary, the product development imperative transcends and replaces any need for adaptation. In a pure RPS, supplying a specialised set of established products to group networks, the need for standardised quality meeting the needs of a wide market area precludes subsidiary-level product adaptation, although some adaptation of processes to improve the effective use of local inputs (both in terms of quantitative availability and qualitative characteristics) might be allowed where the MNE does not manage *a priori* to allocate goods to locations that already suit their existing production techniques. However, our earlier analysis shows that subsidiaries with a predominant TMR orientation still exist in the UK, and also that where WPM/RPM or RPS motivation has emerged these subsidiaries often still embody significant secondary elements of TMR behaviour. Thus the possibility of adaptation as an element in subsidiary-level technological motivation still persists. Three questions in the survey of producing subsidiaries investigated this.

The first of these questions was addressed to subsidiaries which produced (at least as part of their role) already commercially established products of their MNE group, and sought an evaluation of the extent to which they adapted the characteristics of the product and the form of the associated production process. Of 162 respondents who replied to the first part, 28 (17.3 per cent) said they altered the product characteristics 'extensively', 91 (56.2 per cent) that they did so 'moderately' and 43 (26.6 per cent) 'not at all'. With regard to adaptation of production process, 28 (17.4 per cent) of 161 respondents did so 'extensively', 93 (57.8 per cent) 'moderately' and 40 (24.8 per cent) 'not at all'. The similarity between these two frequencies, resulting in near identical average responses in Table 4.4, reflects the fact that 98 of 161 respondents rated product and process adaptation at the same level of intensity. Nevertheless, the differential responses do provide for some quite distinctive results at the industry level (Table 4.4). Product and process adaptation differ very little by home country, but the modestly greater degree of relative commitment to process change by Japanese subsidiaries may still be indicative of a particular concern to optimise the application of effective production techniques as a key element in building up the successful European transplant of their established sources of competitiveness.

The next question asked subsidiaries which carried out some adaptation of any existing goods that they undertook to produce, to say whether or not certain stipulated factors contributed to the need for this. A generalised need 'to respond to differences in consumer tastes' was a motivation for product adaptation for 74.2 per cent of relevant respondents (Table 4.5), with this being of substantial importance to subsidiaries in all industries (except instruments) and from all home countries. It can be observed, however, that the notably pervasive relevance of this factor to subsidiaries of European MNEs is in line with interpretation (Chapter 3) of their particularly strong (compared to US and Japanese) focus on (and presumed responsiveness to) the UK market. Also widely pervasive as motives for product adaptation were the needs 'to meet technical standards (for example, power supply)' (relevant to 66.1 per cent of respondents) and 'to meet national or EU regulations' (63.7 per cent). Here the relatively low relevance of these factors to European subsidiaries (by contrast to their high response to perceived taste differences) suggests that such technical or regulatory factors may be sufficiently standardised throughout the EU (in particular) for goods designed in continental home countries to often be readily acceptable in the UK (in a way that those innovated outside Europe by US or Japanese companies are more frequently not). A relatively low 30.6 per cent of these subsidiaries felt that they needed to adapt their products 'to respond to climatic differences'

Table 4.4 Extent of adaptation of technology by MNE subsidiaries in the UK

	Extent of adaptation (average response)[1]	
	Product	Process
By industry		
Food	2.11	1.89
Automobiles	1.57	1.93
Aerospace	1.50	1.33
Electronics and electrical appliances	2.00	1.90
Mechanical engineering	2.26	2.09
Instruments	1.78	1.89
Industrial and agricultural chemicals	1.85	1.85
Pharmaceuticals and consumer chemicals	1.63	2.50
Metal manufacture and products	1.88	1.88
Other manufacturing	1.70	1.90
Total	1.91	1.93
By home country		
USA	1.93	1.92
Japan	1.88	1.95
Europe	1.87	1.89
Total[2]	1.91	1.93

Notes:
1. Respondents who produced (at least as part of their role) already established products of their MNE group, were asked if they adapted (i) extensively, (ii) moderately, (iii) not at all, either (a) the characteristics of the product, (b) the production process. The average response was then calculated by allocating replies of 'extensively' the value 3, 'moderately' the value 2, 'not at all' the value 1.
2. Includes subsidiaries of MNEs from Australia and Canada.

Source: Survey of producing subsidiaries.

(although attitudes or needs conditioned by climate may be subsumed into the pervasively influential 'consumer tastes').

When asked to evaluate reasons for adapting production processes 58.0 per cent of respondents (Table 4.6) endorsed the relevance of doing so 'to save costs by using more of relatively cheap factors of production'. This then suggests that where subsidiaries produce products that are standardised within

Table 4.5 Reasons for adaptation of existing products by MNE subsidiaries in the UK

	Reason for product adaptation (per cent of respondents)[1]			
	A	B	C	D
By industry				
Food	87.5	25.0	0	75.0
Automobiles	77.8	66.7	33.3	77.8
Aerospace	75.0	100.0	25.0	75.0
Electronics and electrical appliances	78.9	78.9	36.8	81.6
Mechanical engineering	61.9	66.7	42.9	52.4
Instruments	16.7	100.0	0	33.3
Industrial and agricultural chemicals	81.0	57.1	28.6	57.1
Pharmaceuticals and consumer chemicals	66.7	33.3	16.7	50.0
Metal manufacture and products	75.0	75.0	25.0	50.0
Other manufacturing	100.0	43.0	43.0	29.0
Total	74.2	66.1	30.6	63.7
By home country				
USA	69.6	63.0	32.6	63.0
Japan	74.4	74.4	32.6	69.8
Europe	79.3	55.2	31.0	48.3
Total[2]	74.2	66.1	30.6	63.7

Reasons for adaptation of product:
A To respond to differences in consumer taste.
B To meet technical standards (e.g. power supply).
C To respond to climatic differences.
D To meet national or EU regulations.

Notes:
1. Subsidiaries that adapted an established product were asked to endorse any of the offered reasons for doing so that were relevant to their operations.
2. Includes subsidiaries of MNEs from Australia and Canada.

Source: Survey of producing subsidiaries.

the group they are aware of a quite crucial need to take local responsibility for pursuing any available sources of cost efficiency.

Table 4.6 Reasons for adaptation of existing production processes by MNE subsidiaries

	Reasons for process adaptation (per cent of respondents)[1]						
	A	B	C	D	E	F	G
By industry							
Food	50.0	0	50.0	12.5	0	50.0	50.0
Automobiles	36.4	9.1	27.3	72.7	0	27.3	54.5
Aerospace	25.0	0	0	25.0	50.0	25.0	25.0
Electronics and electrical appliances	42.9	22.9	37.1	60.0	17.1	45.7	50.0
Mechanical engineering	52.9	5.9	23.5	35.3	11.8	35.3	64.7
Instruments	37.5	12.5	12.5	87.5	12.5	37.5	75.0
Industrial agricultural chemicals	57.9	21.1	52.6	73.7	10.5	15.8	52.6
Pharmaceutical and consumer chemicals	57.1	0	57.1	57.1	28.6	42.9	57.1
Metal manufacture and products	25.0	0	25.0	75.0	0	25.0	50.0
Other manufacturing	67.0	17.0	33.3	66.7	17.0	66.7	100.0
Total	47.1	13.4	35.3	58.0	13.4	37.0	56.8
By home country							
USA	50.0	17.4	30.4	56.5	8.7	37.0	58.7
Japan	51.2	17.1	36.6	58.5	14.6	43.9	62.5
Europe	34.6	3.8	34.6	65.4	15.4	34.6	50.0
Total[2]	47.1	13.4	35.3	58.0	13.4	37.0	56.8

Reasons for adaptation of production process:
A To meet technical standards (e.g. power supply).
B To respond to climatic differences.
C To meet national or EU regulations.
D To save costs by using more of relatively cheap factors of production.
E To use a larger proportion of skilled production workers.
F To use a smaller proportion of skilled production workers.
G To incorporate established local production processes that seem relevant.

Notes:
1. Subsidiaries that adapted an established production process were asked to endorse any of the offered reasons for doing so that were relevant to their operations.
2. Includes subsidiaries of MNEs from Australia and Canada.

Source: Survey of producing subsidiaries.

A pair of options offered for evaluation related to a need 'to use a larger/smaller proportion of skilled production workers' as motives for adaptation of production technology. The fact that 37.0 per cent of respondents indicated that they made such adjustments to accommodate a smaller proportion of skilled workers, compared with only 13.4 per cent who said they did so to utilise more, may carry worrying implications for the quality of the UK labour force with regard to effective supply of these established goods.

Surprisingly significant (endorsed by 56.8 per cent of respondents) and with much more positive implications, was the adaptation of production technology 'to incorporate established local production processes that seem relevant'. These subsidiaries seem to perceive the potential to enrich their supply of established goods through the interjection of elements of local technologies into their production processes, and also feel that they possess the creative flexibility to do so effectively without compromising their position in group supply programmes. This facet of technological dynamism within types of subsidiaries that could easily settle for a hierarchical knowledge dependency, seems indicative of the intra-group competition that seeks sources of a localised foundation for a creative transition to a higher-value-added positioning.

Compared to the previous four factors, which provoke adaptation of production processes in response to an ability or need to sharpen competitiveness in the light of positive or negative aspects of the local input situation, the remaining three (Table 4.6) relate to aspects of external conditions. The most prominent of these was the need 'to meet technical standards (for example, power supply)' endorsed by 47.1 per cent of respondents, whilst 35.3 per cent also responded to a need 'to meet national or EU regulations' in their production technologies. Relatively unimportant was a desire 'to respond to climatic conditions' with 13.4 per cent overall, where alarm about the UK's weather proved almost irrelevant to subsidiaries of MNEs from home countries elsewhere in Europe.

CONCLUSIONS

The material analysed in this chapter builds on that of the previous one by broadening our understanding of the technological content of the subsidiary evolution process. As expected, the creative transition from ESTPROD to DEVELPROD roles involves a widening of the sources of technology that need to be accessed, and also a crucial upgrading of in-house capacity in order to assimilate and coordinate these more creative inputs. Nevertheless, it also seems that certain elements of technology persist in importance through the creative transition process, and help to serve the key purpose of grounding the wider scope of emerging DEVELPROD subsidiaries in a cohesive (rather than incoherent or anarchic) expansion of the group's technological trajectory. Most important among these were the technologies of past (or persisting) products (that is, ESTPRODTECH) and the tacit knowledge capacities of engineers and shop-floor personnel (that is, ENGUNIT). The key factor that seems to underpin the distinctive scope of DEVELPROD subsidiaries in the most decisive way is the presence of an in-house R&D unit. The next two chapters analyse in detail the position of R&D laboratories in MNE UK operations, and seek to delineate how decentralised approaches to R&D are crucial to the technological and commercial progress of companies seeking to compete globally.

NOTES

1. 'New technology' Hedlund and Rolander observe (1990, p.32) 'seems to entail a lot of combining developments in seemingly unrelated fields, and building a human and social infrastructure enabling the realisations of such synergies. The enlargement of perspective to the global arena means a quantum jump in possibilities for creating development blocks, and the MNC is one of the critical actors with a catalytic role in this respect'.
2. Hedlund and Rolander (1990, p.36), however, have little concern in this regard. Thus 'the trauma of projects spinning off from the core is not so great. In fact, this is part of normal developments. Successes which do not fit well into the guiding thrust of the firm take on their own life in the periphery of the company, or completely outside it. Thus, although aiming for dynamism and change, heterarchically structured learning does not try to internalise all new developments'.
3. The concept of a technology audit is well developed in Contractor and Narayanan (1990).
4. There were 12 Swedish, 14 Japanese and 16 US companies, all of which were considered technology-based and multinational. In all, 91 interviews with technology executives were carried out. These executives seem likely to have been sufficiently senior to have an adequately broad base understanding of group priorities to provide a meaningful relative evaluation of technology-based issues in wider decision making.
5. In Grandstrand and Sjolander's results 'escalating R&D spending' rated well below average for the technology issues for US, Japanese and Swedish respondents.
6. Giddy (1978) noted the way in which the product cycle was becoming 'highly compressed' into a series of near simultaneous innovations in several major markets. Harrigan (1984) documented a similar process and drew attention to its relation to MNE organisational structures.
7. 'The new winners are the companies that are sensitive to market or technological trends no matter where they occur, creatively responsive to the opportunities and threats they perceive worldwide, and able to exploit their new ideas and products globally in a rapid and efficient manner' (Bartlett and Ghoshal, 1990, p.216).
8. Presumably Bartlett and Ghoshal's 'international' corporation would attempt a compromise of the two traditional approaches, with overseas subsidiaries allowed extensive scope to apply essentially centrally-generated innovations to their local environment in quite distinctive forms.
9. Papanastassiou and Pearce (1997b, p.16) and Pearce (1998).
10. Nelson and Winter (1982), Cantwell (1991b) and Dosi (1988).
11. In the US subsample (Papanastassiou and Pearce, 1997a), the relationship between ESTPROD/EUR and GROUPTECH is significantly positive, indicating clearly the possibility

that this type of new group knowledge may be accessed to sharpen the characteristics of products already supplied to the European market by the subsidiary, as well as provide a basis for a more complete innovation process.

12. See, for example, Dunning (1993b), Chesnais (1988) and Hagedoorn (1993) for discussion of strategic technology alliances.
13. Hagedoorn and Schakenraad (1991) provide evidence on the status of R&D-driven associations amongst all strategic technology alliances.
14. See Pearce and Singh (1992a).
15. Food, instruments, chemicals, pharmaceuticals.

5. Multinationals' research and development in the UK

INTRODUCTION

Earlier chapters have already suggested that decentralised R&D now plays important roles in the *strategic* evolution of MNEs, providing a crucial basis for the differentiation of subsidiary roles and occupying key positions as these companies develop an increasingly globalised approach to innovation.[1] Several important pioneering survey-based analyses of R&D in MNEs did indeed discern the presence of a range of roles for overseas laboratories (Cordell,1973 1971; Ronstadt, 1978, 1977), and that the extent and nature of such decentralised activity would depend on the strategic orientation of the companies' global operations (Behrman and Fischer, 1980a, 1980b). Nevertheless, the pervasive conceptual background to an early wave of empirical investigations of the determinants of R&D decentralisation in MNEs[2] took a somewhat different perspective, based on rather less ambitious expectations for the roles of overseas laboratories.

These analyses of the determinants of R&D decentralisation used a dependent variable that was usually defined as the proportion of MNEs' total R&D performed outside their home countries.[3] This aggregate variable was then, in effect, perceived as the result of the summation of a number of separate bilateral decisions that determined whether or not particular potential host countries were able to attract an R&D facility. Thus an MNE was perceived as determining 'the location of its R&D by reconciling centripetal and centrifugal forces' (Hirschey and Caves, 1981, p.117). Whilst certain factors might enable an overseas subsidiary to pull some R&D work into its operations, the dominant view was that it would do this against a pervasive gravitational force that tended to favour the retention of the MNE group's more creative activity at the centre. This expectation, of course, reflects the centralised approach to innovation that was enshrined in the traditional 'centre for global' alternative delineated by Bartlett and Ghoshal (1990).[4]

Against this background the traditional role for overseas R&D in MNEs was then perceived as the limited, and essentially *tactical*, one of supporting the ability to apply the group's well-established centrally-created technology effectively in new market environments and production locations. This short-term function therefore merely involved quite peripheral adaptations of existing products and production processes. To measure the strength of this centrifugal force these studies usually included a variable in terms of the share of overseas sales or production in total group production.[5] However, some studies[6] also incorporated the expectation that the degree of need for R&D support of overseas sales or production may depend on the market to which goods are expected to be sold and include variables to account for this qualifying factor. Thus Behrman and Fischer (1980a, 1980b) suggest that sales on the host-country market may have different needs for R&D support than exports, and that exports to the MNE's home country may have different need for support than those to third countries. This line of argument thus anticipates the more thorough attempts to relate subsidiary-level R&D to the strategic (including market-orientation) positioning of such overseas operations in recent investigation of MNE global technology programmes.

The early discussion of R&D location in MNEs attributes a strong centripetal influence to economies of scale. Thus it was felt that these companies would be reluctant to consider the dispersal of significant R&D work until the main home-country (central or parent) laboratory was fully utilising its key indivisible assets, such as specialised equipment, balanced research teams or uniquely talented individual personnel. Although this perception supported much of the hypothesising in these pioneering studies it rarely proved feasible to test it directly, mainly due to difficulties in formulating an adequate measure of research economies of scale. Nevertheless, Hirschey and Caves (1981) found the predicted negative relationship between overseas R&D and a proxy measure of research economies of scale. Hewitt (1980) found two proxy measures to be insignificant in his tests, although this actually confirmed the expectations of his rather differently modelled approach (reviewed below). Finally, mixed evidence on economies of scale in R&D decentralisation of Swedish MNEs was found in case study analyses of Håkanson and Zander (1986).

Discussion of internationalisation of R&D has often invoked the influence of agglomeration, that is forces that make it desirable to locate laboratories where they can benefit from a synergistic position in a community of research institutions (including laboratories of other firms) with similar ongoing research interests and specialisms (Cantwell, 1991c). In the early studies, agglomeration was usually perceived as a decisively centripetal force in the dichotomous centralisation versus decentralisation choice. In a contemporary context, however, in which MNEs may be able to evaluate the distinctive research capacities, knowledge traditions and general creative competences of many of the countries in which they operate, the forces of agglomeration may take on a new relevance, instead helping to determine *which* locations are accessed as parts of decentralised networked programmes of specialised R&D facilities.[7] Taggart (1991) finds evidence of such agglomeration factors influencing location of R&D units in pharmaceutical MNEs. Thus a high number of new drugs developed in a target country emerged as a positive determinant of new MNE R&D (that is, 'firms clearly see that a good record of new drug development in a particular country is a good indicator of future success for a new R&D facility in that location' (Taggart, 1991, p.236).

Other centripetal forces indicated in early thinking on R&D location in MNEs include avoidance of potential problems of control and coordination that could be generated by decentralisation. It was felt that companies that considered that they had benefited from a carefully controlled and balanced growth of research scope within a central laboratory feared that trying to further enrich this capacity through the addition of overseas facilities could set up new problems of coordination. These could lead to dislocation and loss of focus in the overall programme. Thus Håkanson and Nobel (1993a, p.370) observe that 'R&D tasks are typically unstructured and involve negotiations, persuasion and joint problem solving, activities requiring personal, face-to-face contacts. The cost of such contacts will be reduced by geographical proximity between involved parties'. Although never investigated by a separate variable, the potential problems of coordination influenced the manner of articulation of some of the independent variables in several early studies (for example, Hirschey and Caves, 1981; Lall, 1979).

The concerns over control and coordination took on a very specific manifestation in terms of worries over the security of technology that is created or applied in internationalised R&D programmes. Thus it was feared that the much more widespread need for communication in dispersed programmes would massively increase the danger of the unwanted external diffusion of the probably new and valuable technology involved, compared with the tighter security that should be available in a centralised facility. Rugman (1981, p.606) suggests a theoretical basis for such concerns that 'centralised control of R&D is an implication of [the internalisation] theory of the MNE. Unless the R&D is centralised in the parent its firm-specific advantage is at risk. The MNE prefers to control the rate of its knowledge advantage, and it is afraid of dissipation'.

Within the wave of pioneering studies, the work of Hewitt (1983, 1980) provides the strongest bridge to the concerns and perceptions of contemporary analysis of R&D in MNEs. In general terms, Hewitt sees his modelling as being less concerned with the 'optimising' aims of balancing centripetal and centrifugal forces, and as more compatible with a 'satisficing' or 'behavioural' approach that views the emergence of overseas R&D in MNEs as being an integral part of the evolution of their overall strategic attitude to the positioning of their wider global operations. At any point in time, Hewitt argues, the extent and nature of overseas R&D will depend on, firstly, the stage of evolution of the firm's globalisation strategy (exports; autonomous subsidiaries; international division; geographical area division or global product division) and, secondly, on their basic approach to competitiveness (marketing orientation or R&D orientation). Amongst the possibilities then opened up within his multidimensional scenario, Hewitt drew attention to two potential developments that have received considerable emphasis in subsequent work. Firstly, that overseas subsidiaries may compete to secure the right to develop products (by applying 'local original R&D') and, secondly, that parts of global R&D programmes might be carried out in countries with specialised resources, personnel or traditions (that is, applying 'global original R&D'). Thus, by pointing to product development and participation in MNE global R&D programmes as potential roles of decentralised laboratories, Hewitt moves their positioning towards support of their MNEs' pursuit of strategic competitiveness to a degree that was not envisaged by the more conventional early studies.

The key emphasis of the contemporary view of the internationalisation of R&D in MNEs is, therefore, that it is integral to the pursuit of strategic competitiveness by these companies. From the earlier emphasis on the provision of tactical support for the localised application of established commercial technology, the current perspective now sees overseas R&D as making crucial contributions to the strategic evolution of the technology itself. In the medium term, dispersed R&D units can contribute to the development of strategic competitiveness by taking key positions in the commercial evolution of existing core technologies, through their enhanced embodiment in major new generations of globally-competing products. In the longer term perspectives, overseas R&D units can also play vital roles in the regeneration and revitalisation of the MNE group's core technology itself, through participation in programmes of basic or applied research. Although this new positioning clearly enriches the scope of individual overseas R&D units, it does so by substantially placing their activity within programmes and networks that support the overall strategic evolution of the technological competitiveness of the parent MNE groups.[8] Thus, although the new generation of MNE laboratories have the potential to originate highly distinctive in-house competences, it can also be suggested that they will still be expected to exercise this individualism in ways that involve strong interdependencies with other operations of their MNE group (Papanastassiou and Pearce, 1998a).[9]

These perspectives on R&D in the contemporary MNE will be elaborated and documented as the central themes of the next chapter. The remaining sections here provide evidence on the extent of commitment to in-house R&D in MNE UK subsidiaries and information on institutional and organisational characteristics of such laboratories.

EXTENT OF R&D IN MNE SUBSIDIARIES

As was discussed in detail in the previous chapter, a question in the survey of producing subsidiaries asked them to evaluate each of seven sources of technology in terms of their relevance to their operations. That discussion provided a broad introduction to 'R&D carried out by our own laboratory' (OWNLAB) as a source of technology. The first three tables in this chapter help us to extend the analysis of that data in indicating the extent and positioning (in terms of types of subsidiaries supported) of MNE R&D laboratories in the UK.

Overall, Table 5.1 shows that 3.4 per cent of responding subsidiaries considered OWNLAB to be their only source of technology, whilst 35.8 per cent rated it as a major source and 20.1 per cent as a secondary source. Thus very slightly more than two-fifths of the subsidiaries indicated that they do not use an in-house R&D unit.[10] Support from an R&D laboratory is least prevalent in the ESTPROD/UK subsidiaries, where the need for such support would normally be limited to adapting technology that is already embodied in established products to host-country conditions.

However, it might initially be expected that ESTPROD/EUR subsidiaries would have even less need for in-house R&D support than ESTPROD/UK, since their role of supplying standardised products to wider group networks (here mainly in Europe) would remove even the need for adaptation to local (UK) needs.[11] In fact, Table 5.1 indicates a greater significance for in-house R&D in ESTPROD/EUR than ESTPROD/UK subsidiaries, both in that fewer operate without laboratories (35.6 per cent compared to 48.1 per cent) and that more report OWNLAB as a major (or only) source of technology (40.2 per cent compared with 32.9 per cent).

The unexpected level of persistence of R&D units in ESTPROD/EUR subsidiaries may reflect the selection process through which they acquire this role during their MNE rationalisation programmes. Thus it may be that in assembling a network of specialised supply facilities, MNE group planners view the presence of R&D and other creative attributes as reflecting favourably on the capability and potential of an (at that stage TMR) subsidiary, even though there is no obvious use for these elements of functional scope in the new (RPS) position that the unit is expected to take. If this is so, then the process of rationalising these subsidiaries into their networked role might still be expected to eventually see the decline of those R&D units that may (perhaps for reasons of morale or relations with host-country governments) have been allowed to persist into the early phases of accession to this role. Sensing this vulnerability (and reflecting subsidiary-level competitive ambition engendered by an enhanced awareness of

Table 5.1 In-house R&D (OWNLAB) as a source of technology in MNE subsidiaries in the UK

	Importance of in-house R&D (percentage of subsidiaries)[1]				
	Only source	Major source	Secondary source	Not a source	Total
By industry					
Food		75.0		25.0	100.0
Automobiles		38.9	5.6	55.6	100.0
Aerospace		16.7	16.7	66.7	100.0
Electronics and electrical appliances	2.2	30.4	30.4	37.0	100.0
Mechanical engineering	3.8	26.9	19.2	50.0	100.0
Instruments	9.1	45.5	9.1	36.4	100.0
Industrial and agricultural chemicals	6.9	44.8	20.7	27.6	100.0
Pharmaceuticals and consumer chemicals		50.0	30.0	20.0	100.0
Metal manufacture and products	9.1	27.3	9.1	54.5	100.0
Other manufacturing		21.4	28.6	50.0	100.0
Total	3.4	35.8	20.1	40.8	100.0
By home country					
USA	1.5	46.2	18.5	33.8	100.0
Japan	4.7	21.9	20.3	53.1	100.0
Europe	4.7	37.2	23.3	34.9	100.0
Total[2]	3.4	35.8	20.1	40.8	100.0
By subsidiary type[3]					
ESTPROD/UK		32.9	19.0	48.1	100.0
ESTPROD/EUR	3.4	36.8	24.1	35.6	100.0
COMPART		50.0	16.7	33.3	100.0
DEVELPROD	7.9	58.7	11.1	22.2	100.0

Notes:
1. The percentage of respondents who graded 'R&D carried out by our own laboratory' at each level as a source of their technology.
2. Includes subsidiaries of MNEs from Australia and Canada.
3. Subsidiaries that said a particular role was either their only one or their predominant one. For definitions of subsidiary types, see Table 3.1.

Source: Survey of production subsidiaries.

dependent intra-group status that becomes perceptible to networked ESTPROD/EUR management), genuine roles may be sought for surviving laboratories, which may then generate forward-looking potentials. One obvious aim of major in-house R&D in an ESTPROD subsidiary is to build the knowledge basis for evolution to the DEVELPROD role. Alternatively it could be that whilst the rationalisation of a regional supply network does indeed remove the need for each RPS to have its own R&D unit, it would be necessary for at least one to retain this scope in order to support the whole system.[12] Building the laboratory competence to play this role (and thereby assert a key position in the network) could again explain the more than nominal scope of R&D in many ESTPROD/EUR subsidiaries.[13]

Although one-third of COMPART subsidiaries operates without in-house R&D support, Table 5.1 also shows that half of them rated such laboratories as a major source of their technology. While the former figure is compatible with some of these COMPART facilities undertaking the routine cost-effective supply of existing intermediate goods, the latter provides further support for the view that many now operate through a creative interdependence with DEVELPROD subsidiaries, and utilise their own R&D unit to help with the generation of new components as part of a wider product development process. Finally, the expectation that in-house R&D would be a key driving factor in DEVELPROD subsidiaries is substantially confirmed, with only 22.2 per cent of them reporting the absence of a laboratory and precisely two-thirds rating the output of one as a major (or only) technology input for their work.

Table 5.2 presents average responses for the significance of R&D by industry and home country of subsidiary (these summary measures taking account of both whether an R&D unit is present and, if so, the intensity of its contribution). By this measure R&D is notably weakest in Japanese subsidiaries, with this in fact deriving from (see Table 5.1) the relatively small number of them that both possessed R&D units and considered their output to be a major source of technology when available. This lack of R&D scope seems likely, however, to be due to the relative newness of both the subsidiaries themselves and the internationalisation process in Japanese companies generally, so that considerable expansion may be a logical expectation.[14] Of the four industries that reported the highest ARs for OWNLAB in Table 5.2, all derived this from both above-average proportions of subsidiaries with laboratories (although only modestly so for instruments) and a strong (major or only source status) for their output. The perhaps surprisingly low AR for automobiles derives mainly from the large proportion of subsidiaries without laboratories (Table 5.1), whilst that in electronics is rather more related to the high number of those that considered their laboratory's output to be only a secondary technology source. The very weak status of OWNLAB in aerospace reflects the fact that only one-third of these

Table 5.2 Importance of in-house R&D (OWNLAB) as a source of technology in MNE subsidiaries in the UK

	Home country of subsidiary (average response)[1]			
	USA	Japan	Europe	Total[2]
By industry				
Food	2.60		1.00	2.50
Automobiles	2.11	1.71	1.00	1.83
Aerospace	1.60			1.50
Electronics and electrical appliances	2.10	1.86	2.14	1.98
Mechanical engineering	1.88	1.56	2.11	1.85
Instruments	2.29	2.00	3.00	2.27
Industrial and agricultural chemicals	2.33	1.75	2.42	2.31
Pharmaceuticals and consumer chemicals	1.75	3.00	2.20	2.30
Metal manufacture and products	2.00	1.75	3.00	1.91
Other manufacturing	3.00	1.63	1.60	1.71
Total	2.15	1.78	2.12	2.02

Notes:
1. Respondents were asked to grade 'R&D carried out by our own laboratory' (OWNLAB) as a source of their technology as being either (i) our only source, (ii) a major source, (iii) a secondary source, (iv) not a source. The average response was then derived by allocating a value of 4 to 'only source', 3 to 'major source', 2 to 'secondary source' and 1 to 'not a source.'
2. Includes subsidiaries from Canada and Australia.

Source: Survey of production subsidiaries.

subsidiaries had laboratories and only half of these rated the overall output as a major source of technology.

Some further indication of the strategic positioning of subsidiaries' R&D is shown in Table 5.3, which presents regression tests in which OWNLAB serves as the dependent variable. Along with dummy variables for the subsidiary's industry (other industries serving as the omitted dummy) and for the home country (continental Europe as the omitted source region) in the full sample, the four subsidiary roles were included as independent variables. The view that the DEVELPROD role now provides the most obvious rationale for the commitment to in-house R&D is comprehensively confirmed through a highly significant positive relationship with OWNLAB in all three (US, Japanese and European firm) subsamples. The significant positive sign on ESTPROD/EUR for subsidiaries of European MNEs means that the more they play the RPS role the stronger the status of in-house R&D. Here the probable natural tendency to fight off R&D decline in subsidiaries taking on this role seems to acquire an especially virulent form that may reflect particular circumstances in these firms that we have already suggested. Thus it may be that the processes of reacting to European integration are encouraging rationalisation programmes, part of the technological implications of which are to centralise the more creative and high-value-added work in the continental home-country (parent) operations.[15] To fight against this may provide an extra impetus to the retention of technological autonomy in their UK subsidiaries through in-house R&D units. One aspect of that (to some degree indicated in Chapter 3) may be to result in a relatively strong tendency of European MNE subsidiaries in the UK to target export markets outside Europe. Where these subsidiaries are also supplying established products to European markets (ESTPROD/EUR), the attempt to generate greater autonomy by turning some of these towards markets outside Europe may involve quite extensive adaptive R&D work, in order to remove specific European characteristics and build in elements that appeal to tastes of the new target customers.

Those subsidiaries that possessed R&D laboratories were asked to report if they expected growth or decline in these facilities in the near future. The results reported in Table 5.4 generally indicate a continued momentum in decentralised R&D in these companies, with 39.8 per cent of respondents anticipating laboratory growth and only 11.9 per cent expecting decline. Both Japanese and US subsidiaries recorded a decisive net expectation of growth in their R&D laboratories, but subsidiaries of European MNEs provided a net expectation of decline. For the Japanese and US subsidiaries, the reported expectation is compatible with growing intra-subsidiary creativity as they seek to claim leading positions in their group's strategic approach to the European market (that is, as regionalised dimensions replace localised ones for these units, more R&D emerges as an important element in building the appropriate functional scope). We have already suggested that European MNEs also increasingly adopt a regional technology strategy, but that this more often tends to embody a desire to focus the key creative elements of this on home-country (continental parent) operations.[16] This then seems to result in a sense of vulnerability relating to existing R&D facilities in their UK subsidiaries. The regression tests reported in Table 5.5 confirm these results, with both US and Japanese subsidiaries significantly more likely to expect growth, and US subsidiaries significantly less likely to predict decline, than

Table 5.3 Regressions with OWNLAB as dependent variable – home country sub-samples

	Dependent variable (OWNLAB)[1]			
	USA	Japan	Europe	Total
Intercept	2.2614†	0.7880	−0.1955	0.9336‡
	(2.67)	(1.14)	(−0.34)	(2.61)
Food	−0.2734		−0.1303	0.0313
	(−1.41)		(−0.87)	(0.41)
Automobiles	−1.8791†	−0.1679	−0.6341	−0.2593
	(−2.08)	(−0.34)	(−0.95)	(−0.85)
Aerospace	−0.9643†			−0.2760
	(−2.12)			(−1.34)
Electronics	−0.3650	0.0364	0.0611	0.0246
	(−1.65)	(0.36)	(0.58)	(0.38)
Mechanical engineering	−0.2883*	−0.0359	0.0474	−0.0246
	(−2.20)	(−0.55)	(0.78)	(−0.61)
Instruments	−0.2572*	0.0613	0.1518	0.0276
	(−1.68)	(0.57)	(1.23)	(0.47)
Chemicals	−0.4999	0.0077	0.2433*	0.0861
	(−1.67)	(0.04)	(1.86)	(0.93)
Pharmaceuticals	−0.1744	0.0930	0.0788	0.0359
	(−1.62)	(0.84)	(1.42)	(0.91)
Metals	−0.2125*	0.0059		−0.0236
	(−1.79)	(0.08)		(−0.55)
USA				−0.0025
				(−0.15)
Japan				−0.0311†
				(−2.02)
ESTPROD/UK[2]	−0.0856	0.0323	0.1740	−0.0509
	(−0.64)	(0.21)	(1.29)	(−0.69)
ESTPROD/EUR	0.0798	0.1072	0.2722†	0.1626†
	(0.56)	(0.67)	(2.09)	(2.12)
COMPART	0.2011	−0.2118	−0.1693	−0.0596
	(1.29)	(−1.07)	(−0.70)	(−0.59)
DEVELPROD	0.5432‡	0.4357‡	0.6112‡	0.4799‡
	(4.27)	(2.95)	(5.18)	(6.70)
R^2	0.3987	0.2102	0.6496	0.3279
F	2.45†	1.26	4.89‡	5.14‡
n	62	64	41	174

Notes:
1. For full definition of the dependent variable, see Table 4.1.
2. For definition of independent variables, see Table 3.1.
n Number of observations; ‡significant at 1%; † significant at 5%; *significant at 10%;.

the European subsidiaries (which serve as the omitted home-country variable).

The regressions of Table 5.5 also included the roles of the responding subsidiaries as independent variables. The significant results for the DEVELPROD role again confirm that (for US and Japanese operations in particular, we suggest) there is a momentum towards in-house R&D that supports the strategic focus on product development in these subsidiaries as they seek to assert their status in regionalised operations. Although not achieving significance in either 'growth' or 'decline' regressions, the signs on ESTPROD/EUR suggest that the more prevalent is this role in a subsidiary the more likely is a decline in its R&D capacity perceived to be. This is in line with our interpretation of earlier results as suggesting that many ESTPROD/EUR subsidiaries may be carrying R&D capacity in excess of their logical needs. Although we have indicated ways in which they may be seeking to provide validation for this R&D scope, it seems that many of these units admit a persisting sense of its vulnerability. This scenario can, in turn, be considered as having some worrying implications for the UK as host country. Thus subsidiaries with a certain degree of creative (potentially high-value-added) scope (in an earlier, mainly ESTPROD/UK, role) may gain the more emphatically cost-based ESTPROD/EUR positioning and often then have to shed those characteristics that could individualise their situation in the MNE (and more thoroughly and distinctively embed the operation in the UK economy). Once this R&D has gone, the subsidiary can only sustain its networked position through a low-cost supply of standardised inputs, since a need to avoid 'unnecessary' overheads in retaining the ESTPROD/EUR status makes it increasingly implausible to generate or revitalise elements of creative scope that cannot yield immediate dividends (that is, the DEVELPROD role slips increasingly far out of reach).

AGE OF LABORATORIES

Both surveys included questions that sought information on the age profiles of MNE laboratories in the UK. Only 13.5 per cent of the R&D units reported by producing subsidiaries had been set up before 1950 (Table 5.6), with 17.7 per cent added in the next two decades. The creation of 15.6 per cent more during the 1970s may suggest that it was around that time that overseas R&D in MNEs began the transition from a rather *ad hoc* status (mainly to support the effective decentralised application of centrally-generated product technology) to a more systematically strategic positioning in globalised approaches to technology. This more contemporary perspective then resulted in 31.3 per cent of laboratories being set up in the 1980s and 21.9 per

Table 5.4 Anticipated changes in size of R&D laboratories of MNE subsidiaries in the UK

	Anticipated change[1] (percentage of respondents)	
	Growth	Decline
By industry		
Food	42.9	14.3
Automobiles	42.9	0
Electronics and electrical appliances	55.6	0
Mechanical engineering	46.7	0
Instruments	0	50.0
Industrial and agricultural chemicals	19.0	30.0
Pharmaceuticals and consumer chemicals	37.5	25.0
Other manufacturing	50.0	0
Total	39.8	11.9
By home country		
USA	42.8	4.7
Japan	59.3	7.4
Europe	21.4	29.6
Total[2]	39.8	11.9

Notes:
1. Responding MNE subsidiaries that possessed an R&D laboratory were asked if they anticipated its growth or decline in the near future.
2. Includes laboratories of MNEs from Australia and Canada.

Source: Survey of production subsidiaries.

cent more since 1990. The generalised surge in MNE R&D laboratories in the UK probably reflects two tendencies. Firstly, new subsidiaries are now likely to incorporate R&D right from their initiation, or at least to possess a clearly defined plan for a quick addition of this to their functional scope.[17] Secondly, well-established subsidiaries that traditionally felt able to operate without in-house support now feel impelled to add such activity. This new R&D may merely be intended to allow them to continue their traditional role with increased security or instead may aim to provide the basis for potential upgrading within evolving group strategy.[18]

The replies from the survey of laboratories themselves indicate essentially the same pattern (Table 5.7). Thus 29.8 per cent had been set up before 1965 and 44.7 per cent since 1986. Both surveys supply decisive evidence for a substantial relatively recent emergence of overseas R&D in Japanese MNEs.[19] US and European MNEs were both relatively strongly committed to the creation of R&D laboratories in the UK in the earlier time periods, mainly to support the effective localisation of operations. In line with our interpretation

Table 5.5 Regressions with anticipated changes in size of R&D
laboratories as dependent variables

	Dependent variable	
	Anticipated growth	Anticipated decline
Intercept	−0.1869	0.1648
	(−0.60)	(0.87)
Food	0.0713	0.0390
	(1.23)	(1.12)
Automobiles	0.0900	0.0592
	(0.31)	(0.33)
Electronics and electrical appliances	0.1037*	−0.0096
	(1.77)	(−0.27)
Mechanical engineering	0.0553	−0.0014
	(1.52)	(−0.06)
Instruments	−0.0511	0.1501‡
	(−0.97)	(4.72)
Industrial and agricultural chemicals	0.0434	0.1028†
	(0.54)	(2.11)
Pharmaceuticals and consumer chemicals	0.0452	0.0212
	(1.45)	(1.13)
USA	0.0266†	−0.0210‡
	(2.37)	(−2.98)
Japan	0.0404‡	−0.0083
	(3.35)	(−1.13)
ESTPROD/UK[1]	0.0077	−0.0332
	(0.12)	(−0.84)
ESTPROD/EUR	−0.0713	0.0575
	(−1.09)	(1.44)
COMPART	−0.0327	0.0397
	(−0.41)	(0.82)
DEVELPROD	0.1098*	−0.0744*
	(1.78)	(−1.93)
R^2	0.2820	0.4323
F	2.17†	4.11‡
n	99	97

Notes:
1. For definition of independent variables, see Table 3.1.
   n number of observations; ‡ significant at 1%; † significant at 5%; * significant at 10%.

of less need for this in European MNE subsidiaries, in particular, there is
indeed a notable slowdown in their creation of new laboratories over the last

10 to 15 years. With the exception of a considerable fall in new laboratories reported by US subsidiaries in the 1990s (Table 5.6), the tables tend to suggest that (compared to the European MNEs) these companies continued a steady growth in UK-based R&D as they moved towards a regionalised competitive strategy. Reflecting in particular the prevalence of Japanese units, electronics emerges as an industry with a large proportion of relatively new laboratories. Recently created facilities also prevail somewhat in the pharmaceutical industry as depicted in the laboratory survey (Table 5.7), though less clearly in the replies of subsidiaries (Table 5.6). This modest discrepancy could reflect the presence in the laboratory survey of several

Table 5.6 Dates of establishment of R&D laboratories of MNE subsidiaries in the UK

	Dates of establishment (percentage of cases)					
	Before 1950	1950 to 1969	1970 to 1979	1980 to 1989	1990 and after	Total
By industry						
Food	16.7	50.0	16.7	16.7		100.0
Automobiles	14.3		28.6	14.3	42.8	100.0
Electronics and electrical appliances		11.5	15.4	30.8	42.3	100.0
Mechanical engineering	28.6	14.3	14.3	21.4	21.4	100.0
Instruments	16.7			83.3		100.0
Industrial and agricultural chemicals	15.0	35.0	20.0	15.0	15.0	100.0
Pharmaceuticals and consumer chemicals	25.0	12.5	12.5	37.5	12.5	100.0
Other manufacturing	11.1	11.1	11.1	66.7		100.0
Total	13.5	17.7	15.6	31.3	21.9	100.0
By home country						
USA	15.8	26.3	18.4	34.2	5.3	100.0
Japan			7.4	37.0	55.6	100.0
Europe	23.1	19.2	23.1	19.2	15.4	100.0
Total[1]	13.5	17.7	15.6	31.3	21.9	100.0

Note:
1. Includes laboratories of MNEs from Australia and Canada.

Source: Survey of production subsidiaries.

stand-alone precompetitive units of pharmaceutical companies, set up recently as part of the emergence of a dispersed approach to this phase of research. By contrast, industrial chemicals reveals a relatively weak participation in the recent wave of decentralised R&D, compared to quite pronounced involvement in the earlier era (perhaps up to 1980).

MEANS OF ESTABLISHMENT

The survey of laboratories asked them to say which of four possibilities best described their means of original creation or entry into their MNE group's operations. By far the most prevalent of these means of establishment was a 'fresh installation of the laboratory', which was endorsed by 81.6 per cent of respondents. All of the US units were created in this way, along with 78.9 per cent of the Japanese ones and 70.6 per cent of the European. MNEs in the chemicals industry used this means of achieving UK-based R&D most strongly (88.9 per cent) and the miscellaneous other manufacturing group least (75.0 per cent), with pharmaceuticals (82.4 per cent) and electronics (81.8 per cent) both close to the average.

The 'acquisition of an existing independent R&D facility' accounted for only 8.2 per cent of cases, being relatively strong in laboratories of European MNEs (17.6 per cent) compared with the Japanese ones (5.3 per cent). No electronics MNEs acquired an existing independent UK laboratory, with the figures for pharmaceuticals, chemicals and other manufacturing being 11.8 per cent, 11.0 per cent and 8.3 per cent, respectively. Laboratories that were 'acquired as part of a company involved in a merger or take-over' accounted for another 8.2 per cent of all cases, with Japanese (10.5 per cent) and European (11.8 per cent) companies making very similar use of this means. Electronics MNEs were the strongest users of this route, with 18.2 per cent of their laboratories secured in this way, compared with 8.3 per cent in other manufacturing, 5.9 per cent in pharmaceuticals and no cases in chemicals. Finally, only one laboratory (a Japanese unit in other manufacturing) emerged 'as a collaboration in a R&D joint venture with another company'.

R&D BUDGETS OF LABORATORIES

Respondents to the laboratory survey were asked to report their most recent annual R&D budget, with 41 able to provide this information. As Table 5.8 shows 41.4 per cent reported annual R&D expenditure of less than £2 million, a further 41.5 per cent up to £10 million, and 17.1 per cent £10 million or over. In fact the average R&D budget of the respondents in the top expenditure group was £42.3 million. The longer-established European and, to a

Table 5.7   Dates of establishment of MNE laboratories in the UK.

	Dates of establishment (percentage of cases)			
	Before 1965	1966 to 1985	1986 and after	Total
By industry				
Electronics	30.0	20.0	50.0	100.0
Pharmaceuticals	17.7	29.4	52.9	100.0
Chemicals[1]	33.3	55.6	11.1	100.0
Other	45.5		54.5	100.0
Total	29.8	25.5	44.7	100.0
By home country				
USA	38.5	30.8	30.8	100.0
Japan	11.1	11.1	77.8	100.0
Europe	43.8	37.5	18.7	100.0
Total	29.8	25.5	44.7	100.0

Note:
1. Includes petrochemicals and petroleum.

Source: Survey of laboratories.

Table 5.8   Budgets of MNE laboratories in the UK

	Expenditure - £m (percentage of cases)					
	Less than 1	1 to 1.9	2 to 2.9	3 to 9.9	10 and over	Total
By industry						
Electronics	11.1	33.3	11.1	33.3	11.1	100.0
Pharmaceuticals	12.5	25.0	25.0	18.8	18.8	100.0
Chemicals[1]		14.3		57.1	28.6	100.0
Other	33.3	33.3	22.2		11.1	100.0
Total	14.6	26.8	17.1	24.4	17.1	100.0
By home country						
USA		18.2	36.4	27.3	18.2	100.0
Japan	18.8	37.5	18.8	18.8	6.3	100.0
Europe	21.4	21.4		28.6	28.6	100.0
Total	14.6	26.8	17.1	24.4	17.1	100.0

Note:

1. Includes petrochemicals and petroleum.

Source: Survey of laboratories.

somewhat lesser degree, US laboratories provided the greatest proportion of their cases in the largest expenditure groups, with the newer Japanese recording a larger share in the smaller budget categories. Chemicals was the industry with the strongest tendency to reveal large laboratories in terms of expenditure.

Table 5.9 R&D budgets of MNE laboratories in the UK as a percentage of the total R&D expenditure of their groups

		Per cent of group budget (percentage of cases)				
		Less than 1	1 to 1.9	2 to 9.9	10 and over	Total
By industry						
Electronics		14.3	57.1	14.3	14.3	100.0
Pharmaceuticals		14.3	28.6	35.7	21.4	100.0
Chemicals[1]		14.3		42.9	42.9	100.0
Other		16.7		66.7	16.7	100.0
	Total	14.7	23.5	38.2	23.5	100.0
By home country						
USA		22.2	22.2	33.3	22.2	100.0
Japan		8.3	41.7	33.3	16.7	100.0
Europe		15.4	7.7	46.2	30.8	100.0
	Total	14.7	23.5	38.2	23.5	100.0

Note:
1. Includes petrochemicals and petroleum.

Source: Survey of laboratories.

The UK-based laboratories were also asked to express their budgets as a proportion of the total R&D expenditure of their MNE groups. Thirty-four provided this information, which is summarised in Table 5.9. Overall, 38.2 per cent of them felt they accounted for less than 2 per cent of their group's research expenditures, another 38.2 per cent for less than 10 per cent and 23.5 per cent for over 10 per cent. Reflecting their large absolute expenditures, the laboratories of European MNEs were most likely to account for over 2 per cent of the group budget, whilst in parallel fashion the small Japanese units were most likely to account for less than 2 per cent. UK-based laboratories in chemicals were most likely to report a relatively significant share of their group's total R&D budgets, and electronics was the industry most likely to have achieved only a relatively limited position.

Regression tests (reported in Table 5.10) were run with absolute R&D expenditure (£ million) and share of group budget (per cent) as dependent

Table 5.10 Regressions with R&D budget as dependent variable

	Dependent variable	
	Level of R&D budget	Percentage of group R&D budget
Intercept	−3.2935	−3.0634
	(−0.37)	(−0.35)
USA	3.8079	2.3076
	(0.50)	(0.31)
Japan	−0.1606	6.5872*
	(−0.04)	(1.71)
Chemicals	1.0941	4.5367
	(0.34)	(1.45)
Electronics	0.6055	−1.3603
	(0.26)	(−0.53)
Pharmaceuticals	0.9653	−0.6454
	(0.62)	(−0.39)
AGE	0.3836†	0.2682*
	(2.37)	(1.76)
R^2	0.2051	0.2971
F	1.42	1.83
n	40	33

Notes:
n number of observations; † significant at 5%; * significant at 10%.

variables. The independent variables were dummies for industry (miscellaneous other manufacturing as the omitted dummy) and home country of laboratory (Europe omitted) and the age of the unit. In the case of the absolute R&D expenditure, age was significantly positive (at 5 per cent), confirming that laboratories tended to be able to justify extending their budget as their operations evolved over time. All the dummies were very weak in this regression, suggesting that the age of the laboratory (here controlled for) was a key factor determining the expenditure differences in Table 5.8. In the regression with the share of group budget as the dependent variable, age was still significantly positive (at 10 per cent), indicating that the growth of the UK laboratories over time represented an enhancement of their *relative* position in group operations, rather than merely sharing neutrally in a process of overall expansion. In this regression, the Japanese dummy was significantly positive (at 10 per cent) showing that, when age is controlled for, these laboratories were actually relatively more significant in their groups' operations than those of the omitted European group. This indicates the seriousness of the commitment to overseas R&D reflected in this early wave of Japanese laboratories in the UK.

EMPLOYMENT OF LABORATORIES

Levels of employment in the laboratories of producing subsidiaries are reported in Table 5.11. This shows that 33.0 per cent of these laboratories employed fewer than five scientists, but that 41.0 per cent employed over 20. The R&D units of US subsidiaries tended to be the largest, with 30.0 per cent of them having employment levels of scientific personnel of over 40. Again reflecting their relatively recent origins, Japanese MNE laboratories tended to be the smallest, with 44.4 per cent falling in the six to 19 personnel range, and only 18.5 per cent having 20 or more. Regression tests showed no clear tendency for the size of laboratory to be related to the prevalence of particular roles in the subsidiaries with which they are associated.

The survey sent directly to the laboratories also asked them to supply information on their employment. Of the 46 that reported their absolute staff level, 17.4 per cent employed less than 10, 23.9 per cent between 10 and 19, 19.6 per cent between 20 and 39, 17.4 per cent from 40 to 99 and 21.7 per cent 100 or more. The average employment of laboratories in the largest group was 452. European and US laboratories once again tended to be larger employers than Japanese, with chemicals distinctively largest amongst industries. Thirty-two laboratories estimated their employment as a proportion of that in all comparable units in their MNE group. Of these, 40.6 per cent assessed it as less than 3 per cent, 37.5 per cent between 3 per cent and 10 per cent and 21.9 per cent over 10 per cent.

The survey of laboratories also asked respondents to assess the role of four sources of recruitment in the composition of their scientific labour force.[20] The results for the two most relevant of these are summarised in Table 5.12.[21] In line with the expectation (elaborated in the next chapter) that the availability of experienced and competent personnel would be a factor attracting MNE technological activity to the UK, the most prominent of the sources of recruitment was 'UK scientists recruited in the UK'. Thus 36.2 per cent of respondents indicate that 100 per cent of their scientific personnel had been recruited in the UK, with this degree of localisation very prominent in US laboratories and in those of pharmaceutical firms. By contrast, 25.5 per cent of the respondents reported less than 80 per cent local personnel, with this degree of staff diversification most notable in Japanese and electronics facilities.

'Scientists from elsewhere in the MNE' are shown in Table 5.12 as contributing to the staff of almost half of the laboratories surveyed, with 23.4

Table 5.11 Level of employment of scientific personnel in MNE subsidiaries' laboratories in the UK

	Numbers of scientific personnel (percentage of cases)				
	Less than 5	6 to 19	20 to 39	40 or over	Total
By industry					
Food		14.3	85.7		100.0
Automobiles	28.6	42.9	14.3	14.3	100.0
Electronics and electrical appliances	30.8	30.8	15.4	23.0	100.0
Mechanical engineering	53.3	20.0	20.0	6.7	100.0
Instruments	50.0	33.3		16.7	100.0
Industrial and agricultural chemicals	28.6	23.8	28.6	19.0	100.0
Pharmaceuticals and consumer chemicals	25.0	25.0		50.0	100.0
Other manufacturing	40.0	20.0	20.0	20.0	100.0
Total	33.0	26.0	22.0	19.0	100.0
By home country					
USA	30.0	17.5	22.5	30.0	100.0
Japan	37.0	44.4	11.1	7.4	100.0
Europe	35.7	21.4	28.6	14.3	100.0
Total[1]	33.0	26.0	22.0	19.0	100.0

Note:
1.   Includes laboratories of MNEs from Australia and Canada.

Source: Survey of production subsidiaries.

per cent of them indicating that over 10 per cent of their personnel emerged from this source. The presence of scientists from the parent company in particular seems likely to be the major contributing factor in making such group personnel decisively most prevalent in Japanese (and, in a probably complementary fashion, electronics) laboratories. Thus the involvement of such intra-group transfers in the relatively new Japanese units are likely to be related to the need to embed these facilities (and often their also relatively young producing subsidiaries) in the technological and commercial trajectories of their parent MNE.[22] By contrast, three-fifths of the usually mature and experienced (if not necessarily strategically stable) US and European laboratories were able to operate without the intermediation of personnel from elsewhere in the company.

Of the other two sources of personnel covered in the question, only 23.4 per cent of respondents employed 'foreign scientists recruited in the UK'. This was most relevant in laboratories of European MNEs (46.7 per cent of their respondents) and in the chemical industry (50.0 per cent).[23] Employment of 'foreign scientists recruited outside the UK' played some role in 31.9 per cent of the labs, with European units (53.5 per cent) and those of chemical MNEs (62.5 per cent) again most likely to pursue this type of staff diversity.[24]

A supplementary question then asked those laboratories that included scientists from elsewhere in their MNE group amongst their staff to evaluate the relevance of three possible reasons for the presence of these personnel.[25] To 'participate in the scientific work of the laboratory' was reported as the only role of these staff for 15.4 per cent of respondents, a main one for 57.7 per cent, whilst for another 15.4 per cent they partly played it and it was not part of their activity for 11.5 per cent. This suggests that the primary motive for the interjection of these scientists from elsewhere in the MNE is to complement the abilities of UK personnel in order to help achieve the particular aims of the laboratory, which will have already been articulated and operationalised around distinctive elements of localised scope (or needs).

The two other reasons for the presence of MNE personnel in the UK laboratories can often relate more to a group-perceived need to ensure their effective involvement in the achievement of wider aims (that is, to secure their contributions to the pursuit of elements of strategic competitiveness through a well-defined positioning in the current technological trajectory). The first of these was to 'help in the introduction and assimilation of new group knowledge and technology'. This was endorsed as a main role of these personnel in 23.1 per cent of responding laboratories, part of their role in 57.7 per cent and absent in only 19.2 per cent. The other of these roles of MNE personnel was 'to participate in the management of the laboratory'. One respondent (3.9 per cent) considered this the only role of group scientists, and for 23.1 per cent it was rated a major one, whilst it was part of their role for 53.9 per cent and absent in 19.2 per cent. Thus whilst the vast majority of the scientists 'imported' from other parts of the MNE contribute their own specialised expertise on a day-to-day basis as part of the UK laboratories' ongoing research there is nevertheless a tendency for many of them to also play organisational or integrative roles that reflect the need to ensure the effective positioning of those units in the application and/or generation of the groups' wider technological scope.

Table 5.12 Sources of recruitment of scientific personnel of MNE laboratories in the UK

(A) UK scientists recruited in UK; proportion of employment (percentage of cases)

		Less than 80%	80% to 99%	100%	Total
By industry					
Electronics		36.4	45.5	18.2	100.0
Pharmaceuticals		17.7	29.4	52.9	100.0
Chemicals[1]		12.5	75.0	12.5	100.0
Other		36.4	18.2	45.5	100.0
	Total	25.5	38.3	36.2	100.0
By home country					
USA		15.4	30.8	53.9	100.0
Japan		47.4	26.3	26.3	100.0
Europe		6.7	60.0	33.3	100.0
	Total	25.5	38.3	36.2	100.0

(B) Scientists from elsewhere in the MNE group; proportion of employment (percentage of cases)

		0%	1% to 9%	10% or more	Total
By industry					
Electronics		45.5	18.2	36.4	100.0
Pharmaceuticals		64.7	17.7	17.7	100.0
Chemicals[1]		37.5	37.5	25.0	100.0
Other		54.6	27.3	18.2	100.0
	Total	53.2	23.4	23.4	100.0
By home country					
USA		61.5	30.8	7.7	100.0
Japan		42.1	15.8	42.1	100.0
Europe		60.0	26.7	13.3	100.0
	Total	53.2	23.4	23.4	100.0

Note:
1. Includes petrochemicals and petroleum.

Source: Survey of laboratories.

CONCLUSION

Almost three-fifths of the MNE production subsidiaries surveyed in the UK are shown to currently possess in-house R&D units. For US and Japanese subsidiaries, at least, there is also a very strong expectation that such R&D units will grow in significance over time.The ESTPROD/EUR subsidiaries are perceived as carrying more R&D scope than this role needs, and appear to see this as a last defence against decline into the more functionally barren and submissively networked positioning of a pure supply status. The persistence of R&D in these subsidiaries, then, aims to provide a lifeline to the creative and higher-value-added DEVELPROD role. This evolutionary potential of an in-house laboratory is verified by a clear and pervasive relationship between the strength of the DEVELPROD role and use of the output of its own R&D as a subsidiary's source of technology.

These indications seem to be symptomatic of the emergence of decentralised R&D in MNEs as part of a wider structural and organisational transformation, in which they seek to address new challenges and potentials in the globalised dimensions of competition. Probably half the MNE laboratories in the UK are less than 15 years old, and perhaps one-fifth have been set up since 1990. In terms of budgets the size of laboratories grows over the time, and even their *share* of their groups' R&D expenditure is related positively to their age. These results once again point towards a growth in dispersed R&D in MNEs which is increasingly a core element in the ways that these companies are seeking to generate and assert sources of strategic competitiveness that are fully activated in, and for, the newly globalised context. The next chapter turns to the detailed investigation of the various dimensions of the strategic status of overseas R&D laboratories.

NOTES

1. Archibugi and Michie (1995, p.122) divide 'technological globalisation' into (i) the global *exploitation* of technology, (ii) global technological *collaboration*, and (iii) the global *generation* of technology. Our investigation of the positioning of decentralised R&D in MNEs addresses its involvement in, mainly, the first and third of these aspects of the globalisation of technology. Suggestion of a growing need to be aware of the third aspect (in our terms the longer-term dimensions of strategic competitiveness) is also in line with Hedlund and Ridderstråle's (1997) articulation of the aims of the self-renewing MNE. Here, too, it is emphasised that strategic completeness needs not only programmes of *exploitation* ('where the primary aim is the effective utilisation of given resources') but also of *creation* ('where the focus is to seek opportunities for the future') so that 'exploitation aims at capturing the current potential, whereas creation aims at changing the future potential' (Hedlund and Ridderstråle, 1997, p.324).
2. Several of these studies used industry-level data from the US Department of Commerce (for example, Hirschey and Caves, 1981; Lall, 1979; Hewitt, 1980; Pearce, 1989, Chapter 3). Others were able to use firm-level data (for example, Mansfield, Teece and Romeo, 1979, for

US firms; Håkanson, 1981, for Swedish firms; Pearce, 1989, Chapter 4, for firms from several national origins).

3.   An alternative dependent variable, tested in recent studies (Papanastassiou and Pearce, 1992; Kumar, 1996), takes the form of the research intensity (R&D expenditure divided by sales) of US firms' operations, in particular host-country locations.

4 . It is thus a crucial implication of this perspective that technology flows in MNEs would be from the home country (where new knowledge and products were generated) to foreign countries (where original activity would be limited to their local application). A significant exemplification of the changes in positioning of R&D and creativity in MNEs that we shall suggest here is that recent studies (Håkanson and Nobel, 1998a, 1998b; Yamin, 1995, 1997) have pioneered analysis of 'reverse technology transfer' *from* overseas operations to MNEs' home countries.

5.   See Lall (1979), Hirschey and Caves (1981), Mansfield, Teece and Romeo (1979), Pearce (1989), Håkanson (1981), Håkanson and Nobel (1993b).

6.   See Pearce (1989), Hirschey and Caves (1981), Håkanson (1983), Papanastassiou and Pearce (1994a) and Zejan (1990).

7   In an investigation of overseas R&D in Swedish MNEs, Fors (1996, p.92) found that, after controlling for the need to adapt existing products and processes, these firms 'locate a higher share of their R&D expenditures to host countries which are relatively specialised technologically in their industry', which 'may suggest that one additional motive to locating R&Ds abroad is to gain access to knowledge in foreign 'centres of excellence' and to benefit from localised spillovers'. Kuemmerle (1998) investigated the potential for competitor-driven (that is oligopolistically-responsive) elements in timing and location of the establishment of R&D in pharmaceutical and electronics MNEs. This factor emerged as clearly present, though rather less strongly so for home-base-augmenting units (which are generally 'established close to universities or competitors' R&D sites ... to tap into the innovative potential of universities and semi-public research laboratories ... by capturing some of the spillovers these entities create') than for home-base-exploiting units (which 'facilitate the transfer of knowledge from the locus of knowledge creation to the locus of production and revenue generation ... [by helping] the firm identify opportunities for the application of knowledge that already exists within the firm').

8.   Analysis of 220 firms with the highest volume of patenting outside their home country over the period 1990 to 1996 allowed Patel and Vega (1997) to conclude that 'what happens in home countries is still very important in the creation of global technological advantage for even these most internationalised firms', since these companies tended to locate their technology creation abroad in core areas where they are already strong at home. The dominant mode of the overseas patenting analysed by Patel and Vega was in technologies that reflected both the host-country's revealed technological advantage and an area of the MNE's established technological advantage as indicated in its home-country patenting. Thus there was 'very little evidence to suggest that firms routinely go abroad to compensate for their weakness at home'. Rather, in our terms, the Patel and Vega evidence is compatible with overseas R&D to provide a coherent and logical extension of the strengths of the MNE's technological trajectory.

9.   We can also observe that these views of contemporary MNE R&D have resonances in terms of the transnational approaches to innovation discerned by Bartlett and Ghoshal (1990). Thus laboratories' support for decentralised product development operations can be perceived as relating to 'locally-leveraged' innovation, whilst co-opting distinctive host-country scientific expertise in more speculative research can be part of a 'globally-linked' approach to innovation.

10. This impression is almost precisely confirmed here by the number of subsidiaries that replied actively to the questions that requested details of any laboratory that they possessed. In a study of German and Dutch MNE subsidiaries in Spain, Molero, Buesa and Casado (1995) found that 44.2 per cent of the former, and 43.5 per cent of the latter, carried out R&D programmes. For the German respondents, 46.9 per cent said that some of their product technology, and 54.0 per

cent that some of their process technology, was developed in their Spanish subsidiary. The comparable figures for Dutch subsidiaries were 30.4 per cent and 43.5 per cent.

11. Though some adaptation of production processes that had been initiated in other production environments could persist. However, even this would be limited if locations for the subsidiaries are selected to match, as closely as possible, the needs of the extant production technologies.

12. An alternative might be to set up a laboratory that is independent from any production unit. This would serve to establish its neutrality and mitigate tensions that could arise from co-location with one particular production subsidiary.

13. These arguments, of course, also reflect on the results for ESTPROD/UK subsidiaries. Here it may be that a possibly complacent continuation of an apparently secure position in the local market (and a concomitant partial isolation from intra-group competition) does seem to allow for the relative atrophy of absence of R&D commitment.

14 . For analysis of patent data indicating considerable growth (albeit from very low levels) in decentralised approaches to technology creation in Japanese MNEs, see Pearce and Papanastassiou (1996a) and Papanastassiou and Pearce (1995). For discussion of JETRO information on Japanese R&D units in Europe, see Papanastassiou and Pearce (1994b) and Pearce (1997).

15. The same rationalising and/or centralising tendency could occur with US and Japanese MNE European operations. However, since these do not have a 'natural' home country in Europe, the process could bring more high-value-added activity into UK subsidiaries rather than draw it out. Put another way, European ESTPROD/EUR subsidiaries in the UK see a natural impediment to their accession to DEVELPROD status (which US or Japanese ones do not face) and seek ways of generating roles for R&D *within* their RPS positioning (that other subsidiaries need not pursue).

16. The *global* technology strategy of these companies (within which the European element operates) may at the same time involve expansion in R&D outside Europe (for example, in North America and Asia).

17. The presence of this type of 'familiarisation' lag could explain the relative weakness of R&D in Japanese subsidiaries that is observed in Tables 5.1 and 5.2.

18. In a regression test (including dummy variables for industry and home country) of the age of laboratories, the age of the subsidiary was significantly (at 1 per cent) positive, with a coefficient of 0.32. Whilst decisively supporting the predicted relationship between the age of subsidiaries and their laboratories, this also tends to be compatible with a process where, over time, new subsidiaries implement in-house R&D with increasing alacrity.

19. In the subsidiary questionnaire, Japanese laboratories accounted for only 4.4 per cent of those set up before 1980 but for 49.0 per cent of those created since that date. The survey of laboratories themselves revealed that Japanese MNEs were responsible only for 15.4 per cent of those set up before 1986 but for 66.7 per cent of those put in place since that year.

20. Overall, 47 of the 48 provided this information.

21. For more detailed analysis, see Papanastassiou and Pearce (1998b).

22. Kuemmerle (1997) notes that the presence or not of home-country personnel in a laboratory's top-level management during its start-up period is likely to depend on its role. In a home-base-augmenting (H-B-A) laboratory (that is, 'one designed to gather new knowledge for the company'), the initial leaders 'should be prominent local scientists so that they will be able to fulfil their primary responsibility: to nurture ties between the new site and the local scientific community'. By quickly, through the auspices and contacts of these well-known local leaders, becoming part of the local scientific community, the H-B-A laboratory will 'be able to generate new knowledge for the company'. By contrast, the initial leaders of home-base-exploiting sites (that is, 'established to help a company to effectively commercialise its R&D in foreign markets') should be 'highly regarded managers from within the company ... who are intimately familiar with the company's culture and systems'. These managers can then help to both secure the transfer of relevant knowledge from the company's home base to the R&D site and forge close ties between the new laboratory's engineers and those allied manufacturing and marketing

facilities that seek the effective local exploitation of the home-base knowledge (Kuemmerle, 1997, pp.64–5).

23. Only twice did the proportion of scientific personnel recruited in this way exceed 10 per cent, with the highest level being 20 per cent.

24. In one case, one-third of personnel were reported as having been recruited in this way, though only two more reported over 10 per cent.

25. Although only 22 respondents reported the presence of such staff in the question reported in Table 5.12, 26 replied to this one.

6. Roles and motivations of MNE laboratories

INTRODUCTION

The past two decades have seen a considerable rise in the decentralised R&D of MNEs, both specifically into the UK and as a more generalised global phenomenon (Pearce and Singh, 1992a).[1] In terms of the traditional analytical approach outlined at the start of the previous chapter, this could be interpreted simply as reflecting an increase in the relevance of centrifugal forces and/or a decline in the centripetal ones. Although explanations articulated in this way may be valid, we also suggested in the previous chapter that more fundamental qualitative driving forces can be perceived as lying behind the quantitative trend towards R&D decentralisation. Thus MNEs are adopting new strategic approaches to the pursuit of global competitiveness. As discussed in Chapter 2, this can involve the restructuring of the roles of individual subsidiaries and a reformulation of intra-group interdependencies in order to support this new positioning. Whereas the traditional views of the status of decentralised R&D depended on decisions within a bilateral relationship between a parent (home-country) unit and an individual subsidiary, the newer viewpoints emphasise the positioning of distinctive operations within interdependent networks of mutually-supportive facilities.

Overseas R&D units now often play crucial roles in supporting the ability of individual subsidiaries to stake a claim to a unique product development position within their MNE's wider innovation and supply programmes. Although we have noted that home-country parent-company planners will still seek to retain decisive scrutiny over the balance and coherence of global operations (with regard to both technological evolution and production), the lines of interdependency and the dimensions of dispersed decision making are now much more multifaceted. Overseas R&D units are no longer merely an outlet for the effective application of centrally-generated product technology, but instead play increasingly powerful roles in the creative processes themselves. In fact as early as 1985, Perrino and Tipping's (1989) discussions with 16 major technology-oriented MNEs led them to conclude that 'perhaps the most significant challenge of the next decade for the world's leading technology firms' was likely to be to create 'multidisciplinary R&D cores in each market – each with its own mission – and [to] learn how to manage these cores as a network, *not* as isolated technology outposts from the home office' (p.19).

The investigation of the positioning of foreign companies' laboratories in the UK, which occupies the bulk of this chapter, can be seen as relating to four themes that can be considered to derive from the contemporary view of R&D in MNEs. The first of these represents the qualitative enhancement of the major traditional centrifugal force, in that it is argued that when R&D occurs within overseas production subsidiaries it is now increasingly likely to assist in a substantial product development process rather than merely support the localised application of existing products. This deepens the decentralised involvement in the commercial evolution of MNE technology, since it is now envisaged that overseas laboratories help subsidiaries to address new knowledge (either created locally or accessed from group-level sources, as in a global-innovation strategy) in a disembodied form (as distinct from being already embodied in established products) and develop from it products that are fully responsive to the subsidiaries' particular market environments (regional or global).

The second theme suggests a greatly enhanced relevance, as another centrifugal force, of supply-side factors in the form of the technological characteristics of host countries (that is, the distinctiveness of their knowledge heritage and the quality of their current research capacity). An important element in this is, of course, simply that many more countries can now demonstrate the possession of capacities in these areas to an extent that can attract knowledge-seeking companies. Equally relevant, however, is that the reformulation of the competitive strategies of MNEs provides increased opportunities for the technological characteristics of individual countries to influence location decisions. Obviously this is strongest where a laboratory's main motivation is to provide distinctive basic and applied research inputs into centrally-coordinated global precompetitive programmes. However, since product development subsidiaries are likely, as shown in Chapter 3, to supply market areas that cover many nations, then where in that wider region they are located can reflect *inter alia* a potential host country's ability to supply relevant creative inputs. Thus for these subsidiaries, support for the ability to create (and sustain the competitive evolution of) their products may be more important host-country attributes than the ability to produce them cost effectively.

The third change in the positioning of overseas R&D laboratories suggested by the earlier discussion is that they move from predominantly dependent status in the technology programmes of their MNEs to now play significantly interdependent roles. Three elements of this interdependent positioning may be discerned. Firstly, laboratories may help associated subsidiaries to develop distinctive new products, but do so on the basis of key technologies that are derived elsewhere in the MNE group. At its most formalised this interdependence occurs as the second phase of a global innovation strategy, in which the essence of a new product concept is centrally derived with the relevant knowledge then taken up by the dispersed laboratories to enable regional subsidiaries to generate locally-responsive product variants.

Secondly, overseas R&D laboratories may take positions in strongly interdependent networks[2] of laboratories that focus on mainly precompetitive research, seeking to provide MNE groups with a full and balanced range of inputs into programmes of basic and applied work whose ultimate aim is to create an expanded knowledge base (the long-term aim of strategic competitiveness) from which the major new product concepts should emerge. Here the overseas laboratories aim to provide inputs that support the radical but coherent overall expansion of the group's technological trajectory.

The last type of interdependent laboratory role is to make available knowledge, advice and research assistance to other parts of the MNE (that is, beyond the needs of any subsidiary with which it is associated on a day-to-day basis). This type of interdependent positioning might be expected to occur in laboratories that have acquired a wide knowledge of the technology and product heritage of the MNE, or which have distinctive research competence or research capacity that they wish to justify keeping in place.

The fourth theme of a contemporary view of R&D in MNEs is that the traditional centripetal forces have declined somewhat in relevance as factors constraining decentralisation. Central to this is the view that improvements in communications technology, and MNEs' growing experience in using this as they develop group-level procedures to implement global networks of production and marketing facilities, have lessened the problems and concerns relating to control of decentralised R&D.[3] Furthermore, where reliable procedures for intra-group transfer of the (perhaps most vulnerable) fully-commercialised technologies have been in place for some time, MNEs may feel diminished concern over their ability to achieve secure coordination of international programmes in the more speculative phases of R&D (Pearce, 1989, p.2).

In addition, it can be argued (Pearce, 1989, p.39) that emergence of effective mechanisms for communication and coordination in MNEs can also reduce the centripetal effect of economies of scale in R&D, where these derive from indivisibilities in key assets such as uniquely talented scientific personnel or major pieces of research equipment. If such assets, whilst essentially remaining part of the capacity of a central laboratory, can be accessed on a temporary basis by decentralised laboratories (to support distinctive needs of their own work) then there will be less need to concentrate programmes in the central unit in order to secure the full utilisation of these expensive specialised attributes.

ROLES OF LABORATORIES

Building on earlier typologies,[4] both surveys addressed the issue of the roles that could be played by decentralised R&D units in MNEs. Thus those respondents to the questionnaire which was sent to producing subsidiaries that possessed an in-house R&D unit were asked to evaluate the relative strength of each of four possible roles in the work of their laboratory. The results of this are given in Tables 6.1 and 6.3(a). The questionnaire that was sent directly to foreign MNE laboratories in the UK also requested a similar evaluation of the position of four comparable roles in their own work. These replies are summarised in Tables 6.2 and 6.3(b). Differences between the results of the two surveys can be expected to arise from the fact that the respondents to the one that was sent to the laboratories themselves can include stand-alone or 'independent' units (as distinct from those 'associated' with production facilities)[5] in a way that is automatically precluded in the other. Earlier research (Pearce and Singh, 1992a) indicates that a strongly distinctive element in the positioning of stand-alone units is likely to be participation in globally-integrated programmes of precompetitive research serving group-level objectives (that is, the long-term component of strategic competitiveness, or the second type of interdependence noted earlier).

The first role offered for evaluation was that of supporting the operations of an associated UK production subsidiary, by assisting in the adaptation of any established products that it is expected to produce or the processes to be used. This is therefore the original support laboratory role (SL1), emphasising the most traditional centrifugal influence in the form of support for the improved decentralised application of an MNE's established (and probably centrally-created) technology as already embodied in its current products. Overall, the results of both surveys indicated quite a strong continued presence for this role, with almost two-thirds of those subsidiaries that possessed laboratories rating SL1 activity a major part of their work though, by contrast, over one-third of laboratory respondents excluded it (reflecting its irrelevance to the stand-alone units which participated only in that sample).

Table 6.1   Roles of R&D laboratories of MNE subsidiaries in the UK

	Importance of laboratory roles[1] (average response[2])			
	SL1	SL2	LIL	IIL
By industry				
Food	2.71	2.57	3.00	1.57
Automobiles	2.86	1.86	3.00	1.43
Electronics and electrical appliances	2.59	1.89	2.73	1.54
Mechanical engineering	2.60	1.87	3.00	1.40
Instruments	2.20	1.80	3.17	1.60
Industrial and agricultural chemicals	2.81	2.38	2.81	1.86
Pharmaceuticals and consumer chemicals	2.38	1.75	2.50	2.38
Other manufacturing	2.54	1.73	2.82	1.45
Total	2.62	2.00	2.84	1.64
By home country				
USA	2.52	2.19	2.90	1.76
Japan	2.78	1.74	2.93	1.54
Europe	2.59	1.96	2.63	1.56
Total[3]	2.62	2.00	2.84	1.64
By subsidiary type[4]				
ESTPROD/UK	2.53	2.08	2.81	1.81
ESTPROD/EUR	2.68	2.11	2.83	1.73
COMPART	2.57	2.86	3.00	2.29
DEVELPROD	2.67	1.98	2.94	1.60

Roles of laboratories:

SL1 Adaptation of existing products and/or processes to make them suitable to our market and conditions.

SL2 To provide advice on adaptation and/or development to other producing subsidiaries of our MNE group.

LIL To play a role in the development of new products for our distinctive markets.

IIL   To carry out basic research (not directly related to our current products) as part of a wider MNE-group-level research programme.

Notes:

1. Respondents were asked to evaluate each laboratory role as (i) its only role, (ii) a major role, (iii) a secondary role, (iv) not a part of its role.

2. The average response was calculated by allocating a value of 4 to 'its only role', 3 to 'a major role', 2 to 'a secondary role', and 1 to 'not a part of its role'.

3. Includes laboratories of MNEs from Australia and Canada.

4. Subsidiaries that said a particular role was either their only one or their predominant one. For definitions of subsidiary types, see Table 3.1.

Source: Survey of producing subsidiaries

Table 6. 2 Roles of MNE laboratories in the UK

| | | Importance of laboratory roles[1] (average response[2]) | | | |
		SL1	SL2	LIL	IIL
By industry					
Electronics		2.18	1.73	2.09	1.64
Pharmaceuticals		1.35	1.53	1.59	3.00
Chemicals[3]		1.89	2.11	2.00	2.00
Other		2.45	2.00	2.27	1.82
	Total	1.90	1.79	1.94	2.23
By home country					
USA		1.92	1.85	2.23	2.00
Japan		1.84	1.68	1.68	2.16
Europe		1.94	1.88	2.00	2.44
	Total	1.90	1.79	1.94	2.23

Roles of laboratories

SL1 To support UK-based production operations of the MNE by assisting in the adaptation of the products to be produced or processes to be used.

SL2 To support non-UK production operations of the MNE by advising on the adaptation of the products to be produced or processes to be used.

LIL To work with the UK subsidiary's other functions (i.e. management, marketing, engineering, etc.) to develop a distinctive new product that it will produce for its markets.

IIL To operate independently of any producing subsidiary to carry out basic or applied research (not associated with current producing operations) as part of a programme of precompetitive R&D implemented and coordinated by the MNE group.

Notes.

1. Respondents were asked to grade each role as (i) our only role, (ii) a predominant role, (iii) a secondary part of our role, (iv) not a part of our role.
2. The average response was calculated by allocating 'only role' a value of 4, 'predominant role' a value of 3, 'secondary role' a value of 2, and 'not part of our role' a value of 1.
3. Includes petrochemicals and petroleum.

Source: Survey of laboratories.

The second role distinguished is a somewhat more contemporary (or emergent) version of the support laboratory (SL2), in the form of offering advice on product and process adaptation and/or development to non-UK manufacturing subsidiaries of the parent MNE group. The SL2 role, therefore, moves the support laboratory function into the wider competitive context in which many MNEs now require their subsidiaries to operate, by implementing the third type of R&D interdependence suggested earlier.

Table 6.3   Relative strength of roles in MNEs' R&D laboratories in the UK

	Strength of role[1] (per cent of respondents)			
(a) Laboratories in subsidiary survey	SL1	SL2	LIL	IIL
Only role of laboratory	2.0		5.9	1.0
A major role of laboratory	65.3	27.7	75.2	19.0
A secondary role of laboratory	25.7	44.6	15.8	23.0
Not part of the role of laboratory	7.0	27.7	3.0	57.0
Total	100.0	100.0	100.0	100.0
	Strength of role[2] (per cent of respondents)			
(b) Laboratory survey	SL1	SL2	LIL	IIL
Only role of laboratory	2.1	2.1		16.7
A predominant role of laboratory	22.9	14.6	35.4	25.0
A secondary part of laboratory's role	37.5	43.8	22.9	22.9
Not a part of the role of laboratory	37.5	39.6	41.7	35.4
Total	100.0	100.0	100.0	100.0

Notes:
1. For definitions of roles, see Table 6.1.
2. For definitions of roles, see Table 6.2.

Source: Survey of producing subsidiaries (a) and survey of laboratories (b).

Thus we have seen that the needs of the evolving competitive situation often mean that subsidiaries that once supplied a substantial product range mainly to their host-country market now focus on the cost-efficient supply of only a subset of these products, but do so for a wider market (mainly Europe in the case of these UK-based subsidiaries). Those products that exit one subsidiary's range will then become the specialised responsibility of another facility (elsewhere in Europe in this case), as a result of rationalisation of the MNE's supply network. It is this process of subsidiary evolution that provides scope for a potential widening of scope in the support laboratory role.

As individual subsidiaries move towards more substantially export-oriented roles (ESTPROD/EUR here) the need for the services of a dedicated SL1 type of unit will decline (in particular as far as adaptation of products to local tastes is concerned). However, like its associated production facility, such a laboratory may seek to secure its survival by opening itself up to positions in wider group activity (by taking on SL2 responsibilities). In the context of the rationalisation and development processes of MNE operations in Europe, the SL2 role could be acquired by their UK-based laboratories in several ways.

Firstly, where a production subsidiary elsewhere is expected to initiate, or greatly increase its emphasis on, supply of a good that the MNE's UK operation previously had a particular expertise in, then any problems it may face with this new responsibility may be solved by consultation with the UK subsidiary's laboratory, which can apply a well-based familiarity with the product in question. Mutual support between such laboratories, in terms of the relocation and application of this type of tacit knowledge of established group products, may then come to play a quite systematic (SL2) role in the transition to more integrated MNE supply networks.

Secondly, the SL2 role may emerge as a response to a potential general constraint on the effectiveness of MNE moves to rationalised European networks of specialised production subsidiaries. The ability of a subsidiary to realise increased efficiency by exporting a limited range of products to the whole European market depends on a homogeneity of tastes which may not actually exist in the region. If the heterogeneity of national tastes for a particular product is not to be simply overridden (with consumers compensated by lower prices achieved through the greater efficiency), then means of combining responsiveness to decentralised variation in taste with geographically centralised production are needed. Here improved intra-group communications may make this possible if SL2-type activity in a laboratory in a particularly idiosyncratic part of a projected export market can define the product adaptations that are discerned as necessary there. This information can then be passed back to the production facility in another country, which is to be responsible for regional supply of the product, whose SL1 operation can assimilate and help implement the needed adjustments. With scope for flexible production, the subsidiary could then create and supply a range of appropriately adapted variants of its core product in order to react positively to persistent taste differentiation within its target regional market.

Nevertheless, as MNEs achieve the effective rationalisation of the supply of those parts of their product ranges that were already well established in Europe, they may decide that many of the product sites no longer need to retain individualised R&D support for their relatively routine production operations. Instead, with the generation of good communications and improved understanding of the needs of particular segments of a regional market, it may become possible to use a considerably reduced number of SLs to provide R&D support to the whole rationalised production network. Thus a third SL2 role is for high-quality examples of such laboratories to take an enhanced position in support of a wide constituency of geographically-dispersed supply facilities. Often, in order to avoid accusations of favouritism, this type of SL2 may operate independently of any particular production unit.

A fourth possible situation in which significant SL2–type activity can emerge is within labs (the locally integrated laboratories [LILs] to be discussed below) whose main role is to help development (DEVELPROD) subsidiaries in the creation of their new products. However, when such UK subsidiaries succeed in creating very effective new goods (with a strong Europe-wide market emerging) it may be decided that some of the supply of these should be undertaken by factories in other countries. If this happens, the laboratory in the UK product development subsidiary will be likely to have a strong SL2- type responsibility for assisting these continental production units in assimilating the relevant technology and, if necessary, in adapting it to local production conditions or tastes.

Finally, we have suggested earlier that those subsidiaries that focus on supply of component parts (COMPART) often play an active role in product development programmes, by taking strong responsibility for creating the technology relevant to the inputs they will supply for the new good. If this happens, then the component suppliers' laboratories may build collaborative interdependencies with other component suppliers in the programme and/or with the MNE subsidiary ultimately requiring the input. This can often involve the COMPART laboratories in providing SL2-type advice to associated parts of their MNE's supply network.

In the main these various potential SL2 roles suggest secondary positions in laboratories, helping the international dissemination of either experience accumulated in long-established SL1-type units or new product technology recently created in LILs. This is clearly confirmed in Table 6.3, where SL2 work is considerably less prevalent than SL1 or LIL in terms of 'only' or 'predominant/major' status in both surveys, but is the most pervasive of all roles in terms of 'secondary' positioning in both samples. The emerging significance of this type of support for technological interdependence and knowledge diffusion in increasingly networked MNE operations may also be reflected in its absence from only one-quarter of the laboratories covered by the production subsidiary questionnaire, whilst the comparable figure of two-fifths in the laboratory survey is not substantively different from that of the other three roles.

When summarised in terms of average responses, the status of the SL2 role is relatively much closer to that of the other two subsidiary-associated roles (SL1 and LIL) in the laboratory survey (Table 6.2) than in that sent to production units (Table 6.1). This may reflect the presence of stand-alone units in the former survey. Thus, although a laboratory within a particular subsidiary in an MNE's rationalised European programme of production facilities could take responsibility for providing R&D support to the whole integrated network, we have suggested that this might be compromised if it led to suspicion that that laboratory might favour its associated subsidiary in terms of network development. To alleviate this, some UK-based laboratories providing SL2-type support to a full European network may operate independently of any UK production subsidiary and attempt to emphasise that this underwrites their commitment to fairness and neutrality in the supply of advice and services. As this role is likely to need a high level of technological competence and a clear grounding in the group's technology (backward interdependency with group knowledge as well as forward interdependence with the production network) it could sometimes be undertaken as a secondary role in the stand-alone laboratories that participate in precompetitive research programmes.

In Table 6.1, the SL2 role emerges as strongest within the operations of the COMPART subsidiaries. Taken with the complementary strength of the product development (LIL) role in COMPART subsidiaries' laboratories, this further reinforces the perception that a distinctive element in the activity of the component supply units is to generate creative interdependencies supporting the work of subsidiaries that are seeking to develop new final products (DEVELPROD). Thus here the strong involvement of COMPART subsidiaries in providing SL2 advice and information to other subsidiaries seems likely to be part of a mutually-supportive product development operation to which they will ultimately supply custom-created component parts.

The third laboratory role involves working with the other functions (that is, management, marketing, engineering, and so on) of an associated UK production subsidiary in order to develop a distinctive new product that it will then supply to its markets. This moves the laboratory's motivation towards a more contemporary version of the centrifugal influence (that is, localised product development rather than adaptation), so that it is likely to address technology in a disembodied form (that is, applied research results, either derived directly from its own work or imported from other sources within the group) and then collaborate closely with other subsidiary functions in order to create new goods from it. Thus this LIL role supports a much wider creative scope within subsidiaries, with the objective of developing a product that adds an additional dimension to the overall range of the MNE, rather than merely seeking the more effective application of well-established group products through SL-type work. In order to achieve this level of creative competence within an individual subsidiary, the in-house R&D unit needs to work in a closely integrated fashion with marketing personnel, engineering and general management. From this collaboration it should be hoped to ensure that a new good meets originally-perceived market needs, can be effectively produced in local conditions and supports wider managerial views of the subsidiary's desired process of evolution.

In the replies to the questionnaire that was sent to laboratories themselves, the LIL role is clearly stronger than that of the SL1 (that is, the two roles associating laboratories directly with local producing subsidiaries' activity) in terms of 'only' or 'predominant' status (Table 6.3b), but notably less prominent in terms of evaluation as a secondary activity. This may suggest that where LIL activity emerges in a laboratory it quickly takes the strongest or defining position in its work, whilst traditional SL1 operations perhaps reveal a propensity to persist even though reduced to secondary status. This can then be tentatively perceived as compatible with the hypothesis of a current evolutionary process in which LIL activity is tending to usurp the leading position of SL1 work in the UK-based MNE laboratories. Nevertheless, when these results are summarised into average responses (Table 6.2) the positions of SL1 and LIL remain closely comparable. Replies to the questionnaire sent to producing subsidiaries once more suggest some degree of predominance of LILs over SL1s in terms of the 'only' or 'major' role, with the position again reversed for secondary role status (Table 6.3a). Here, however, the average responses derived (Table 6.1) do reflect an at least modest overall leadership role of the LIL over the SL1.[6]

The degree of prevalence of the LIL role over that of the SL1 just noted appears somewhat unexpectedly tentative seen in the light of the decisive relationship noted earlier (Table 5.1) between the degree of commitment to product development in a subsidiary and the likelihood of possession of an in-house R&D unit. It would appear, therefore, that an R&D unit is much more likely to appear (or persist) in subsidiaries that begin to focus on product development as their main role, with LIL activity then emerging as the laboratory's primary commitment in support of this. However, where laboratories are present for this reason they are often also expected to apply some resources to help with the adaptation of any established products whose supply remains a secondary function of the DEVELPROD subsidiary. In those subsidiaries where the main role is the supply of established products, the earlier evidence suggests that this provides less scope for (or ability to justify) an in-house R&D unit. This may suggest the ironical result that the most effective supply of established products may emerge in those DEVELPROD subsidiaries for which it is only a secondary role, but where it is likely to get support from high-quality laboratories.

The previous argument may sharpen the sense of vulnerability in those subsidiaries whose dominant current role is the supply of well-established products and, where they possess an in-house R&D unit, thereby increase their resolve to retain it and provide it with a key position in reinforcing or redefining their status. In particular, this is likely to involve putting into place the technological capability and scope to underpin a move towards a product development role. Thus Table 6.1 shows that in the laboratories of both ESTPROD/UK and ESTPROD/EUR subsidiaries, LIL-type work is modestly more prevalent than the more logical SL1−type. This may again suggest that for a manufacturing subsidiary the possession of an R&D unit is often not only vital to how it plays its role in the current competitive programmes of the MNE group, but is also a crucial element in how it asserts its own position within the internal competitive processes that help define the evolution of group-level strategy.[7]

The final type of R&D role may be designated as that of an international interdependent laboratory (IIL), in which it operates independently of any producing subsidiary in order to carry out basic and/or applied research as part of a wider programme of precompetitive R&D that is implemented and coordinated by the MNE group (thus epitomising the second type of interdependency suggested earlier). This characterisation of IILs suggests three ways in which they are distinctive by comparison with the other roles in the typology.

Firstly, they focus on basic and/or applied research in a way that LILs and SLs would not be expected to do, but are not then normally required to themselves carry this through to the development stage. Thus it is the unique responsibility of IILs to contribute to the regeneration and reinforcement of the group's core of scientific knowledge through speculative precompetitive research that is not directly motivated by reaction to immediate commercial problems or needs,[8] but instead targets the longer-term evolution of the MNE's technological trajectory (thus also addressing the second need of strategic competitiveness).

Secondly, the need to support high-quality precompetitive research, but the lack of any systematic involvement with subsidiaries responding to local market conditions (as prevails in LILs and SL1s), means that IILs will be uniquely responsive to supply-side location factors in the form of the distinctive strengths of host-countries' current research capacity and accumulated technological heritage. Thus they would embody most strongly our second theme regarding contemporary trends in MNE global R&D strategies, as another increasingly relevant centrifugal influence.

Finally, the IIL's defining interdependency is not with other functions (either in the same country or elsewhere) but instead with similar precompetitive laboratories of the MNE group located in other countries. Although on occasion an IIL's basic or applied output might be taken up for development by LIL operations in the same country, it is more likely to operate as a specialised component of an international programme of mutually-supportive precompetitive research facilities. Such a programme would aim to generate new scientific knowledge that can underpin the continued technological distinctiveness of the MNE, and thus contribute to its successful evolution and revitalisation by providing the basis for new generations of products that allow it to sustain a commitment to innovation as a key source of competitiveness. In line with the supply-side influence noted above, it is suggested that such a programme of precompetitive investigation would need to tap into the best-available sources of knowledge in a wide range of scientific disciplines, which may well be located in a number of different countries. Through IILs in each of the relevant national science bases, an MNE seeks to generate a coordinated programme that provides it with the scope to access top-quality sources of each of the areas of knowledge that are expected to be relevant to technological progress in its industry. Thus we can see IILs as the key participants in the first phase of a global innovation strategy, and also as potentially contributing to Bartlett and Ghoshal's globally-linked approach to innovation.

The distinctive characteristics that we have just discerned for IILs again point to the suggestion that it is this role that is most likely to require the creation of independent (stand-alone) R&D units by MNEs. This perspective can immediately be seen to be reflected in the replies from producing subsidiaries (Table 6.3a) who see the IIL role as being absent from almost three-fifths of their associated laboratories, making it by far the most likely role to be totally excluded from the work of these units. This may reflect the fact that the nature of the specific competences created in these laboratories, to target their primary LIL or SL aims, often provide little scope for spin-off inputs into the rather differently focused precompetitive programmes or that, even when such potential does exist, the associated production unit prefers them to concentrate on their uncompromised in-house support to current supply effectiveness and localised product development.

Nevertheless, it also seems that a quite significant proportion of the laboratories whose predominant objective is to support directly the immediate aims of a UK production subsidiary, do find scope to also operate within group-level precompetitive programmes as a secondary or (in one-fifth of cases) even a major commitment. By contrast with the possible diversion from a subsidiary's current commercial objectives, the supplementary presence of such basic/applied work could then serve to emphasise its distinctive R&D scope and thereby strengthen its claim to an enhanced position in the group's higher-value-added creative activities.

As would be predicted, however, the status of the IIL role is decisively enhanced when we observe the replies to the laboratory sample, moving from the clearly lowest position in the previous case (Table 6.1) to the decisively first position here (Table 6.2). Although over one-third of responding laboratories still omitted IIL work (here, however, a figure comparable to that of other roles) it emerged as somewhat ahead of LILs in terms of 'predominant' and (especially) 'only' role status and clearly ahead of the two forms of SL positioning. This clear shift in emphasis points to a significant position amongst foreign MNE R&D activity for stand-alone units whose objective is to co-opt distinctive high-quality elements of UK technology and research capacity to support longer-term global programmes whose results are not therefore likely to strengthen the competitiveness of UK-based industry directly.

TYPES OF WORK DONE IN MNE LABORATORIES IN THE UK

Further perspectives on the strategic positioning of MNE R&D operations in the UK were sought in a question in the laboratory survey, which asked respondents to evaluate the relative importance in their activity of six types of scientific investigation or technological support.

The first two types of work defined represent the precompetitive phase, covering speculative scientific investigation that seeks to expand the MNEs' core knowledge in those disciplines that are expected to be relevant to their industry's technological evolution. Such pure research is not implemented to in any way seek solutions to currently defined commercial problems, but the ultimate objective is rather to provide the scientific basis for radical new commercial potentials. We have suggested that programmes of this type of precompetitive research contribute to the first phase of a global innovation strategy, by seeking to put into place the scientific foundations of a major new product concept. Thus it targets the long-term component of strategic competitiveness by securing a decisive and distinctive evolution in the scientific core of the MNE group's technological trajectory.

Of these types of precompetitive work, the totally pure and speculative 'basic research' emerged as relatively rare (Table 6.4), being reported as absent from 47.9 per cent of responding laboratories' activity and rated as a predominant (or only) function in merely 18.9 per cent. Part of the sparseness of basic research in MNE UK laboratories could certainly reflect a persistence of the traditionally-argued tendency to prefer to centralise such work, in response to the standard centripetal influences (Chapter 5). In addition, however, it could also be related to a relatively low tendency to perform such work at all in-house (Pearce and Singh, 1992a), instead substituting a quite strong propensity to acquire such pure scientific inputs externally through associations with university laboratories or independent research institutes. If this is so, and building on earlier arguments, then MNEs seeking to access an effective programme of basic research in this collaborative fashion would still have a strong motivation to do so in ways that respond to the international diversification of scientific competences. The articulation of such basic research collaborations with local universities in particular host countries may then be an important role of MNE overseas laboratories, albeit one that seems to provide only limited scope for complementary work of this type in their own operations. In this case, overseas laboratories (and a decentralised approach to technology acquisition generally) may contribute more to the ability of MNEs to operationalise and sustain programmes of basic research than is suggested by their in-house work. This is further investigated in Chapter seven.

The second facet of precompetitive work was defined for responding labs as 'applied research aimed at creating a possible commercially applicable concept from basic research results available in the group'. Whereas we have suggested that basic research is carried out with no specifically defined commercial objective yet in mind, applied research is then seen as beginning when elements of knowledge that arise within MNE basic programmes begin to be perceived as possibly providing the basis of an important new dimension of competitive scope. The work here is still essentially scientific research, but now focused on addressing issues that have been distilled from the more open-ended basic programmes as possibly embodying specific commercial potentials that it is hoped to bring into clearer focus during this stage.

The successful completion of applied research is then considered to result in the broad definition of the characteristics of a significant new product concept. This puts into place a clear understanding of the nature of the new service the good is expected to supply to customers and provides full definition of the scientific knowledge relevant to its effective production (that is, completes phase one of a global innovation strategy), without yet setting out full details of its ultimate commercial format (which becomes the target of a later development phase and of closer association with production subsidiaries).

Table 6.4 Types of scientific work carried out in MNE laboratories in the UK

		Types of scientific work[1] (average response[2])					
		A	B	C	D	E	F
By industry							
Electronics		1.64	2.00	2.45	2.40	2.00	1.60
Pharmaceuticals		1.94	2.18	2.00	2.12	1.35	1.18
Chemicals[3]		1.67	2.44	2.44	1.78	2.00	1.67
Other		1.55	2.00	2.73	1.91	2.09	1.91
	Total	1.73	2.15	2.35	2.06	1.79	1.53
By home country							
USA		1.54	2.46	2.69	2.08	2.00	1.67
Japan		1.74	1.74	2.05	2.26	1.79	1.42
Europe		1.88	2.38	2.44	1.81	1.63	1.56
	Total	1.73	2.15	2.35	2.06	1.79	1.53

Types of scientific work.
A Basic (precompetitive) research.
B Applied research aimed at creating a possible commercially applicable concept from basic research results available in the group.
C Development work aimed at helping to create a commercial product for particular market(s) from new ideas resulting from our own laboratory's applied research.
D Development work aimed at helping to create a commercial product for particular market(s) from new ideas resulting from applied research carried out in other laboratories in the MNE group.
E Work to adapt current products for particular markets.
F Work to adapt current production processes to particular conditions.

Notes.
1. Respondents were asked to grade each type of scientific work as either (i) our only type of work, (ii) a predominant type of work, (iii) a secondary part of our work, (iv) not a part of our work.
2. The average response was calculated by allocating 'only type' the value of 4, 'predominant type' the value of 3, 'secondary type' the value of 2, and 'not a part' the value of 1.
3. Includes petrochemicals and petroleum.

Source: Survey of laboratories.

Applied research was rated a predominant role by 35.4 per cent of responding laboratories and as a secondary one by 43.8 per cent more, which (Table 6.4) makes it clearly the more pervasive of the two precompetitive types of work in MNEs' UK-based laboratories. This may come about because applied research in UK laboratories not only builds on their own in-house basic results, but also derives from the internalisation of the further investigation of ideas emerging from their collaborations with UK university laboratories. It may also occur by acquiring the mandate to carry out the more applied and focused further pursuit of scientific results that derive from the group's perhaps relatively dispersed programmes of basic work.

The next two types of work envisaged for MNE laboratories related to their potential positioning in the product development process. The first of these was defined as 'development work aimed at helping to create a commercial product for particular market(s) from new ideas resulting from our own laboratory's applied research'. This emerged as the most prevalent type of work overall (Table 6.4), being assessed as their predominant (or only) type by 48.0 per cent of responding laboratories, a secondary one in 35.4 per cent more and, therefore, as only absent from 16.6 per cent. This suggests a distinctively localised development competence in MNE UK-based operations, in which their own applied research scope, reflecting in-house technological capability, is supported by similar strengths in complementary functions (for example, marketing, engineering, strategic planning) to achieve a unique addition to the group's product range. This strategic positioning for the work of these MNE laboratories is supportive of the second theme outlined in the introduction to this chapter in that it indicates that technological supply-side factors can have a strong influence on where in such groups high-value-added product development subsidiaries might emerge.

The second of the two types of product development work is less self-contained, perhaps locating the activity within phase two of a global innovation strategy by accepting the first of the types of interdependency suggested earlier. Thus this type of activity was defined as 'development work aimed at helping to create a commercial product for particular market(s) from new ideas resulting from applied research carried out in other laboratories in the MNE group'. Here a new product concept becomes available within the group (perhaps in a 'parent' laboratory that has coordinated the programmes of precompetitive research from which it derives) and it is then decided that its effective global commercialisation requires the immediate creation of several regional product variants, each of which responds to the distinctive needs of a significant segment of the international marketplace. Again working with local inputs in other functional areas, the UK laboratory may take up the defining technology of the new concept and generate its own (predominantly European-market-focused) version of the product. There is quite strong evidence for the emergent status of this type of positioning in MNE laboratories, since it was present in the work of all except 29.8 per cent of respondents, although as a predominant (or only) type of work in only 32.0 per cent it does not yet match the former approach to product development as a key role.

The final pair of types of lab work relate to the more traditional ideas on the positioning of these units, taking the form of 'work to adapt current products for particular markets' and 'work to adapt current production processes to particular conditions'. Here product adaptation was rated a predominant part of their work by only 17.0 per cent of respondents, although 44.7 per cent considered it did take a secondary position. This, though, was somewhat stronger than process adaptation (which may often be more effectively performed by experienced engineering personnel on the shop floor), which was absent from the work of 53.2 per cent of respondents and took a predominant position for only 6.4 per cent. Table 6.4 shows that when converted to average responses, the two adaptation roles fall well below the status of product development work, which provides stronger evidence for our first theme of evolutionary processes in MNE R&D than we could derive from the previous section.

We have placed considerable emphasis on the positioning of decentralised R&D activity in MNEs within processes of evolution in these companies' strategic approach to global competitiveness. As different stages of development in global strategy may lead to different priorities within overseas R&D, the analysis of this, and the previous, section provides us with an opportunity to attempt to discern such variations between labs of MNEs from different home countries and competing in different industries.

The relative maturity of US MNE operations in the UK seems to have allowed them to provide their R&D units with a coherent division of responsibilities within emerging group-level approaches to technology creation and product development. Thus Table 6.4 reveals a quite limited position for basic research in UK laboratories that may reflect the US companies' confidence in the continued ability of their home-country science base to supply a large part of the range of inputs required at this stage. However, both applied research and the complementary type of product development that builds on in-house technology then emerge into distinctively strong positions. This suggests that a high assessment of UK creative competences does lead US MNEs to allow their laboratories there to pick up new centrally-generated knowledge at a relatively early stage in order to take it forwards towards distinctive European product development. The importance of these two types of work, embodying the applied *research*/product *development* interface, is reflected in the above-average presence of LILs (especially in the laboratory survey) and of IIL work when reported by producing subsidiaries (which might have a clearer perspective on its integration with this type of in-house development process).

Although the second type of product development (that is, that building on centrally-generated applied research and product concepts) was of only average relevance, both product and process adaptation took on relatively high significance in the work of US laboratories (Table 6.4). Very speculatively it can then be suggested that US MNEs have two rather differently phased approaches to seeking product competitiveness in the European market. In the one already discerned, new scientific possibilities (US-generated basic research output) are addressed very early by European operations for a locally-integrated process that combines applied research and product development. Alternatively, a more decisively centralised product development approach may see the full definition of details of a new product achieved in US-based operations, with European (here UK) subsidiaries and laboratories then only expected to carry out rather traditional adaptation to sharpen its competitive entry into that new market area. Thus, whilst SL1-type laboratories retain a moderate significance in US MNEs, SL2s are now of distinctively above-average relevance (especially in the replies of laboratories, where the role could be a strong secondary responsibility of stand-alone IILs), suggesting the progressive emergence of a propensity for the UK-based laboratories to support the Europe-wide competitive application of already successful US products. Overall, then, US laboratories in the UK seem to often take positions as strategic technology leaders in their MNE European operations, with a distinctive commitment to the development of technology and products and also a notable secondary responsibility to provide support and advice to other parts of the group in the region.

In Table 6.4, basic research emerges as of average importance in Japanese laboratories, which may reflect two factors. Firstly, a desire to access this phase of research scope abroad in response to perceived weakness in their home-country competence in pure science and, secondly, a current reluctance to actually do so that reflects a limited experience of potential host countries and of organising dispersed scientific programmes. A substantial expansion of such work within the growing overseas commitment of Japanese MNEs is thus a very plausible trend as the experience of their laboratories deepens and their organisational confidence grows. Applied research and, therefore, that type of product development that builds on it in-house, are of well-below-average relevance in the work of Japanese laboratories in the UK. This may suggest two patterns in the technological behaviour of these MNEs. Firstly, such basic research as is done in the UK is unlikely to fuel applied research and product development there, but perhaps rather to be integrated into group precompetitive programmes as envisaged by phase one of a global innovation strategy. Secondly, and to some degree reflecting this, the derivation of a new product concept *is* a stage of the innovation process that home-country operations do feel confident to take clearcut responsibility for (that is, centralised completion of the first phase of a global innovation strategy).

The patterns suggested above, then, lead to a very strong position for the second type of product development in Japanese laboratories in the UK. Thus, in a way that is compatible with the second phase of a global innovation strategy, they pick up the technological outlines of the new product concept and play a key role in the generation of a distinctive European-market variant of the good.[9] The relative stature of the first four types of work in Japanese laboratories leads to a modest assessment of the positions of IILs (Tables 6.1 and 6.2), whilst LILs are evaluated much more strongly in the subsidiary survey than in that deriving from the laboratories themselves (where clearer perception of the interdependence of the product development process with centrally-derived knowledge may lead them to downplay this role).

Product adaptation is of average significance in the work of these laboratories, although process adaptation is quite sparse (perhaps indicating a particular confidence in, and therefore commitment to, established Japanese production methods). The SL1 role, then, is quite strongly endorsed in the subsidiary survey, though less strongly so by laboratories. SL2 status is, however, relatively rare in both surveys, probably reflecting the pioneering position of UK subsidiaries in the first wave of European operations of Japanese MNEs, so that there is often as yet little activity elsewhere in the region to need this type of intra-group support. Thus, overall, in the absence of fully-developed European networks of these Japanese companies, the UK-based operations seem to act as bridgeheads for the regional application of existing products (adaptation in SL1s) and new technology (development in LILs). Alongside the desire to sustain a position in a growing commitment to decentralised basic research, it seems likely that defence of this current position in the high-value-added product development and competitiveness-enhancing activity of Japanese MNEs should be a concern of UK inward investment policy, as these companies increasingly investigate the potential for widening the geographical scope of their European operations.

The distinguishing characteristic of the work in UK-based laboratories of European MNEs (Table 6.4) is a somewhat above-average commitment to each of the first three types (that is, basic and applied research and the approach to product development that builds on them in-house) but a notably low involvement in the second, group-coordinated, form of product development. The high evaluation of IIL status by the laboratories themselves (Table 6.2) parallels the strong presence of basic and applied research and may reflect the perception of the researchers in these units that the UK science base can still support a distinctive input into group programmes of such work. This, we have suggested, may however then represent inputs to an emerging home-country orientation of creative work in continental MNEs, where the ultimate product development work that emerges from such precompetitive knowledge-generating programmes is focused increasingly in parent operations.

A feared removal of product development scope from decentralised operations may already be reflected in the relatively low evaluation of LIL work reported in the subsidiary survey (Table 6.1). The quite strong persistence of the more self-contained and locally-integrated form of product development may then be an attempt to keep in place, and sustain, the individualised vitality of UK creative scope (diverting at least some basic/applied work away from group programmes). This may then support product creation that explicitly targets the local UK market, or even markets outside Europe. Although both forms of adaptation are of little importance, the SL2 role is reported as of some relative significance (especially by the laboratories). This may reflect a distinctive knowledge of some of their groups' more established technologies, which the laboratories may then seek to leverage as at least a temporary basis for asserting an involvement in these MNEs' European technological scope.

Pharmaceuticals emerges as the industry with the most decisive commitment to decentralised programmes of precompetitive research, reflected in the distinctively strong presence of IILs. That the above-average performance of basic and applied research is followed by a very weak position for the first type of product development (Table 6.4), indicates that the precompetitive work supports mainly group objectives rather than further localised creativity. Although the second form of product development is of some significance, neither type of adaptation has any real importance in pharmaceutical laboratories' work, and a low evaluation of LIL and SL status reinforces the view of a predominantly science-oriented drive in these facilities.

In chemicals, precompetitive work (especially applied research) is again quite important and here (compared to pharmaceuticals) feeds through to support a quite modest degree of local in-house development. Whilst there is little involvement with the other form of product development, both types of adaptation are relatively significant in these chemical laboratories. These responsibilities are reflected in the quite strong presence of IILs (ranked second to pharmaceuticals in both surveys) and average commitment to both LIL and SL1 roles. Quite distinctive, however, is the well-above-average status of SL2 in the chemical industry's UK operations. This may help with the effective extension into other market areas of product-related technology generated in these laboratories' rather self-contained development efforts.

Electronics has a relatively limited commitment to precompetitive research in its UK laboratories, but then reveals an above-average presence of all four remaining types of work (with a distinctive emphasis on the group-programme type of product development, though, it should be noted, this does not uniquely reflect the activity of Japanese enterprises). Through the work of LILs and SL1s (at least in the perception of laboratory respondents), the UK-based technological operations of electronics MNEs seeks mainly to sharpen the competitiveness of existing products and achieve the European application of new group-level knowledge.[10]

INFLUENCES ON THE STRATEGIC POSITION OF R&D LABORATORIES

It is the central theme of this analysis that decentralised R&D operations in MNEs are playing roles that are increasingly integral to the ways in which these companies are pursuing the objectives of globalised strategic competitiveness. A question in the survey of UK-based MNE laboratories attempted to detect the view of such units on the nature of the forces currently affecting the evolution of their own positioning within such globalised technological strategies of their group. Thus they were asked to evaluate the relative strength of four influences on either the decision to set up their facility (where this was sufficiently recent to define the laboratory's current strategic motivation) or the nature of its recent growth or evolution.

One of the key potential positions for decentralised R&D units within the global competitive evolution of MNEs relates to the sharpening of the commercial application of their existing technologies, through an enhanced responsiveness to any idiosyncratic elements in the needs of dispersed (regional or national) markets. This can involve the tactical adaptation of products or production processes that embody long-established group knowledge, or the more strategic development of new products either from original technology recently derived from precompetitive work or through the radical reapplication of knowledge from the group's established competences. These may be distinguished as demand-side influences in that they derive from the requirements of a laboratory in a particular location to provide support to other local functions (production and marketing) in their need to respond to their competitive market pressures.

The first factor offered for evaluation relates to the more traditional (tactical) of these demand-side influences, being defined as 'increased competition in its main markets leading our production subsidiary to adapt its product or production processes to improve effectiveness'. This emerges as of relatively limited relevance (Table 6.5), being rated as irrelevant by 43.5 per cent of responding laboratories, a minor influence by 21.7 per cent and a major (or only) influence by 34.8 per cent. However, its more strategic equivalent, 'increased competition and pressure for effective product innovation leading our subsidiary to need to develop new products for its key markets', emerges as the most powerful of all four influences, with 8.7 per cent of respondents believing it to be the only relevant factor, 50.0 per cent more rating it a major one and only 17.4 per cent considering it to be irrelevant. These results indicate clear support for our first theme, by placing product development ahead of adaptation in the laboratories' demand-side responsibilities, with this emerging within the context of a need to sharpen decentralised elements of the innovation process as the companies build procedures to respond better to intensified global-market pressures.

The two other influences covered by this question may be considered as supply-side factors in that they relate to the ability of a laboratory to take on and fulfil particular objectives within the technology programmes of an MNE. To a large degree the ability of a lab to generate the relevant in-house competences is then expected to reflect the quality and distinctiveness of its host country's research infrastructure and traditions and its level of commitment to scientific education. Another of our themes, suggested in the introduction to this chapter, is that the repositioning of overseas R&D in MNEs provides enhanced scope for such supply-side factors to become relevant in determining the location and scope of laboratories. Two elements in this repositioning provide the context for this suggestion. Firstly, where laboratories take on the IIL role in international networks of precompetitive work, they will be decisively attracted to those countries whose technological heritage and research traditions are distinctively strong in one or more of the scientific disciplines that need to be accessed. Secondly, where an LIL needs to support an associated subsidiary in a product development process the relevant market area is likely to be a wide one and the ability of potential host countries in the region to provide a high-quality scientific environment for the laboratory may be a major influence on where the activity is ultimately located.

The first of these two supply-side influences offered for the evaluation of laboratories was 'to make effective use of a strong UK technological capability in areas of science particularly relevant to our industry'. The ability to access this type of specialised research capacity and technological heritage was supported as another very significant factor affecting the positioning of MNE laboratories in the UK (Table 6.5), with 4.4 per cent of respondents considering it the only relevant influence, 52.2 per cent a major one and 23.9

Table 6.5 Evaluation of influences on the decision to set up an MNE laboratory in the UK, or on its recent growth or evolution

		Influence[1] (average response[2])			
		A	B	C	D
By industry					
Electronics		2.20	2.40	2.40	1.70
Pharmaceuticals		1.59	2.18	2.53	2.29
Chemicals[3]		2.22	2.89	2.33	2.11
Other		2.00	2.80	2.30	1.90
	Total	1.93	2.50	2.41	2.04
By home country					
USA		2.00	2.62	2.08	2.00
Japan		1.78	2.39	2.56	2.00
Europe		2.07	2.53	2.53	2.13
	Total	1.93	2.50	2.41	2.04

Influences.

A Increased competition in its main markets leading our producing subsidiary to adapt its products or production processes to improve effectiveness.

B Increased competition and pressure for effective product innovation leading our subsidiary to need to develop new products for its key markets.

C To make effective use of a strong UK technological capability in areas of science particularly relevant to our industry.

D To make effective use of the general strong UK technological and research infrastructure.

Notes.

1. Respondents were asked to grade each influence as (i) the only influence, (ii) a major influence, (iii) a minor influence, or (iv) irrelevant.
2. The average response was calculated by allocating 'only influence' the value of 4, 'major influence' the value of 3, 'minor influence' the value of 2, and 'irrelevant' the value of 1.
3. Includes petrochemicals and petroleum.

Source: Survey of laboratories.

per cent more a minor one. The other supply-side factor was 'to make effective use of the general strong UK technological and research infrastructures'. This broadly-based ability to support high-quality scientific work (perhaps in LILs), as distinct from the leading-edge knowledge and research capacity in specialised disciplines (more relevant to IILs), was of rather diminished relevance but still a quite pervasive influence. Thus 32.6 per cent of respondents rated it a major (or only) influence, 37.0 per cent rated it a minor one and only 30.4 per cent believed it was irrelevant. These results are certainly compatible with the theme of emerging supply-side influences in MNE R&D decision making.[11]

In Table 6.5, US laboratories suggest a strong emphasis on the demand-side influences, reinforcing the view of a predominant drive to achieve the best commercial application of available technology (especially through product development in LILs) rather than seek inputs that help reinforce such knowledge scope. Of the supply-side factors it is the first (strength in specialised disciplines) that is relatively of least influence, which is compatible with the earlier perception that US companies (confident of home-country scope) have limited commitment to basic research in their UK laboratories. Although need for product development is a quite relevant influence in Japanese laboratories, the most significant overall is the more distinctive of the two supply-side influences. More decisively than emerges from results in the previous section, this may support the view of a strong drive in the internationalisation of Japanese companies' R&D that responds to a perceived weakness in home-country basic research capacity in several key scientific disciplines. The results for European laboratories in Table 6.5 are compatible with our earlier speculative interpretation of the motivations of these units. Thus a high valuation of a general technological infrastructure, which in particular includes some areas of very distinctive capability, by these UK-based units leads to an attempt to defend their continued use of it (during processes of rationalisation in these European MNE regional operations) by building it into strong localised product development and adaptation activities (which may not be fully comprehended or authorised by technology planners at group headquarters).

Very much in line with earlier perceptions of their science-oriented strategic positioning, laboratories in pharmaceuticals combine the highest evaluation of both supply-side factors and the lowest rating of both those on the demand side. The moderate relevance of supply-side factors in chemicals supports a strong influence from both product development (especially the type that builds on complementary in-house applied research; Table 6.4) and adapt-ation. Once again, demand-side factors seem to be the more decisive forces, driving laboratory evolution in electronics MNEs, though, perhaps surprisingly, on the supply side it is distinctive attributes that carry the greater influence.

Alongside the broad influences that help to define the strategic positioning of MNE laboratories (Table 6.5) responding R&D units were also requested to assess the relevance of a number of more detailed factors. Thus two questions in the laboratory survey asked whether or not respondents considered that a range of factors were likely to influence growing roles for their facility (Table 6.6) or to operate as potential causes of decline (Table 6.7).

Bearing in mind that some responding laboratories took research-oriented stand-alone positions, there is rather strong support (47.8 per cent of replies) for a 'desire to develop a distinctive product for our production subsidiary's market' as a significant evolutionary force in the positioning of overseas R&D in MNEs (Table 6.6). The especially strong status of this motive in Japanese laboratories is in line with a view that after establishing a position based on the commercial effectiveness of existing centrally-generated goods, there is a clear expectation of a move towards a more distinctive application of group technology to European-market needs through local product development. The continued basic/applied research orientation of pharmaceutical laboratories is indicated by their uniquely low evaluation of this influence.

Despite their quite strong product development commitment, only 26.1 per cent of laboratories rated 'to support our subsidiary's increasingly independent role in MNE-group activity' as a factor likely to drive their own growth. By contrast, 73.9 per cent believed that growth would be a response to their own desire 'to support an increasing role for our own laboratory in the group's scientific activity'. Thus it seems that (especially in US and European MNEs, and those in the pharmaceutical and chemical industries) the laboratories tend to see their progress as more likely to derive from the ability to assert an individualised position in the group's overall technological evolution than from a status that is mainly responsive to the market-focused needs of associated production subsidiaries. This certainly reinforces the view of strengthening technological interdependence in the positioning of de-centralised R&D units of MNEs, which in turn derives from a willingness and ability to individualise their competences in ways that respond as much to local supply-side factors as to demand-side needs. The very strong response to the second of this pair of factors in US laboratories may represent a certain frustration with and, therefore, reaction to, the perception that the MNE group still considers that home-country (US-based) inputs can support most of its needs for core knowledge generation. By contrast, the above-average prevalence of the former of these two factors, and the relatively low response to the latter, in Japanese laboratories may indicate that the original establishment of these (mostly relatively new) units benefits initially from a role within producing operations and that an attempt to position themselves rather more in the group's technology networks requires the gradual emer-gence of a more precise understanding of how their in-house scope (reflecting growing familiarity with distinctive local capabilities) takes on original dimensions that it can contribute to this wider knowledge environment.

Table 6.6 Evaluation of factors that might influence the growing roles of MNE laboratories in the UK

	Influence (percentage of respondents[1])					
	A	B	C	D	E	F
By industry						
Electronics	63.6	36.4	45.5	63.6	18.2	9.1
Pharmaceuticals	11.8	17.6	76.5	52.9	47.1	17.6
Chemicals[2]	62.5	25.0	100.0	12.5	37.5	25.0
Other	80.0	30.0	80.0	20.0	30.0	10.0
Total	47.8	26.1	73.9	41.3	34.8	15.2
By home country						
USA	38.5	23.1	92.3	23.1	38.5	15.4
Japan	55.6	33.3	55.6	66.7	11.1	11.1
Europe	46.7	20.0	80.0	26.7	60.0	20.0
Total	47.8	26.1	73.9	41.3	34.8	15.2

Influence:

A Desire to develop a distinctive product for our production subsidiary's market.
B To support our subsidiary's increasingly independent role in MNE-group activity.
C To support an increasing role for our own laboratory in the group's scientific activity.
D Availability of local scientific personnel.
E Financial support from UK government (for example, tax incentives).
F Pressure from UK government policies.

Notes:

1. Respondents were invited to endorse any influence they felt to be   relevant.
2. Includes petrochemicals and petroleum.

Source: Survey of laboratories.

The 'availability of local scientific personnel' was rated a potential influence on the growing stature of laboratories in 41.3 per cent of replies, indicating that the ability of the UK science base and education system to provide an adequate supply of technical personnel is likely to influence the degree of commitment of MNE creative operations. This factor was of greatest relevance to Japanese laboratories and, partly reflecting this, to laboratories in electronics. 'Financial support from UK government (for example, tax incentives)' was endorsed by 34.8 per cent of respondents, and tended to be strongest for European laboratories and of least relevance to Japanese ones. It may be, therefore, that such support can play a role in the incremental evolution of well-established laboratories (perhaps even as a response to

Table 6.7 Evaluation of factors that might cause a diminished role in MNE laboratories in the UK

	Potential cause of diminished role (percentage of respondents[1])						
	A	B	C	D	E	F	G
By industry							
Electronics	9.1	63.6	54.5	54.5	36.4	63.6	18.2
Pharmaceuticals	0	70.6	52.9	17.6	58.8	70.6	58.8
Chemicals[2]	22.2	77.8	66.7	11.1	66.7	77.8	55.6
Other	10.0	70.0	70.0	10.0	50.0	90.0	30.0
Total	8.5	70.2	59.6	23.4	53.2	74.5	42.6
By home country							
USA	0	75.0	66.7	16.7	75.0	66.7	66.7
Japan	10.5	57.9	42.1	31.6	31.6	78.9	21.1
Europe	12.5	81.3	75.0	18.8	62.5	75.0	50.0
Total	8.5	70.2	59.6	23.4	53.2	74.5	42.6

Influence:
A Less need to provide support to our subsidiary's production operations.
B Parent company decisions to limit the role of this laboratory (perhaps transferring some of its work to another group laboratory).
C As a result of group rationalisation in response to market conditions (e.g. recession, increased competition, etc.).
D A lack of scientific personnel.
E Negative external financial situation (e.g. tax increases).
F Negative internal financial situation (e.g. declining profits, increased wages).
G Unfavourable pressure from UK government policies.

Notes:
1. Respondents were invited to endorse any cause they felt to be relevant.
2. Includes petrochemicals and petroleum.

Source: Survey of laboratories.

perceived vulnerability), but is taken into account less by those (for example, Japanese ones) that are more concerned with their initial strategic positioning. Only 15.2 per cent of the laboratories believed that their growth prospects were likely to be affected by 'pressure from UK government policies'. This may reflect more the relative lack of positive UK policies in this area than a generalised immunity of MNE scientific operations to possible host-country intervention.

Of the seven possible influences on a diminished laboratory role (Table 6.7) that were offered, the least relevant (endorsed by only 8.5 per cent of replies) was 'less need to provide support to our subsidiary's production operations'. Therefore there remains a clear understanding on the part of laboratories that are currently associated with production subsidiaries that operating within such units will continue to provide a decisive influence on their own evolution, even if this is exercised in the light of increasingly relevant supply-side factors and awareness of involvement with the group's technological trajectory.

The increasing interdependence of globalised R&D in MNEs provides laboratories with the potential to earn powerfully specialised positions in group-level programmes of knowledge generation and product creation. This means, though, that however well such a laboratory builds its own individualised competences and however much distinctive product scope this may help endow on an associated production subsidiary, its position becomes increasingly vulnerable to external decision making concerning the evolution of the group's overall networked programmes. Thus, new commercial priorities or technological potentials may lead an MNE to refocus its R&D programmes, with some laboratories losing size or status and others acceding to new responsibilities with enhanced resource scope. We have already noted (Table 6.6) that many respondents see increased involvement in group networks as a potential source of their growth, but the continued restructuring of such programmes is also acknowledged as a notable source of vulnerability. Thus 70.2 per cent considered 'parent company decisions to limit the role of this laboratory (perhaps transferring some of its work to another group laboratory)' as a possible cause of a diminished role.

Furthermore, 59.6 per cent of responding laboratories believed a decline in their position could come about 'as a result of group rationalisation in response to market conditions (for example, recession, increased competition, etc.)'. This can reflect the possibilities that the need for short-term retrenchment in MNE groups may often in fact target longer-term programmes, with R&D then an especially vulnerable target, and that the contributions of overseas laboratories are still perceived as marginal when such cuts are necessary.[12] Japanese laboratories were somewhat less concerned about both of these types of intra-group rationalisation than were their US or European counterparts. This was likely to reflect their perception of a position in programmes that were seen as part of a current extension of strategic scope (new dimensions of globalisation) in their MNE groups (Pearce and Papanastassiou, 1996a, pp.52–5), and which therefore still seemed likely to provide clear potential for further expansion. By contrast, many of the European and US laboratories may feel under rather more pressure to defend an established position in mature networks that embody less obvious inherent growth momentum. Where the buoyancy of the whole technology commitment can be perceived as open to question, individual laboratories may be more likely to see their own growth (Table 6.6) as likely to derive from the ability to assert a stronger individualised position (European and US laboratories) in the programmes.

Only 23.4 per cent of laboratories believed 'a lack of scientific personnel' was likely to provide a source of decline in their status. Just as Japanese (and therefore electronics) laboratories perceived the availability of such personnel as a factor that would strongly support their growth (Table 6.6) so they were relatively most likely to feel seriously constrained were a shortage to occur. These laboratories, therefore, seem quite distinctively sensitive to access to high-quality scientific personnel as a supply-side influence on their evolution.[13]

Adverse aspects of their financial environment were clearly distinguished as potential sources of vulnerability by the surveyed laboratories. Thus 53.2 per cent of them felt that a 'negative external financial situation (e.g. tax increases)' might cause a diminished role, whilst 74.5 per cent considered such declines could derive from a 'negative internal financial situation (e.g. declining profits, increased wages)'. This perception by such laboratories indicates that they still feel especially at risk in periods of financial downturn where, as previously noted, R&D may be the function most likely to face cutbacks and decentralised units may be the most vulnerable. The latter aspect of this view, at least, should over time be mitigated where the overseas laboratories achieve their objective of asserting a strongly individualised competence that contributes uniquely to group scope and cannot, therefore, be quickly replicated in another unit.

'Unfavourable pressure from UK government policies' was viewed as having a possible adverse influence in 42.6 per cent of replies. In some cases this may reflect the reaction to specific aspects of constraint on their activities which derive from UK government policies, or it may instead indicate a wider perception of a lack of support for the supply-side environment (science and education funding) from which these laboratories would expect to derive the potential sources of individualised scope from which they can defend their position.

SUBSIDIARIES THAT DO NOT HAVE LABORATORIES

Some rather different perspectives on the positioning of overseas R&D in MNEs were sought through investigation of the attitudes of those UK-based

*Table 6.8 Evaluation by MNE subsidiaries in the UK without an R&D
laboratory of reasons for not having one*

	Reason for not having a laboratory (percentage of respondents)[1]					
	A	B	C	D	E	F
By industry						
Automobiles	33.3	83.3	58.3	0	16.7	8.3
Electronics and electrical appliances	44.0	52.0	48.0	4.0	16.0	8.0
Mechanical engineering	63.6	63.6	45.5	0	27.3	0
Industrial and agricultural chemicals	45.5	72.7	81.8	18.2	9.1	0
Other manufacturing	66.7	70.0	46.7	13.3	16.7	3.3
Total	52.8	66.3	52.8	7.9	16.9	4.5
By home country						
USA	58.6	62.1	44.8	10.3	24.1	6.9
Japan	46.3	63.4	53.7	4.9	14.6	4.9
Europe	58.8	76.5	64.7	11.8	11.8	0
Total[2]	52.8	66.3	52.8	7.9	16.9	4.5

Reasons for not having an R&D laboratory.

A Our operations do not require enough adaptation or development to need one.
B We can obtain adequate adaptation/development advice from other laboratories of our MNE group.
C R&D economies of scale in our industry mean our operations are not large enough to justify a laboratory of effective size.
D Our group believes technology is too sensitive to risk decentralisation of important scientific work.
E Our group centralises creative work because it believes communications and coordination problems make decentralisation of R&D ineffective.
F We believe it would be difficult to recruit adequate local personnel to staff a laboratory to meet our needs.

Notes.

1. MNE subsidiaries without an R&D laboratory were asked to indicate which of the offered reasons they believed were relevant to the decision to omit such a facility from their operations.
2. Includes subsidiaries of MNEs from Australia and Canada.

Source: Survey of producing subsidiaries.

production operations that did not currently have an in-house laboratory. Two questions in the survey of the production subsidiaries were thus addressed explicitly to those without an R&D unit. The first of these (Table 6.8) asked respondents to say whether or not they believed each of six factors had contributed to the decision not to have their own R&D unit.

A majority (52.8 per cent) of the respondents to this question endorsed the view that a significant factor in not having a laboratory was that 'our operations do not require enough adaptation or development to need one'. Alongside this, even more (66.3 per cent) believed 'we can obtain adequate adaptation/development advice from other laboratories of our MNE group'. Bearing in mind that earlier evidence (Chapter 5) indicated that the majority of the subsidiaries without laboratories are predominantly focusing on the manufacture of established products, these results suggest that as the supply of such goods becomes an increasingly specialised and networked position (that is, the ESTPROD/EUR role replaces ESTPROD/UK), there is likely to be decreasing need for in-house R&D to support such production units. This confirms the increasing significance of the third type of research interdependency in MNEs' decentralised R&D that we outlined in the introduction to this chapter. Although this means that some ESTPROD/UK subsidiaries with laboratories may retain them in an upgraded, network-supporting, form (that is, to play the SL2 role) on their transition to ESTPROD/EUR status, it also provides a basis for the earlier suggestion that ESTPROD/EUR subsidiaries feel that in-house R&D may be considered an expendable luxury. They believe, then, that unless they can actively target the more substantial enhancement of creative competence needed to facilitate the incorporation of the product development role they are in danger of, instead, suffering a 'hollowing out' of functional scope that reduces them to a technologically-limited and strategically-vulnerable cost-based position.

Another well-supported reason for not having R&D (52.8 per cent of respondents) was that 'R&D economies of scale in our industry mean our operations are not large enough to justify a laboratory of effective size'. Although we earlier suggested that emerging interdependent approaches to the internationalisation of technology in MNEs can often provide means of overcoming the potential constraints of economies of scale, these results indicate that there remain some limits to this with national operations sometimes still being too small to justify separate R&D scope.

Our suggestion of diminished relevance of traditional centripetal forces constraining overseas R&D in MNEs received rather more support with respect to the other two such factors investigated in this question. Thus only 7.9 per cent of the respondents endorsed 'our group believes technology is too sensitive to risk decentralisation of important scientific work' as a reason for the absence of R&D from their activity, whilst only 16.9 per cent considered that 'our group centralises creative work because it believes communications and coordination problems make decentralisation of R&D ineffective'. Although both these factors may well constitute matters of valid organisational concern for MNEs, it seems that the benefits of decentralised approaches to technology are such that procedures have been developed to mitigate these concerns and minimise the risks. The availability of these procedures seems to be understood by those subsidiaries that do not yet have a laboratory, so that they are unlikely to feel the presence of such organisational constraints when more positive motivations became apparent. Finally, only 4.5 per cent of respondents believed they did not have R&D because 'it would be difficult to recruit adequate local personnel to staff a laboratory to meet our needs'.

The second of these questions to subsidiaries without in-house R&D asked them to consider whether or not each of four factors might influence them to set up a laboratory in the future (Table 6.9). Here there was widespread support (69.1 per cent of responding subsidiaries) for the view that a factor that could positively affect the desire for an R&D laboratory was that 'our subsidiary wishes to increase the degree of independence it can exercise within the MNE group'. Recalling again that most of these subsidiaries currently play ESTPROD roles, this response shows a strong awareness of the vulnerability that can arise from the functionally-constrained dependency of this position and therefore the desirability of in-house R&D as a crucial element in individualising their scope. That a formal incorporation of R&D may be a key factor in operationalising undercommitted subsidiary-level competences was quite strongly endorsed (27.3 per cent of replies) in the view that 'we feel the creative potential of our personnel (e.g. in management, marketing, engineering) is currently stifled and could be better used for the group if combined with additional local technological inputs (i.e. our own scientists)'.

The possible addition of R&D therefore appears to be viewed by many subsidiaries as a key way in which they can augment their scope sufficiently to accede to a less dependent role within the creative programmes of their MNE group. However, such ambitious producing subsidiaries seem to accept that their new position will be one that is interdependent with the commercial evolution of the mainstream of their MNE (that is, the medium-term objectives of strategic competitiveness), rather than one which helps the group to access more radical new scientific inputs (that is, the longer-term objective). Thus only 12.7 per cent of respondents considered that 'the UK has a strong science

Table 6.9 Evaluation by MNE subsidiaries in the UK without an R&D laboratory of factors that could influence them to set one up

	Factor (percentage of respondents)[1]			
	A	B	C	D
By industry				
Automobiles	50.0	16.7	0	0
Electronics and electrical appliances	80.0	25.0	5.0	10.0
Mechanical engineering	87.5	25.0	25.0	0
Industrial and agricultural chemicals	66.7	33.3	50.0	16.7
Other manufacturing	53.3	33.3	6.7	0
Total	69.1	27.3	12.7	5.5
By home country				
USA	46.7	26.7	13.3	13.3
Japan	83.9	29.0	9.7	3.2
Europe	71.4	28.6	28.6	0
Total[2]	69.1	27.3	12.7	5.5

Reasons for considering an R & D laboratory.

A Our subsidiary wishes to increase the degree of independence it can exercise within the MNE group.
B We feel the creative potential of our personnel (e.g. in management, marketing, engineering) is currently stifled and could be better used for the group if combined with additional local technological inputs (i.e. our own scientists).
C The UK has a strong science base in our industry and we could use this on behalf of the MNE group if we had our own laboratory.
D We would recommend our MNE group to use talented local scientists in a basic research oriented laboratory, even if this does not contribute to this subsidiary's current operations.

Notes.
1. MNE subsidiaries without an R&D laboratory were asked to indicate which of the offered reasons they felt might influence them to set one up in the near future.
2. Includes subsidiaries of MNEs from Australia and Canada.

Source: Survey of producing subsidiaries.

base in our industry and we could use this on behalf of the MNE group if we had our own laboratory' was a factor that might encourage them to set up a laboratory. Similarly, only 5.5 per cent viewed 'we would recommend our MNE group to use talented local scientists in a basic research oriented laboratory, even if this does not contribute to this subsidiary's current operations' as being a viable reason for a future R&D unit.

SOURCES OF FUNDING FOR R&D LABORATORIES

An organisational issue that also has a significant relationship with the strategic positioning of R&D laboratories in MNEs is the sources of funding used to finance their operations. The UK laboratories surveyed were asked to evaluate the relative position in their budgets of five sources of funding. Decisively, the most pervasive of these sources was 'funds from the parent company of the MNE group', with 25.5 per cent of respondents who evaluated this source reporting it as their only one, 29.8 per cent more rating it as a major source, and 17.0 per cent a supporting source, whilst the fact that only 27.7 per cent did not access it at all made this the only type of funding that was used by more than half the laboratories. Although 'funds from an associated UK producing subsidiary' emerged overall as clearly the second most relevant source of laboratory finance, it was rated far behind parent company support. In fact, its status was somewhat dichotomous; absent from the majority of laboratories' budgets but usually of considerable importance when present. Thus 57.8 per cent of respondents who judged its relevance reported it as absent, but 15.6 per cent said it was their only source of funding and 17.8 per cent more a major one (so that the 8.9 per cent who rated it as merely a secondary source amounted to only 21.0 per cent of those who used it).

When expressed in terms of average responses in Table 6.10 pharmaceuticals emerges as emphatically the industry where UK-based laboratories tended to depend most strongly on parent (group-level) funds and at the same time made least use of finance from associated local producing subsidiaries. This clearly reflects the strategic positioning of these laboratories. Thus their strong focus on the IIL role (Table 6.2) and relative commitment to basic research and, to some degree, applied research and the more group-dependent type of product development (Table 6.4), suggests a clearcut commitment to work that contributes to, and/or builds on, the wider technological programmes of the MNE. That is, these pharmaceutical laboratories, in particular, embody those precompetitive aspects of interdependent individualism that provide limited immediate connections with current commercial UK-based activity and, therefore, need funding from group sources that support the longer-term objectives of strategic competitiveness.

Electronics provides the strongest case of the contrasting position of alternative sources of funding, with the most notable use of finance from associated production subsidiaries and well-below-average dependence on the

Table 6.10   Sources of funding for MNE laboratories in the UK

		Source of funding (average response)[1]				
		A	B	C	D	E
By industry						
Electronics		2.20	2.18	1.82	1.30	1.20
Pharmaceuticals		1.69	3.18	1.25	1.06	1.00
Chemicals[2]		1.89	2.33	1.89	1.11	1.11
Other		2.00	2.20	1.20	1.10	1.10
	Total	1.91	2.53	1.50	1.13	1.09
By home country						
USA		2.18	2.42	1.33	1.27	1.18
Japan		1.74	2.63	1.58	1.05	1.05
Europe		1.93	2.50	1.53	1.13	1.07
	Total	1.91	2.53	1.50	1.13	1.09

Sources of funding

A Funds from an associated UK producing subsidiary.
B Funds from the parent company of the MNE group.
C Funds from elsewhere in the group.
E Funds from UK government.
F Funds from EU budget.

Notes:
1 Respondents were invited to evaluate each source of funding as (i) the only source, (ii) a major source, (iii) a supporting source, (iv) not a source. The average response was then derived by allocating a value of 4 to 'only source', 3 to 'major source', 2 to 'supporting source' and 1 to 'not a source'.
2. Includes petrochemicals and petroleum.

Source: Survey to laboratories.

MNE parent. This then emerges as reflecting particularly localised aspects of the positioning of these laboratories, with strong status for SL1 and LIL units (Table 6.2) and for development and adaptation (Table 6.4). Parent funding prevails over that from a local subsidiary in chemicals, but with both activated at more moderate levels (Table 6.10). This perhaps reflects the importance of the SL2 role (Table 6.2) and group support for applied research (although, as Table 6.4 suggests, this seems to feed through to a local product development process).

Japanese labs are the most likely to build their budgets around central-group funding, and to have least dependence on the support of a UK-based production subsidiary. Although the presence of basic research and the group-related type of product development (Table 6.4) may relate to the prominent status of parent funding, it is also likely that this reflects the newness of the laboratories and, indeed, of producing operations in Europe. Thus parent funds may be particularly prevalent in the early stages of these Japanese facilities, partly because their initial role is the transfer of extant (and so far centrally-controlled) technology into the new environment and partly because the UK-based production subsidiaries do not yet have either the independent financial scope or the in-house creative momentum to support laboratories properly. At the early stage it is the home-country headquarters in Japanese MNEs that seem to drive and, therefore fund, decentralised R&D (although this is often related mainly to application of existing technology) even where this is applied through association with a UK-based production subsidiary.

US MNE laboratories are somewhat the least likely to access parent funds and clearly the strongest users of subsidiary finance (even though the former source is still rather the more influential). This reflects the pervasive involvement of these units in the effective commercialisation of technology for US MNE European operations (notably through the LIL role and both applied research and product development, but with adaptation work also prevalent) and the relatively limited status of basic research and IIL positioning. The strong status of IILs and precompetitive research in European laboratories might have indicated an even more powerful position for central funds than actually emerges in Table 6.10. An explanation for this derives from our earlier speculations about the status of the UK laboratories (and of subsidiary positioning) in continental MNEs. Thus it can be suggested that the more ambitious and higher-value roles in these laboratories, which would normally provide strong justification for central-funding, are here more often the result of local initiatives that perhaps have only grudging support (or perhaps active disapproval) from HQ and thus are required to depend to a much greater degree than usual on support from an associated UK subsidiary.

Regression tests were run using the sources of funds as dependent variables and incorporating dummy variables for industry and home country of the MNE and the roles of laboratories (as reported in Table 6.2) as independent variables. These regressions were quite weak overall and provided relatively few significant results (which can partly reflect the relationship between industry/home country and the laboratories' role). Nevertheless, some indicative patterns emerge. Although well short of significance in both cases, the IIL role is positively signed for parent funds and negatively so for subsidiary finance, supporting the expectation that this is a positioning that supports longer-term group-level aims. More decisively, SL2 status is significantly positively related to parent finance and significantly negatively to funding from an associated UK subsidiary. This is clearly in line with the fact that SL2 work supports other (non-UK) subsidiaries of the MNE, but also indicates that laboratories playing this role seem to do so in a way that is often systematically recognised (and therefore funded) centrally by the parent group rather than representing an *ad hoc* transaction with another part of the group. Finally, the SL1 role approaches positive significance in terms of subsidiary funding, although the negative sign on parent funding is very weak.

A third type of intra-MNE laboratory financing covered in the question was 'funds from elsewhere in the group', that is mainly sister subsidiaries in countries other than the MNE home countries. Overall, 63.0 per cent of laboratories considered that none of their budget derived from this source and only 10.9 per cent rated it as more than a secondary one. This type of funding was especially sparse in pharmaceuticals, paralleling the limited use of local subsidiary finance and again indicating the decisive influence in these laboratories of precompetitive work that supports group-level objectives. In the regression, SL2 provided the expected positive sign (all other roles were very weakly negative) although well short of significance. Taken with the generally restrictive relevance for this type of finance the weak result for SL2 is compatible with our suggestion that this laboratory role is often one that is centrally mandated and funded (as a manifestation of group-level support for interdependent approaches to globalisation in their technology programmes) rather than the result of occasional agreements between dispersed laboratories and/or subsidiaries.

Responding laboratories were also requested to evaluate the importance of two sources of R&D funding from outside their MNE group, namely 'funds from the UK government' and 'funds from the EU budget'. In neither case did the relevance of these sources exceed the secondary and in both the vast majority of respondents (86.7 per cent for the UK government, and 91.1 per cent for the EU, funds) said the source was not accessed. This contrasts somewhat with the result in Table 6.6, which found that around one-third of these labs felt that 'financial support from UK government (for example, tax incentives)' was a factor that might influence their future growth. This may indicate unrealised potential for policy support of this type. These sources of finance were most used by electronics laboratories (the only positively signed industry dummy in both regressions, and significantly so for 'UK government funds'), which may suggest that they are most readily available for the product development (or even adaptation) work that is strong in these units. The very weak accessing of these sources in pharmaceuticals can then support the complementary perspective that these types of finance tend not to be available for precompetitive work. That these sources of funding would be most readily available to support commercially-oriented work is compatible with their relative prevalence in US laboratories' budgets (and clearly positive US dummies in both regressions, which approaches significance for UK government funds).

CONCLUSIONS

The analysis of MNE R&D units in the UK, presented in this chapter, indicates that the positioning of these laboratories is increasingly as part of integrated programmes of technological progress and implementation that support global strategic objectives which are comprehended and supported at the group level. One vital facet of this type of repositioning of overseas R&D in MNEs involves an expansion and upgrading of the roles that decentralised laboratories can now play. Moving forward from an earlier adaptation of existing product and process technology, laboratories in the UK emerge as now playing two roles that seek to expand, in more fundamental ways, the commercial and knowledge horizons of their MNE groups. These roles involve, firstly, precompetitive work (basic and, especially, applied research) which aims to expand the core of knowledge available to the group and, secondly, participation in the increasing decentralisation of the product creation (innovation) process itself.

Paralleling the two approaches to localised innovation evaluated by product development *subsidiaries* in Chapter 4, the *laboratories'* evidence also indicates their participation in similar alternatives. Thus many of them (especially those of US and European MNEs) provide their inputs into new product generation by building on their own applied research activity. However, there is also evidence of the presence (most notably in Japanese laboratories) of the alternative approach (envisaged in the procedures of a global innovation strategy) where the laboratory picks up, and then seeks to work with other subsidiary functions to commercialise locally, the technology of a new outline product concept that has been defined elsewhere in the group's operations. The corollary of these alternatives in the product development process can then be found in the positioning of UK laboratories' precompetitive work. Thus even though this research is often carried through the interface with development into a sequentially-integrated localised innovation process, this is not always the expected outcome, with the precompetitive work sometimes being carried out in a stand-alone (pure IIL) facility which then feeds its inputs into external (group articulated and coordinated) scientific programmes.

These newly enhanced dimensions of expectation for the *output* of MNE UK laboratories implies the second key facet of their repositioning detected in the analysis, namely the significantly increased importance in decision making relating to their existence and status of the quality and scope of locally-available scientific *inputs*. The positive interpretation of the UK's scope in this regard appears to be manifest in both the forms addressed in the analysis. Firstly, in the form of a world-class tradition in certain areas of science, so that MNEs can perceive a major value in tapping into this heritage and, mainly through precompetitive research, benefiting from participation in its further evolution. Secondly, in the more generalised quality of the current science base (as reflected, for example, in the knowledge and competence of new graduates) which can adequately support the effective activation of the technological component of innovation processes (that is, more the ability to comprehend, assimilate and operationalise the new knowledge that is generated through the more specialised scientific capacities of the first type).

Ultimately, then, the analysis suggests that localised R&D is a crucial element in involving an economy in the higher-value-added processes of MNEs and in building a position that can share in, influence and benefit from the technological and commercial evolution that is at the core of these companies' ability to survive and flourish in globalised competition. Support for the local science base, both through its research capacity and through education and training, is then an obvious and vital prescription. An appropriate balance within this support should, however, be informed by the more detailed understanding of MNEs' potential use of dispersed R&D.

One area of concern could occur if policy focused excessively on support for high-profile precompetitive research with a concomitant neglect of development activity. This would tend to attract MNE basic and applied research but limit the extent to which output of this feeds through to localised product creation, and thereby to an upgrading of the supply profile of subsidiaries located in the same economy. Thus MNEs would tend to use mainly pure (stand-alone) IILs with their research output flowing out into group-coordinated programmes rather than being retained within locally-integrated product creation processes. In a similar manner, this form of bias in R&D support would also lessen MNE enthusiasm for involving subsidiaries in the types of product development that build on new group-generated product concepts.

By contrast, an overcommitment to mechanisms supporting development, which ultimately withdraws support from basic/applied research, can also be detrimental, especially if this eventually also leads to the atrophy of those areas of science where a strong tradition (and available stock of knowledge) had previously been an attracting factor. Certainly a well-supported development culture can still be activated by MNEs which can, as noted, implement (through LILs) the local variants of new group-originated product concepts (as conceptualised for the second phase of a global innovation strategy). Ultimately, though, there is a danger that this situation could be seen as replicating in the modern context the types of technological dependency that limit the potential of some economies to a lower-level or 'peripheral' status. Thus whilst considerable benefits derive from participation in the innovation programmes of MNEs, both through the supply of new and highly-profitable goods and through the provision of well-rewarded work for local creative personnel, this is not based on a degree of originality in local inputs that helps to actually define the direction of these groups' technological and commercial trajectories (and therefore embed the decentralised operation in a more secure, and potentially more rewarding, fashion in the further evolution of these companies' core capabilities). It is also possible that, even when only envisaging LIL-type development work in a country, MNEs may be considerably influenced in their location decision by the presence of currently highly reputed basic research programmes (for example, employing individual scientists of outstanding stature).

In essence these perspectives on the roles played by foreign MNE R&D units, and indeed the revealed scope for knowledge-related expansion in the strategic positioning of production subsidiaries, represent ways in which these global companies interact with national systems of innovation (NIS).[14] It would be hoped that the interjection of MNE operations into an NIS would complement and strengthen its current effectiveness. For a mature industrial economy, such as the UK, it would be logical to pursue the continued evolution of what would be expected to be a rich and wide-ranging NIS, encompassing both the institutions that can provide for precompetitive research that helps to build on strong areas of scientific leadership and mechanisms that support dynamic processes of product development.

Normally it would be logical to want MNE operations to be involved in many elements of such an NIS and to thereby underwrite its continued balanced evolution, and we have noted above how distorted policies (either generally or specifically towards MNEs) could constrain the benefits a country gets from the technological activity of foreign firms. Finally, however, we can also note that the variegated roles of MNE laboratories, and the way in which this allows for the potential decoupling of research and development in particular parts of their global network, can provide an alternative policy perspective for countries that are aware of a distorted or incomplete NIS. Here, host-country policies towards technology and MNEs may be able to actively encourage the regeneration or revitalisation of the particular areas of weakness (or imbalance) that may be compromising the overall effectiveness of the NIS, through support for particular facets of MNE R&D and innovation programmes.

NOTES

1. See also Pearce and Papanastassiou (1996a) for JETRO data on increased numbers of Japanese laboratories in Europe.
2. The increased networking and interdependence of R&D operations are discussed by De Meyer (1991, 1993); Håkanson (1990); Håkanson and Laage-Hellman (1984); Howells (1990a); Pearce and Papanastassiou (1996b); and Pearce and Singh (1992a, 1992b).
3. See Howells (1990a, 1990b) for discussion of developments in communications and organisational techniques in globally-competing enterprises.
4. Cordell (1971, 1973); Ronstadt (1977, 1978); Haug, Hood and Young (1983); Pearce (1989); and Pearce and Papanastassiou (1996a).
5. The separation of independent and associated laboratories in the JETRO surveys of Japanese companies' operations in Europe has facilitated useful documentation of the extent and implementation of the distinction. See Papanastassiou and Pearce (1994b, 1995), Pearce and Papanastassiou (1996a), and Pearce (1997).
6. In analysis of German subsidiaries' R&D operations in Spain, Molero and Buesa (1993) found that 70.0 per cent of these included 'development of new products' in their aims. Although this was matched by 'product improvement' it exceeded all other aims (that is, 'development of new manufacturing processes' [40 per cent]; 'process development' [48.0 per cent]; 'adaptation of imported technologies' [26.0 per cent]).
7. It has been suggested (Håkanson and Nobel, 1993a, p.381) that where MNEs have loose and informal control systems (as might be the case with growing heterarchy) local R&D can be created or retained above the level formally authorised from headquarters (see also Håkanson, 1990; Håkanson and Zander, 1986, 1988).
8. The desire of laboratories carrying out this type of work to remove themselves from the day-to-day pressures of production support has been noted previously (Pearce and Singh, 1992a). However, attention has also been drawn (Håkanson and Nobel, 1993a) to the danger that this isolation may lead to laboratories' work failing to contribute to the coherent development of the group's technological trajectory.
9. This role was especially strong in some industries where Japanese companies are not yet clearcut market leaders. This may suggest a supply-side influence (alongside market responsiveness) in that here European inputs are being sought to supplement those from the home country, whose competence is less trusted than in the industries of accepted Japanese leadership.
10. Distinctive market-related ideas emerging from LIL and SL types of work may then also support the ability of these electronics subsidiaries to develop products independently of new group technology (the first type of product development) despite limited in-house precompetitive research. This could, for example, involve deriving radical new product dimensions from the technology embodied in existing goods.
11. In their analysis of overseas R&D in Swedish MNEs, Håkanson and Nobel (1992) found what we may consider to be supply-side factors to be mainly only moderately important in absolute terms. However, they included three of the five determinants (out of a total of 21) that had significantly increased their relevance between 1970 and 1985, that is, 'monitor the development of technology and competition abroad', 'proximity to foreign research centres', 'acquisition of

technologies new to the group'. In his study of Swedish MNE overseas R&D Fors (1996) found that, after controlling for factors relating to adaptation, a significant positive relationship emerged between the share of a company's total R&D expenditure carried out in a particular country and the extent to which that country specialised technologically in the firm's industry (which may equate to the first of our supply-side indicators). However, in the same test a variable formulated as 'researchers, scientists, engineers and technicians per one thousand inhabitants' for each country, and intended to serve as a general scientific skill level (and thus equating to our second supply-side indicator) was not significantly related to Swedish MNE R&D in that country.

12. Brockhoff and Pearson (1998) indicate that R&D budget cuts are likely only in the case of deep recessions, but are then likely to be implemented through the elimination of 'marginal' projects. The quite strong response to factor C in Table 6.7 could then suggest that, despite the arguments for much decentralised R&D in MNEs now being embedded within *strategic* programmes with group-level implications, many overseas laboratory managers still see their status as somewhat marginalised.

13. Serapio (1993, pp.212–13) draws attention to evidence on a projected slowing in the growth of supply of Japanese scientists and engineers. This may engender the sensitivity of Japanese MNEs to the availability of such personnel in their overseas operations.

14. See Lundvall (1992), Nelson (1993) and Freeman and Soete (1997, Chapter 12). Cantwell and Iammarino (1998) have also demonstrated the validity and value of analysing MNE operations within regional (in the sub national sense) systems of innovation.

7. Scientific collaborations of MNE research laboratories in the UK

INTRODUCTION

The previous two chapters have analysed extensively the strategic positioning of MNE R&D units' operations in the UK. The dominant emphasis has thus been on the factors motivating and facilitating these laboratories' status in intra-group programmes for generation and use of knowledge. We have also noted, however, that the ability of an overseas laboratory to play a distinctive role in its MNE's technological evolution is likely to reflect its presence in another unique knowledge community, that is that of the host country. One facet of the operationalisation of this potential is, of course, the ability to internalise parts of the host-country science community in the laboratory itself, by recruiting talented local personnel as the core of its research scope. The laboratory will thus seek to embody in its own activity the tacit knowledge of these scientists, which will itself encompass vital elements of those idiosyncratic aspects of the local technological heritage and current research competence that are most valuable to support the MNE's expanding technological trajectory. Complementing this, however, is the potential for an externalised access to other facets of the scope of the local science base through collaborative arrangements with independent local research institutions. These associations were analysed through questions in the survey of MNE laboratories in the UK, and this chapter focuses on a discussion of this aspect of their tapping into local knowledge potentials.

EXTENT OF LABORATORIES' SCIENTIFIC COLLABORATIONS

This section evaluates the extent of the MNE laboratories' collaborative associations with various UK scientific institutions, using evidence from the questionnaire that was sent directly to those R&D facilities. It can be recalled (Chapter 4) that when producing subsidiaries were asked to evaluate the significance to their operations of various sources of technology less than half of these respondents rated 'R&D carried out for us by local scientific institutions (e.g. universities, independent labs, industry labs)' as of any

189

relevance and only 3.2 per cent rated it as of more than secondary importance. We did, however, indicate two reasons why these replies might have understated the contribution of R&D acquired externally in the UK. Firstly, when the replies derived from the production subsidiaries, the respondents may have been able to evaluate with some precision the status of any technology inputs that are received directly from their in-house laboratories, but could have been much less clear about how much of that knowledge had resulted, in turn, from their laboratories' collaborative associations with other UK research institutions. The survey of laboratories themselves can often assess that from a more direct experience in the articulation and implementation of these shared R&D arrangements. Secondly, local research collaborations may be strongest in areas of work that are more often the province of stand-alone MNE laboratories than those associated with producing subsidiaries. These independent units are included in the survey directed to laboratories but, by definition, are not reported by the manufacturing subsidiaries. Thus we may well expect a more substantial recognition of the presence and significance of these local R&D associations in the laboratory survey that provides the input to this chapter.

The first type of collaborative link addressed in the survey was with 'universities in the UK'. Here 14 (29.2 per cent) respondents said that such collaborations were 'extensive', 25 (52.1 per cent) rated them as 'moderate' and only nine (18.7 per cent) considered they were 'non-existent'. When converted into an average response in Table 7.1, this indicates that collaborations with universities were the most prevalent type for these MNE laboratories. It also suggests immediately, a stronger perception of scientific links than reported by the production subsidiaries.

An *a priori* expectation would be that university laboratories are likely to do work of a predominantly precompetitive type (that is, with no immediate commercial problem or potential in mind)[1] in technological disciplines that reflect a long-term tradition of top-quality specialisation of the country's science base. This would lead us to expect that such collaborations would be strongest for MNE laboratories whose own specialisation and role is towards the longer-term aims of strengthening the group's technological trajectory through a precompetitive research focus. Thus university collaborations emerge as strongest (Table 7.1) for those MNE laboratories where basic and/or applied research are a strong priority. However, such links are also very important for laboratories that help subsidiaries to develop products based on their own research (DEVLAB), with this notably ahead of their relevance to laboratories that help with the creation of new products based on group-level research (DEVGROUP). Thus where MNE subsidiaries create products that

Table 7.1 Extent of collaboration between MNE laboratories in the UK and other scientific institutions

		Institution (average response[1])						
		A	B	C	D	E	F	G
By industry								
Electronics		1.82	1.18	1.45	1.64	1.82	1.27	1.27
Pharmaceuticals		2.29	1.65	1.29	1.41	1.47	1.29	1.29
Chemicals[2]		2.33	1.89	1.44	1.67	1.44	1.44	1.56
Other		1.91	1.55	1.73	1.27	1.36	1.27	1.45
	Total	2.10	1.56	1.46	1.48	1.52	1.31	1.38
By home country								
USA		2.08	1.69	1.54	1.38	1.46	1.23	1.31
Japan		2.05	1.37	1.32	1.42	1.74	1.16	1.21
Europe		2.19	1.69	1.56	1.63	1.31	1.56	1.63
	Total	2.10	1.56	1.46	1.48	1.52	1.31	1.38
By type of laboratory[3]								
SL1		1.83	1.58	1.42	1.42	1.58	1.17	1.58
SL2		2.14	1.71	1.29	1.57	1.71	1.43	1.57
LIL		2.12	1.53	1.47	1.65	1.59	1.18	1.24
IIL		2.20	1.55	1.35	1.25	1.30	1.50	1.40
By type of R&D[4]								
BASIC		2.22	1.56	1.44	1.33	1.44	1.44	1.44
APPLIED		2.24	1.71	1.47	1.47	1.47	1.47	1.59
DEVLAB		2.18	1.55	1.59	1.68	1.55	1.32	1.41
DEVGROUP		1.93	1.40	1.27	1.40	1.73	1.13	1.00
PRODADAPT		1.88	1.50	1.25	1.38	1.63	1.00	1.25
PROCADAPT		2.00	2.00	1.33	1.33	1.67	1.00	1.33

Institution:

A Universities in the UK.
B Independent research laboratories in the UK.
C Industry research laboratories in the UK.
D Other UK firms.
E Other independent firms overseas.
F Universities overseas (e.g. as part of an EU-supported programme).
G Government and other public laboratories.

Notes:
1. Respondents were asked to grade collaborations with particular institutions as (i) extensive, (ii) moderate, (iii) non-existent. The average response was calculated by allocating extensive the value of 3, moderate the value of 2, non-existent the value of 1.
2. Includes petrochemicals and petroleum.
3. Average responses calculated for laboratories that said they were 'predominantly' or 'only' that type. For definition of laboratory types, see Table 6.2.
4. Average response calculated for laboratories that said the type of R&D was their 'only' or 'predominant' work. For definition of types of R&D, see Table 6.4.

Source: Survey of laboratories.

are based on a sustained in-house (subsidiary-level) scientific effort this seems to reflect an interaction with local knowledge specialisms (as embodied in university research traditions) that is continued into the actual product development process. Where the subsidiary picks up new group-level technology as the basis for its product development, the local technology heritage is less relevant to support of the innovation process, and university links are rather less prevalent. University collaborations are also of well-below-average significance for laboratories doing mainly adaptive work.

In line with the above results and interpretation, university collaborations are most relevant to IIL-type units and least so to the SL1 type. Such university links also support LILs quite strongly (probably especially those with a DEVLAB product creation focus) and also SL2-type units (suggesting that support of a wider constituency by SL2, compared to SL1, demands higher-quality work, and perhaps the solving of *ad hoc* problems beyond the scope of their immediate in-house knowledge or research competence). Laboratories of European MNEs, and those in chemicals and pharmaceuticals, were the most likely to have formulated collaborative arrangements with UK universities.

Our initial surmise is that 'independent research labs in the UK' base their ability to market themselves to potential customers/collaborators around a heritage of research experience within the most powerful of the acknowledged technological specialisms of the host country. Although this might provide slightly less flexibility of range than university laboratories, it would involve the same precompetitive-research-related appeal to potential MNE collaborators. Overall, reported links with such independent laboratories are much less prevalent than with universities, with only one MNE respondent reporting that these are extensive, 25 (52.1 per cent) rating them as moderate and 22 (45.8 per cent) describing them as non-existent. As was the case for universities, collaborations with independent laboratories are notably prevalent for chemicals and pharmaceuticals and in European-controlled laboratories, though US laboratories also use them to an above-average degree (in a way that they did not use university collaborations).

Apart from a somewhat inexplicably strong result for process adaptation the results in Table 7.1 are compatible with the view that independent laboratories provide high-quality locally-specialised technological inputs, albeit exercised somewhat more closely to commercial problems and priorities than we hypothesised (which would be compatible with their enhanced position for US laboratories). Thus MNE laboratories focusing on applied research now clearly prevail over those doing basic research, in terms of their collaborations with UK independent laboratories, and those developing products locally in a technologically self-contained fashion (DEVLAB) still prevail over those creating products in a group innovation programme (DEVGROUP). Here IIL-, LIL- and SL1-type units differ little in their propensity for collaborations (a relative enhancement of the SL1 position compared to university laboratories), whilst SL2s emerge as most likely to establish such associations with independent laboratories. Overall it may be the case, therefore, that independent laboratories can provide specialised inputs that complement the competences of the MNE facilities, but which are accessed and exercised in a relatively more *ad hoc* problem-solving fashion (that is, in more ambitious types of support laboratory activity) than as integral parts of ongoing programmes of product development (LIL) or precompetitive (IIL) work.

The third scientific institution offered for evaluation in terms of degree of collaboration with MNE laboratories was 'industry research laboratories in the UK'. Here we envisage UK laboratories that have a tradition of providing support (often substantially funded at the industry level) for particularly focused sectors and which, therefore, have a strong background in those areas of science especially relevant to 'their' industry. Crucially, this is then expected to be combined with a greater knowledge of, and commitment to, the problems and potentials of the commercial application of this specialised competence than would be the case for university or even independent laboratories. No MNE laboratories felt they had extensive collaborations with industry laboratories in the UK, but 45.8 per cent did perceive such associations to exist to a moderate degree. Pharmaceuticals is the industry that is distinctively least oriented to this type of collaboration, which again reflects its generally stronger commitment to those more purely scientific elements of precompetitive investigation that are better articulated through research links with universities and independent laboratories. As was also the case with independent laboratories (though less decisively so for universities), Japanese laboratories are least likely to establish associations with those in industry laboratories. This may reflect either unfamiliarity with such institutions in an environment to which they are relatively new, or perceived lack of a need to seek outside advice on their currently very effective commercial technologies and products.

The strong links of LILs with industry laboratories are compatible with the latter's anticipated expertise in the commercial application of technology. In a similar way, the stronger links of SL1s compared with SL2s (reversing the position for independent laboratories) is likely to reflect a particular knowledge of the localised (here UK) market conditions for commercial applications of technology as a distinctive competence of these industry laboratories. The leading position of laboratories doing DEVLAB work, in terms of degree of links with industry laboratories, may relate to the ability of such local facilities to assist these MNE units (and their associated producing subsidiaries) in nurturing not only the distinctive technological scope that derives from the local scientific tradition but also, most crucially, its application to product development that is responsive to local conditions.

Research collaborations with 'other UK firms' were rated as extensive by two (4.2 per cent) of responding MNE laboratories and as moderate by another 19 (39.6 per cent). The relative prevalence of such collaborations in units focusing on DEVLAB and APPLIED work, and those substantially taking on the LIL role, suggests these links are entered into as an element of a product development process. Since we shall show in the next chapter that MNE product development subsidiaries in the UK make considerable use of independent UK input suppliers, we may suggest that this creative relationship underpins many of the interfirm research collaborations found here. By contrast, pure scientific research seems sparse in such collaborations (low values for BASIC and IILs). Although (as noted earlier, in Chapter 4) there has been much discussion of inter firm collaboration in this precompetitive phase of research, in terms of strategic technology alliances, it seems likely that such relationships (precisely because of their often strategic implications) are most clearly articulated at the parent (rather than subsidiary) level.

'Other independent firms overseas' provided extensive research collaborations for four (8.3 per cent) of the MNE laboratories and moderate links for 17 (35.4 per cent) more. Once again, precompetitive research appears to be of little relevance to the formulation of such links (low values for IILs, BASIC and APPLIED). Instead, these collaborations were relatively strongest in that type of laboratory (SL2) that is defined to have an international commitment and also in that whose work involves an interdependent position in a group-level innovation programme (DEVGROUP). Although the associations defined for SL2s and DEVGROUP type work are intra-group (with sister laboratories or subsidiaries of the same group) it appears that expertise in international communications, and the generally more extrovert and cosmopolitan outlook reflected in these commitments, also opens them up rather more to research collaborations with independent firms outside the UK.

The responding MNE laboratories felt that R&D links with 'universities overseas (e.g. as part of EU supported programmes)' were extensive in two (4.2 per cent) cases and moderate in 11 (22.9 per cent) more, but absent from 35 (72.9 per cent). Such links were most prevalent for laboratories of European MNEs which may, indeed, reflect the presence of EU support. A strong precompetitive element in such programmes would also be compatible with the relative prevalence of such links in IILs and in those laboratories that are oriented towards BASIC and APPLIED work.

Finally, respondents were asked to evaluate their research collaborations with 'government and other public laboratories'. None assessed these as extensive and only 18 (37.5 per cent) believed they were even of moderate relevance. The relatively strong response of European laboratories, alongside quite strong collaborations of IILs and in BASIC and APPLIED work, could again suggest the presence of relationships articulated within the context of EU-supported programmes. The strong results for both types of SL are, however, compatible neither with this possible institutional influence nor with the types of work that provoke such collaborations (for example, low values for adaptation).

TYPES OF WORK INVOLVED IN COLLABORATIONS.

The broad themes of our investigation suggest that the collaborative R&D arrangements scrutinised here involve MNEs tapping into distinctive knowledge and skill competences of host countries in order to secure, in various ways, the enhancement of their own technological scope to support their global competitiveness. As the MNE programmes both to create new core technology (precompetitive research) and to apply it effectively commercially (globalised approaches to innovation) are increasingly articulated through international networks involving strong intra-group research interdependencies and knowledge transfers, it is no longer at all inevitable that high-quality inputs and scientific work that are secured in one country will automatically boost the immediate competitiveness of that economy. Therefore significant issues have been seen to arise concerning the value to host countries of allowing MNEs the scope to access and work with institutions within their scientific community. An important discriminating element in understanding the issues that are involved here is the nature of the work that is done within collaborations between MNEs and host-country institutions. Therefore the questionnaire sent to MNE laboratories asked them to state whether each of five different types of work played a role in their collaborations with UK-based scientific institutions.

The types of issues just alluded to perhaps take their most stark form in the case of basic research. Although the strong prevalence of the types of subsidiary-level product development that embody ideas and technology uniquely accessed or created by that subsidiary suggests that on occasion locally-derived basic research results can feed through to self-contained in-house product innovation, this is by no means the only viable scenario. Alternatively the basic research done in an MNE's UK laboratory (supported by local collaborations) may be only a specialised part of the group's global programme (with other complementary research done in laboratories in other countries), so that the ultimate output is derived centrally (in a 'parent' laboratory) through the synthetic overview of all the decentralised elements of the programme. Although this may lead to vital new product concepts being implemented globally by the MNE, the extent to which its operations in any country receive a competitive boost through this will not be related in any systematic way to the contribution that country made to the earlier phases of the MNE's research.

However, if the basic research element in local scientific collaborations may well not result in a direct or immediate boost to host-country industrial competitiveness, it could have indirect longer-term benefits. These could accrue if host-country scientific institutions improve their scope, knowledge and experience through collaborations with MNEs. Improved funding, entry into the alternative knowledge community of the MNE and experience of the organisation and implementation of wider R&D programmes may all enhance the scope of host-country institutions and their researchers and technology planners, with this ultimately leading to improvements in the ability of the indigenous scientific community to contribute to growth in the competitiveness of locally-based industry. It is relevant, therefore, to look at the degree of presence of basic research in collaborations, and particularly the context within which it occurs.

Overall, Table 7.2 shows that precisely one-third of MNE laboratories that had links with UK scientific institutions included basic research in such collaborative work. Predictably, basic research was most prevalent in the collaborations of those MNE laboratories that themselves had a predominant focus on this type of work (BASIC), although 37.5 per cent of them used their association with the UK institutions only for applied work.[2] In addition, half of the laboratories that focused mainly on applied work (APPLIED) sought inputs of basic research from local collaborations. These two results parallel the greatest prevalence of basic research in the local links of IILs. Nevertheless, both LILs and SLs, and laboratories doing the DEVLAB variant of product innovation, incorporated basic research to a substantial degree in their collaborations. This points to the presence of a certain amount of UK-based product development by MNEs which seems to derive from semi-autonomous and sequentially-integrated scientific work within subsidiaries that builds on local basic research. Thus it appears that whereas a very clear potential for basic research results derived within MNE collaborations to 'leak' out of the UK through IILs does exist, the alternative possibility of 'capturing' such results for localised product development through LILs (and DEVLAB work) is also indicated in the results.

Table 7.2 Types of work involved in collaborations of MNE laboratories in the UK with other UK scientific institutions

	Types of work (percentage of respondents[1])				
	Basic research	Applied research	Product development	Product adaptation	Process adaptation
By industry					
Electronics	14.3	57.1	28.6	14.3	57.1
Pharmaceuticals	41.2	70.6	29.4	5.9	0
Chemicals[2]	28.6	71.4	14.3	0	28.6
Other	36.4	63.6	27.3	18.2	36.4
Total	33.3	66.7	26.2	9.5	23.8
By home country					
USA	33.3	75.0	41.7	16.7	25.0
Japan	26.7	46.7	20.0	13.3	13.3
Europe	40.0	80.0	20.0	0	33.3
Total	33.3	66.7	26.2	9.5	23.8
By type of laboratory[3]					
SL1	33.3	88.9	11.1	22.2	33.3
SL2	14.3	71.4	28.6	14.3	28.6
LIL	33.3	75.0	41.7	25.0	33.3
IIL	50.0	60.0	10.0	5.0	15.0
By type of R&D[4]					
BASIC	62.5	62.5	0	0	0
APPLIED	50.0	81.3	12.5	6.3	12.5
DEVLAB	38.1	57.1	38.1	14.3	23.8
DEVGROUP	27.3	54.5	27.3	18.2	18.2
PRODADAPT	0	60.0	20.0	40.0	60.0
PROCADAPT	0	33.3	33.3	33.3	66.7

Notes:
1. Percentage of responding MNE laboratories who considered that at least part of their collaboration with another scientific institution was to assist in the particular type of work.
2. Includes petrochemicals and petroleum.
3. Replies for laboratories that said they were 'predominantly' or 'only' that type. For definition of laboratory types, see Table 6.2.
4. Replies for laboratories that said the type of work was their 'only' or 'predominant' work. For definition of types of work, see Table 6.4.

Source: Survey of laboratories.

We have considered the phase of applied research to run from the point where the purely scientific results of basic research are initially perceived to have possible commercial resonances to the point where such potentials have been refined to the state of a new product concept. Successful applied research at the subsidiary level may obviously lead to locally-integrated product development (commercial refinement of the product concept, that is, DEVLAB) within the host country. However, given the technological networking and globalised-innovation perspectives of the contemporary MNEs, applied research results (like basic ones) may migrate for further development elsewhere in the group[3] (that is, the host country may again not get the full benefit of the value-added scope that its technological inputs help to create). Since Table 7.2 shows that two-thirds of MNE laboratory collaborations with UK scientific institutions involve applied research, it is again relevant to scrutinise closely the contexts where this occurs.

Applied research is, again predictably, most prominent in the collaborations of those MNE laboratories that focus on such work as their own predominant motivation (APPLIED). However, its prevalence in links of basic research laboratories, and especially as the most prominent element in the local associations of IILs, opens up the possibility that in some cases the further development of collaborative applied research may occur elsewhere in the MNE group. Nevertheless, the fact that applied research occurs in three-quarters of LILs' collaborations, and in over half of those of both types of laboratories that focused on product creation (as a logical input to DEVLAB, but also as support to DEVGROUP processes that mainly use knowledge from elsewhere in the group), suggests the successful localised appropriation of the results of such research associations in many cases. The strong position of applied research in the collaborations of SLs (and thus of laboratories focusing on product adaptation) may have an explanation in the processes of subsidiary evolution in modern MNEs. Thus we have described in earlier chapters how the types of subsidiaries that traditionally employ SLs to improve their supply of standardised products feel increasingly vulnerable in the contemporary MNE and seek to use their laboratories (whose own survival would otherwise be in doubt) to upgrade and individualise their competences in order to secure a move to high-value-added product development status. Working with local scientific institutions on applied research (which would initially be beyond the in-house scope of their SLs) may secure distinctive new knowledge for the ambitious subsidiary away from the (potentially disapproving) scrutiny of the parent company, and also provide an environment within which the SL's personnel can enhance their own research scope and perspectives. Put another way, SLs implementing applied research collaborations in this way hope to eventually upgrade their own status to LIL, by enriching their own knowledge base and research scope and by endowing their related subsidiary with the technological capacity for individualised product development.

Work on product development occurs only in just over one-quarter of the collaborations reported in Table 7.2. This reflects the fact that the technological input into this type of work needs to be very closely integrated with other in-house functions (for example, marketing, engineering, financial management) and also that the specialised competences of many local institutions (for example, university laboratories) are more focused on the precompetitive research phases. Nevertheless, product development collaborations were most prevalent where they would be predicted (that is, in LILs and those laboratories focused on DEVLAB and DEVGROUP). Also it should be recalled that those MNE laboratories with a predominant product development mandate did have strong collaborations involving basic and, especially, applied research, thereby building their own technological competences prior to the more widely-functioned and carefully-coordinated in-house development process.

Product adaptation work was a predictably rare constituent of the research collaborations covered here, occurring in less than one-tenth of all cases. Even those laboratories for which product adaptation was the main function included such work only in four-tenths of their own collaborations, instead often focusing on rather more ambitious work for reasons suggested above. However, process adaptation subsidiaries did incorporate work of this type in two-thirds of their collaborations which, along with a strong complementary presence in those of product adaptation laboratories, meant that process adaptation work was included in almost one-quarter of all links.

MOTIVATION FOR COLLABORATIONS

The questionnaire also investigated some of the reasons behind the R&D collaborations between MNE laboratories and UK scientific institutions. As Table 7.3 indicates, the vast majority of the laboratories (91.9 per cent) felt that such scientific links served *inter alia* to simply extend the scope of their operations by enabling them 'to secure inputs that we do not have in our own laboratory'. Given the pervasiveness of this motivation it is not surprising that it does not vary at all systematically in relevance between types of laboratory or the nature of the work that they do. It does, however, endorse a more general point about the decentralisation of R&D in MNEs. Thus it suggests that the types of MNE laboratories covered here do not attempt to internalise all the knowledge or skills that they require, but have an innate willingness to complete their scope through externalised relationships with other elements of

Table 7.3 Reasons for collaboration of MNE laboratories in the UK with other scientific institutions

	Reasons for collaboration (percentage of respondents[1])							
	A	B	C	D	E	F	G	H
By industry								
Electronics	75.0	50.0	12.5	12.5	12.5	0	0	12.5
Pharmaceuticals	92.9	42.9	0	0	7.1	0	0	7.1
Chemicals[2]	100.0	71.4	14.3	0	28.6	0	0	28.6
Other	100.0	50.0	0	0	12.5	12.5	12.5	25.0
Total	91.9	51.4	5.4	2.7	13.5	2.7	2.7	16.2
By home country								
USA	100.0	40.0	0	0	10.0	10.0	10.0	20.0
Japan	78.6	42.9	0	0	14.3	0	0	14.3
Europe	100.0	69.2	15.4	7.7	15.4	0	0	15.4
Total	91.9	51.4	5.4	2.7	13.5	2.7	2.7	16.2
By type of laboratory[3]								
SL1	87.5	50.0	0	0	12.5	12.5	12.5	37.5
SL2	100.0	62.5	0	0	0	0	0	12.5
LIL	100.0	41.7	0	0	8.3	8.3	8.3	25.0
IIL	87.5	68.8	6.3	0	18.8	0	0	6.3
By type of R & D[4]								
BASIC	75.0	62.5	0	0	0	0	0	12.5
APPLIED	87.5	68.8	6.3	0	12.5	0	0	12.5
DEVLAB	83.3	44.4	5.6	0	22.2	0	0	27.8
DEVGROUP	88.9	44.4	0	0	11.1	0	0	22.2
PRODADAPT	75.0	0	0	0	0	25.0	25.0	50.0
PROCADAPT	100.0	0	0	0	0	0	0	0

Reasons for collaboration.

A To secure inputs that we do not have in our own laboratory.
B To improve our knowledge of the direction of scientific activity in our research field.
C To improve our production subsidiary's image.
D For financial/tax reasons.
E In response to our group's policy.
F In response to government pressures.
G In response to government incentives.
H To help in the improvement of the quality of life (e.g. environment, nutrition, other social concerns).

Notes:

1. Percentage of respondents who considered that a particular reason played a role in the implementation of their collaboration(s).
2. Includes petrochemicals and petroleum.
3. Replies for laboratories that said they were 'predominantly' or 'only' that type. For definition of laboratory types see table 6.2.
4. Replies for laboratories that said the type of work was their 'only' or 'predominant' work. For definition of types of R&D, see Table 6.4.

Source: Survey of laboratories.

the host-country science base. The collaborations can therefore be seen as strongly indicative of the way that decentralised R&D laboratories in MNEs serve to mediate between these companies' overall scientific needs and an increasingly geographically differentiated and permanently evolving range of sources. Qualitative aspects of the local science base may firstly help to determine what roles an MNE operation in a particular country can claim within its group's programmes, with the laboratory then deciding (with various degrees of parent company intrusion) what elements are best brought within its permanent scope and what may be better performed within supporting collaborations of the types surveyed here.

Just over half (51.4 per cent) of responding laboratories felt that their collaborations also served 'to improve our knowledge of the direction of scientific activity in our research field'. This, too, related to a monitoring function for decentralised R&D in MNEs. As innovation-oriented MNEs find that they need inputs from a wider range of scientific disciplines to support their effective technological evolution, and as an increasing range of countries move to the frontiers of specialised areas (that is, as individual national science bases narrow in terms of their true world class specialisms (Cantwell, 1991c), but more countries have *some* such leading-edge competences), these companies need a means of retaining a sustained contact with the sources of scientific progress in all relevant locations (for example, university and other specialist laboratories). Their overseas R&D laboratories and, in turn, their collaborations with relevant local institutions seem to serve this purpose. The potential pure research (precompetitive) orientation of this behaviour seems to be reflected in the fact that this motivation is endorsed most strongly by IILs and laboratories doing basic and applied work.

Only two of the other reasons for collaboration covered in the survey (Table 7.3) received more than negligible support. Firstly, 16.2 per cent of respondents felt that work within such collaborations enabled them 'to help in the improvement of the quality of life' by addressing issues relating to the environment, nutrition and other social concerns. The concerns were of greatest relevance in laboratories involved with product adaptation and product development and in those that were most likely to be locally responsive (that is, LILs and SL1s). Here it may be that the MNE subsidiaries and their laboratories feel a social and marketing related need to help address particular issues of local public concern, and do so through these collaborations both because local institutions already have a background in the problems and because announcements of such associations provide good public relations.

Finally, 13.5 per cent of respondents felt that their implementation of collaborations was 'in response to our group's policy'. We have already suggested reasons why MNEs might feel potential benefits from their decentralised R&D units' interactions with the local science base. Not too many of these overseas laboratories, however, seem aware of this as a forcefully articulated group policy. Although absent from the perception of basic research laboratories, this motivation tends to otherwise occur where it would seem most relevant (that is, in IILs, applied research laboratories and in units with a product development orientation). These types of units have a level of in-house orientation that provides them with the ability to read and evaluate local scientific trends through collaborative work.

FORMS OF COLLABORATION WITH UNIVERSITIES

The last question in the survey that related to the MNE laboratories' scientific links covered the nature of their collaborations with UK universities. The first of these options related to the presence of 'work proposed and carried out by the university, and funded by us'. Overall, 38.1 per cent of responding MNE laboratories felt that such a situation occurred within their collaborations (Table 7.4). By type of MNE laboratory IILs were clearly most likely to adopt this type of collaboration and SL1s notably least. Furthermore, those laboratories mainly doing basic or applied work used such associations most, followed by both types of product development unit, whilst this form of agreement was absent from laboratories with an adaptation orientation. Clearly the further the natural concerns of the MNE laboratories are from the solution of short-term problems relating to current commercial technology, and the closer they are to the longer-term pure scientific investigation needed to reinforce their groups' core knowledge, the more they rely on host-country universities to discern the most promising lines of (mainly basic) research. This reinforces the view that although precompetitive research is accepted by MNEs as needing to be fully addressed if they are to achieve sustained competitiveness, the natural environment for the proper articulation and pure scientifically-motivated performance of much of the work of this type is within universities.

As already suggested, a significant role of many overseas R&D units in MNEs is thus to monitor and tap into such work where it is being done in their host country, again bearing in mind the increasing tendency for particular countries to develop areas of world leadership in specialised disciplines. It is, then, often the case that in order to evaluate likely local collaborations

Table 7.4 Nature of collaborations with UK universities of MNE laboratories in the UK

| | Form of collaboration (percentage of respondents[1]) | | | | |
	A	B	C	D	E
By industry					
Electronics	57.1	57.1	28.6	28.6	71.4
Pharmaceuticals	47.1	82.4	23.5	41.2	58.8
Chemicals[2]	37.5	75.0	25.0	62.5	62.5
Other	10.0	60.0	40.0	40.0	60.0
Total	38.1	71.4	28.6	42.9	64.3
By home country					
USA	16.7	66.7	25.0	50.0	91.7
Japan	50.0	64.3	14.3	21.4	35.7
Europe	43.8	81.3	43.8	56.3	68.8
Total	38.1	71.4	28.6	42.9	64.3
By type of laboratory[3]					
SL1	22.2	77.8	33.3	44.4	55.5
SL2	42.9	85.7	14.3	28.6	57.1
LIL	38.5	76.9	38.5	30.8	61.5
IIL	52.6	68.4	31.6	52.6	57.9
By type of R & D[4]					
BASIC	44.4	77.8	33.3	44.4	55.5
APPLIED	41.2	76.4	23.5	52.9	64.7
DEVLAB	28.6	71.4	38.1	52.4	61.9
DEVGROUP	27.3	72.7	18.2	45.5	45.5
PRODADAPT	0	80.0	0	20.0	60.0
PROCADAPT	0	66.7	0	33.3	66.7

Form of collaboration.
A Work proposed and carried out by the university, and funded by us.
B Work proposed and funded by us, but carried out by the university.
C Participation in, and coordination of, wider research projects involving several universities.
D Provision of scholarships for research students at universities.
E Employing students in our laboratory as interns.

Notes:
1. Percentage of respondents who endorsed the relevance of a particular form of collaboration to their university links.
2. Includes petrochemicals and petroleum.
3. Replies for laboratories that said they were 'predominantly' or 'only' that type. For definition of laboratory types, see Table 6.2.
4. Replies for laboratories that said the type of R&D was their 'only' or 'predominant' work. For definition of types of R&D, see Table 6.4.
Source: Survey of laboratories.

effectively, and to benefit most decisively from a coherent working relationship with them, the MNE laboratories often incorporate a certain level of in-house basic and, especially, applied research commitment. Although such in-house performance of precompetitive work by MNE overseas laboratories is itself of significant magnitude, the evidence here suggests that it understates the importance of internationalised access to this type of research and knowledge as an element in the globalised technology programmes of these companies.

The complementary type of collaboration, in the form of 'work proposed and funded by us, but carried out by the university', was used by 71.4 per cent of responding MNE laboratories. In absolute terms this format was again very strongly used by IILs and by laboratories with a basic or applied research focus (Table 7.4). In line with the analysis above, this suggests that laboratories with in-house precompetitive competences and priorities can also use this background to articulate, in a more pre-emptive way, programmes of work that can embody complementary expertise of local laboratories. Again, the laboratories are seen as acting as a crucial medium for the creative interaction of an MNE's current technology trajectory with those external (national) science bases that can provide key inputs (output of precompetitive research) to the longer-term enrichment and reinforcement of the group's core technology (that is, help to define the nature of the evolution of the technology trajectory and support the long-term needs of strategic competitiveness).

By contrast with the first form of association, however, development and adaptation-oriented laboratories also make very extensive use of this type of collaboration. In many such cases the problems to be addressed within the university collaboration emerge initially from the inter functional associations of the MNE laboratories (for example, with associated marketing and/or engineering groups within a production subsidiary). Elements of the technology problems discerned in this way may then devolve onto the laboratories' local collaborative links. There may be different grades of this, however. In the case of laboratories addressing local product development (LILs), high-quality in-house abilities may be matched to strong university laboratory competences in a positive (confident) attempt to secure the capacity for sustained localised knowledge input into MNE innovation processes. The laboratory has an expertise in discerning the technological needs of a subsidiary that is seeking to build an individualised product development competence and can skilfully mix internal and external capabilities in dynamic programmes that support these aims. Where the laboratories address difficulties in local application of existing products and processes (SL1) they may be adept at defining the technological issues (good inter-functional communications), but may sometimes lack the scope to actually solve all the problems that arise. Where they cannot get an answer from elsewhere in the MNE (due to a strongly localised element in the problem or perhaps a reluctance to expose their own limitations within the group) they may invoke a more *ad hoc* association with a host-country university.

Only 28.6 per cent of laboratories operated a broader context for these collaborations in the form of 'participation in, and coordination of, wider research projects involving several universities'. The projects articulated by laboratories in this way seem to address both precompetitive and product development aims. The last two forms of scientific link evaluated involve support of students. Although the direct work of such young scientists is unlikely to immediately boost the MNE's technology in uniquely distinctive ways, support of them may provide a key basis for the creation of mutual confidence in its position in the local science base. It also fits with the types of spillovers that may enable MNE laboratories to play a positive role in the broader development of the host-country science base and technology scope. Here, 64.3 per cent of laboratories reported that they were 'employing students in our labs as interns' and 42.9 per cent supported 'the provision of scholarships for research students at universities'.

CONCLUSIONS

It has been argued by Cohen and Levinthal (1989, p.593) that firms invest in R&D not only to pursue directly new process and product innovation, but also to develop and maintain their broader capabilities to assimilate and exploit externally available information. The research on the decentralisation of R&D activities in MNEs reviewed in the previous two chapters clearly suggests the strong presence of both these factors in the motivation for the establishment of overseas laboratories in these companies. The evidence reviewed in this chapter has distinguished ways in which their linkages with local scientific institutions also contribute to the ability of MNE laboratories in the UK to fulfil these twin objectives.

Two important impressions of the survey results scrutinised are that, firstly, precompetitive (basic and applied) research is relatively more prevalent in MNE laboratories' collaborations with UK scientific institutions than in their own in-house work and, secondly, that these types of work are accessed quite strongly by laboratories that work with product development subsidiaries as well as by those that themselves have a mainly precompetitive focus. Therefore we can suggest that these collaborations support the ability of MNE laboratories to achieve both R&D objectives delineated by Cohen and

Levinthal. Certainly we have indicated how the nature and content of their institutional associations enable the MNE laboratories to monitor, access and assimilate the most distinctive elements in the technological progress of the host-country science base. When carried out by IILs, such collaborative basic and applied research enables such units to fulfil their position as an individualised contributor to group-level programmes of research that aim to enrich the longer-term perspectives of the MNE technological trajectories.

However, collaborations with local scientific institutions (including their basic and applied research component) also supports those laboratories that are integrated parts of the product development operations of producing subsidiaries. Although there is a strong in-house scope in these LILs, much of this may be exercised in joint problem solving with other subsidiary functions in the product development process. The ability of the LIL to contribute unique knowledge dimensions, derived from more speculative research activity, to the creative process may then benefit particularly from its externalised technology associations. Thus the research collaborations may serve to underwrite the individualised knowledge scope of the subsidiaries (mediated through their in-house laboratories) and thereby play a crucial role in helping them to assert their distinctive position in their group's product creation programmes.

Overall, we can speculate that externalised access to local research and knowledge capacity, through the types of collaborative arrangement surveyed here, may become increasingly important as ways in which laboratories (and associated subsidiaries) seek to individualise their scope and claim strong high-value-added positions in the increasingly globally-differentiated operations of heterarchical MNEs.[4] If this is so, then these collaborations can be seen as another significant element in the increasingly crucial interdependency between the *global* technology programmes of MNEs and vital components of *national* systems of innovation.

NOTES

1. For detailed analysis of the position of US universities *vis a vis* the knowledge needs of commercial enterprises see Rosenberg and Nelson (1994). They conclude (p.340) that 'what university research often does today is to stimulate and enhance the power of R & D done in industry, as contrasted with providing a substitute for it'.
2. If this suggests that the local institution here gets early acquaintance with new basic research output that has been derived entirely within the MNE laboratory it provides an example of how such links can enrich the knowledge available to the local technological community.
3. See Pearce and Singh (1992a) for evidence on project mobility in MNEs.
4. This may be seen as a process of 'strategic externalisation', thus paralleling and complementing processes of 'strategic internalisation' which involve 'the absorption and

development by the subsidiary of competitive advantages using resources existing in the host-environments' (Papanastassiou and Anastassopoulos, 1997).

8. Subsidiaries' linkages with UK input suppliers

INTRODUCTION

The links of MNE operations with UK scientific institutions, investigated in the previous chapter, can be seen to possess the potential to improve the medium- and long-term competitiveness of UK-based manufacturing by enhancing the context through which local technology can be applied to industrial activity. Comparable linkages of MNE subsidiaries with UK suppliers of components and other intermediate goods may provide more immediate benefits by substantially expanding the market for these companies and facilitating enhanced efficiency through more complete realisation of economies of scale. Here too, however, deeper and more sustained gains may be available if the association with the MNE provides a basis for a qualitative extension of the local suppliers' product range and knowledge capacity, so that economies of scope may emerge amongst the potential benefits that they receive.[1]

Two aspects of these issues were investigated in the survey of producing subsidiaries. Firstly, they were asked to say whether or not a range of potential supply sources were accessed for their operations. In addition to the extension of their supply networks to encompass independent UK companies (the key focus of the spillover issues addressed here) the other sources mainly involved the continuation of established input linkages. Two of these involve independent component suppliers (either from an MNE customer's home country or from a third country) that now operate in the UK, having probably been induced to do so mainly by the need to reproduce locally an existing MNE relationship when that customer extended its own supply base into the new environment. This may have external benefits to UK competitiveness if these specialist input suppliers are now used by local manufacturing enterprises (which had not accessed them before) in ways that expand their own scope or efficiency. Finally, intra-group sources are assessed in terms of other parts of the MNE supply network (either in Europe or elsewhere). Although local-content requirements seek to ensure that use of these and other sources outside a host country do not reach levels that reduce local operations in MNE subsidiaries to mere assembly ('screwdriver' plants), it can also be accepted that some degree of intra-group sourcing is necessary (especially early in a subsidiary's evolution), to achieve security and quality of supply of key components.

The second aspect of the survey investigation of local input linkages related to the provision of technology or other supply-related knowledge to UK component manufacturers as part of a new relationship with an MNE subsidiary. The first facet of this simply related to the frequency with which those subsidiaries that used UK input suppliers transferred advice to them. Then the content of such technology transfer was investigated, in terms of the prevalence of each of three types of knowledge or expertise. A key concern here was the extent to which such transfers were transaction specific, or whether the content was sufficiently generalised to allow spillover benefits into the wider competitive environment of the UK component companies (that is, the extent to which the MNE believes it cannot, or does not need to, secure full appropriation of the changes in supplier efficiency generated by the knowledge or skill passed on).

SOURCES OF INPUTS USED BY MNE SUBSIDIARIES

The respondents to the production subsidiary questionnaire were asked to say whether or not each of six types of input supplier were used in their operations. Table 8.1 summarises the replies to this question. Regression tests were also run using industry and home-country dummies and the roles of subsidiaries as independent variables (Table 8.2). Amongst the suppliers, 'independent UK companies' emerged as notably the most pervasive, being accessed by 90.6 per cent of the responding MNE subsidiaries. Bearing in mind the ubiquitous status of these independent UK suppliers, too much importance should not be placed on their particularly prevalent position for DEVELPROD subsidiaries (Table 8.1), or the significant positive relationship between their use and the degree of commitment to product development in the regression test (Table 8.2).

Despite the previous comment, however, it is certainly an immediately important result to note that subsidiaries that have a commitment to product development *are* very keen to involve independent UK suppliers in such operations[2] (even whilst reluctant to invoke this as a uniquely significant relationship). Thus such an association may carry direct and indirect benefits that should involve a potential for sustained synergies and spillovers. As well as benefiting it directly through any distinctive knowledge or product development insights provided by an independent local input supplier, the profound involvement of such an extra-group partner in its creativity can add an extra dimension to the emancipation that a subsidiary seeks in order to

Table 8.1 Relative importance of sources of inputs in MNE subsidiaries in the UK.

	Importance of input source[1] (per cent of respondents)					
	A	B	C	D	E	F
By industry						
Food	88.9	33.3	44.4	88.9	33.3	0
Automobiles	100.0	11.1	27.8	61.1	44.4	38.9
Aerospace	75.0	20.0	40.0	40.0	40.0	80.0
Electronics and electrical appliances	92.0	4.0	46.0	64.0	20.0	52.0
Mechanical engineering	84.0	8.0	16.0	48.0	32.0	20.0
Instruments	100.0	9.1	27.3	27.3	36.4	63.6
Industrial and agricultural chemicals	92.3	26.9	34.6	76.9	61.5	53.8
Pharmaceuticals and consumer chemicals	81.8	0	27.3	45.5	81.8	54.5
Metal manufacture and products	80.0	10.0	10.0	40.0	30.0	40.0
Other manufacturing	93.8	6.3	12.5	50.0	12.5	37.5
Total	90.6	11.0	30.9	58.0	35.9	43.6
By home country						
USA	89.2	10.8	32.3	55.4	41.5	52.3
Japan	95.5	1.5	37.3	58.2	17.9	52.2
Europe	85.7	21.4	19.0	57.1	57.1	19.0
Total[2]	90.6	11.0	30.9	58.0	35.9	43.6
By subsidiary type[3]						
ESTPROD/UK	89.2	7.1	32.1	61.9	33.3	45.2
ESTPROD/EUR	95.6	11.0	40.7	60.4	31.9	45.1
COMPART	100.0	15.4	61.4	46.2	23.1	30.8
DEVELPROD	98.4	17.2	20.3	56.3	25.0	37.5

Sources of inputs.
A Independent UK companies.
B Previously independent UK companies now part of the MNE group.
C Independent suppliers from the home country of the MNE group now operating in the UK.
D Independent UK-based companies of another nationality.
E Other parts of the MNE group in Europe.
F Other parts of the MNE group outside Europe.

Notes:
1. Respondents were asked to tick any input source that was used in their operations.
2. Includes subsidiaries of MNEs from Australia and Canada.
3. Covers subsidiaries that described themselves as 'only' or 'predominantly' each type. For definitions, see Table 3.1.
Source: Survey of producing subsidiaries.

stake its claim to a unique and individualistic status in the group's overall evolution. From the point of view of the local supplier, its involvement in the product development operations of an MNE subsidiary is likely to extend its own scope and creative skills, through a dynamic engagement with new production trajectories and the opportunity to generate tight cooperative bonds with a leading internationally-competitive enterprise. Beyond the two immediate partners to the transaction, spillover benefits may also accrue to other parts of the indigenous industrial sector if improved efficiency and scope in the independent local supplier company enables it to serve established customers more cost effectively or with better quality inputs, or even as a source of new ideas for product evolution.

Two of the supply sources investigated relate to independent foreign component companies operating in the UK (that is, firms that are themselves subsidiaries of MNEs, but not formally associated with the purchasers of their intermediate goods). The first of these was 'independent suppliers from the home country of the MNE group now operating in the UK'. Such suppliers proved to be of somewhat limited relevance, with only 30.9 per cent of respondents using them. It is notable that this source is least important to DEVELPROD subsidiaries (almost significantly negative in the regression) and notably more important (almost significantly positive) for the ESTPROD/EUR operations.[3] This combination may suggest that independent home-country suppliers to MNEs tend to be cost-effective producers of standardised inputs to well-established final products, so that an efficient replication of the relationship in the UK would be most relevant to those subsidiaries whose primary strategic orientation was to supply such final goods into a relatively price-competitive market area.[4] Such a characterisation of the status of independent home-country suppliers as based around a technologically dependent and strongly hierarchical parent-country relationship with MNEs can then explain why their supportive migration is required by relatively few of these customers, who can normally expect to replicate the quite routine relationship more conveniently with host-country enterprises.

The second type of foreign input supplier operating in the UK was described for respondents as 'independent UK-based companies of another nationality' (that is, not the MNE subsidiary's home country or the UK). Where MNEs use such independent third-country intermediate good suppliers in the UK, it is most likely to be because they are the subsidiaries of major international component part specialists with whom a long-standing relationship exists throughout their mutually dispersed global operations. This source emerged as

Table 8.2 Regressions with sources of inputs as dependent variable

	Dependent variable (type of input supplier)[1]					
	A	B	C	D	E	F
Intercept	0.5850‡	0.1557	0.0352	0.5224†	0.5517‡	0.2179
	(4.75)	(1.13)	(0.17)	(2.33)	(2.79)	(1.03)
Food	-0.0211	0.0421	0.0780*	0.0671	0.0498	-0.0746*
	(-0.87)	(1.53)	(1.91)	(1.51)	(1.27)	(-1.79)
Automobiles	-0.0257	0.0402	0.0787	0.0562	0.3980†	-0.0196
	(-0.26)	(0.36)	(0.53)	(0.31)	(2.47)	(-0.11)
Aerospace	-0.0608	0.0615	0.1316	-0.0639	0.1094	0.1856
	(-0.77)	(0.76)	(1.09)	(-0.48)	(0.94)	(1.50)
Electronics	-0.0258	-0.0034	0.0614*	0.0238	0.0367	0.0216
	(-1.25)	(-0.15)	(1.77)	(0.63)	(1.10)	(0.61)
Mechanical	-0.0264†	-0.0027	0.0009	-0.0059	0.0307	-0.0319
engineering	(-2.00)	(-0.18)	(0.04)	(-0.25)	(1.44)	(-1.41)
Instruments	0.0057	0.0086	0.0308	-0.0322	0.0393	0.0158
	(0.30)	(0.39)	(0.95	(-0.91)	(1.26)	(0.47)
Chemicals	-0.0209	0.0445	0.0694	0.0757	0.1546‡	0.0697
	(-0.68)	(1.29)	(1.35)	(1.35)	(3.13)	(1.32)
Pharmaceuticals	-0.0115	-0.0131	0.0132	-0.0060	0.0734‡	0.0170
	(-0.89)	(-0.90)	(0.61)	(-0.26)	(3.53)	(0.77)
Metals	-0.0076	0.0039	-0.0006	-0.0104	0.0144	0.0013
	(-0.52)	(0.24)	(-0.02)	(-0.39)	(0.62)	(0.05)
USA	0.0000	-0.0152†	0.0080	-0.0045	-0.0121	0.0323‡
	(0.00)	(-2.44)	(0.87)	(-0.45)	(-1.35)	(3.40)
Japan	0.0063	-0.0180‡	0.0123	-0.0035	-0.0220‡	0.0299‡
	(1.23)	(-3.12)	(1.44)	(-0.37)	(-2.66)	(3.38)
ESTPROD/UK[2]	-0.0110	-0.0263	-0.0500	0.0030	-0.0148	0.0229
	(-0.44)	(-0.94)	(-1.20)	(0.07)	(-0.37)	(0.54)
ESTPROD/EUR	0.0768‡	0.0001	0.0671	0.0271	-0.0590	-0.0107
	(3.00)	(0.00)	(1.57)	(0.58)	(-1.43)	(-0.25)
COMPART	0.0545*	0.0478	0.1073*	-0.0160	0.0531	-0.0719
	(1.67)	(1.30)	(1.97)	(-0.27)	(1.01)	(-1.29)
DEVELPROD	0.0742‡	0.0246	-0.0652	0.0011	-0.1064‡	0.0083
	(3.00)	(0.89)	(-1.59)	(0.03)	(-2.69)	(0.20)
R^2	0.1672	0.1697	0.1449	0.0761	0.2411	0.2000
F	2.10†	2.15†	1.79*	0.87	3.35‡	2.63‡
N	173	174	174	173	174	174

Notes:
1. For full description of input sources (dependent variable), see Table 8.1.
2. For full definitions of the independent variables, see Table 3.1.

n number of observations; ‡ significant at 1%; † significant at 5%; *significant at 10%.

clearly the second most relevant of the six, being used by 56.3 per cent of respondents. The strong accessing of these suppliers by subsidiaries playing both ESTPROD roles may suggest the replication in the UK of supply relationships (that is, involving standardised inputs to familiar final products) already established elsewhere in the global networks of both companies. However, DEVELPROD subsidiaries also made use of such suppliers, which may also reflect the transfer to the UK of a tradition of mutually-shared decentralised development processes throughout the global network of both companies.[5]

The last input source located in the UK was described as 'previously independent UK companies now part of the MNE group' and emerged as the least relevant of all, being utilised by only 11.0 per cent of respondents. The relative prominence of this source for DEVELPROD subsidiaries may suggest that internalisation of especially creative local-component-producing enterprises may be a significant motivation. The same factor could then underpin the relatively strong acquisition of local suppliers by European subsidiaries, if we apply the suggestion of earlier chapters that these subsidiaries often seek to sustain sources of creativity in their operations against a trend to repatriate product development to the continental home country. The negligible interest in this mode of supply internalisation by Japanese subsidiaries may reflect the familiarity and ease which these companies feel with externalised sourcing through networks of independent operations.[6]

The remaining pair of input sources investigated involved supply from outside of the UK, but from within the MNE group. Thus 35.9 per cent of respondents were found to obtain inputs from 'other parts of the MNE group in Europe' and 43.6 per cent from 'other parts of the MNE group outside Europe'. Whilst clearly supportive of the view that international intra-group supply networks are a vital component of the strategic behaviour of the contemporary MNE, it can also be observed that these two sources rank behind two of the UK-based sources of inputs (including the implication that the needs of subsidiaries may be a factor in attracting the co-location in the UK of operations of leading independent component supply companies). The DEVELPROD subsidiaries emerge as relatively limited users of these intra-group input sources (just as they were of independent home-country suppliers). This has interesting resonances with their extensive use of independent UK suppliers noted earlier, since it provides a clear indication that the process of pursuing product development responsibility at the subsidiary level not only involves a localisation of creativity but also seems to benefit from not being too closely locked into the trajectories of other parts of the group network (where the norms of existing technologies and standardised products tend to prevail). As would be anticipated, the UK subsidiaries of European MNEs have a relatively strong propensity to be sourced from group operations elsewhere in Europe, with very limited accessing of supplies from outside the region. For both US and Japanese subsidiaries, by contrast, intra-group input supply is rather stronger from sources outside than inside Europe, so that whilst these MNE UK operations have been seen (Chapter 3) as being involved mainly in European supply networks, a significant element of their ability to do this effectively derives from intermediate good networks that extend beyond the region.[7]

TECHNOLOGICAL ADVICE PROVIDED TO SUPPLIERS BY MNE SUBSIDIARIES

The successful operation of foreign companies' subsidiaries in the UK can be expected to be based on the use of technologies that are specific to the MNE group (whether already embodied in established products, or used as a basis for a localised product development effort), so that their output is of distinctive products using specific complementary production processes. The individualised nature of the MNE subsidiaries' production (whether transferred from elsewhere in the group or locally generated) is normally likely to rule out the purchase of existing 'off-the-shelf' components from newly recruited independent UK suppliers.[8] Thus we have observed the way in which many subsidiaries seek to sustain access to intra-group supply sources (which already provide inputs to a standardised final product) or to replicate extra-group ones (with independent home-country or third-country suppliers setting up their own UK subsidiaries). Nevertheless, the vast majority of surveyed subsidiaries also manifest a willingness, for economic and/or political reasons, to extend their supply network to encompass independent local suppliers. The preceding argument then suggests, however, that these local suppliers will need to extend their product range, or at least considerably adjust existing elements of it in very specific ways, to meet the needs of new MNE subsidiary customers. A further implication of this is that there is likely to be some transfer of information or advice from the subsidiary to its local component supplier.

This means that its association with an MNE subsidiary should benefit an independent UK supplier, not only through an expansion of demand but also through learning processes that result from the acquisition of knowledge that represents part of the competitive and technological scope of significant international enterprises. An important issue, then, is how much of the extra information or expertise acquired by the supplier in this way is specific to its relationship with its MNE customer, and how much can provide spillovers into its wider knowledge or skills in forms that benefit its performance in other areas of its market (for example, local UK customers). Two questions in the survey asked MNE subsidiaries about provision of advice to their independent UK suppliers.

The first of these questions (Table 8.3) asked those subsidiaries that used independent UK suppliers to evaluate how often they were likely to provide them with technological advice. This emerged as a fairly common practice within such subcontracting relationships, with 30.8 per cent of subsidiaries considering they offered technological advice 'frequently', a further 47.7 per cent 'sometimes', but only 15.1 per cent 'rarely' and 6.4 per cent 'never'. The offering of advice does not tend to vary to any notable degree between subsidiary roles. Possible variation could have been expected between DEVELPROD and the ESTPROD roles, since the aim of the former to achieve a significant original final product might lead to a need for considerably different inputs and therefore the transfer of new specifications to local suppliers. That this does not appear to be the case may reflect a profound involvement of the supplier in the final-product development process,[9] so that the characteristics of new inputs will emerge within a mutually-shared and cohesive creative programme which the MNE subsidiary partner does not then see as a unilateral 'provision of technical advice' to their local subcontractor. Furthermore, the local input manufacturer will probably have been recruited to the role in reflection of proven competence (reflected in an existing range of successful components) and this may significantly influence the overall development operation, so that what it eventually supplies to the newly-created final product may be well within (and decisively reflect) its existing technological scope.

European subsidiaries emerge as notably the least likely to provide advice 'frequently', but also least likely to 'never' offer it. Thus they seem at least as willing as US or Japanese operations to support suppliers in this way wherever needed, but to find it to be necessary less often. This may reflect a greater degree of common technological and product heritage between the UK industrial sector (including its intermediate goods companies) and those of continental MNE home countries (which may also be associated with the continued strong commitment of European subsidiaries to supply the UK domestic market, noted in Chapter 3), so that there is a degree of innate cohesion between the needs of these final good companies and their UK component suppliers. Frequent supply of technical advice is strongest in three high-technology industries: aerospace, instruments and pharmaceuticals. The prevalence of new scientific knowledge as a key element in progress of these industries may often result in quite radical product changes that prevent relationships with local suppliers from becoming routine or stabilised, so that they are subjected particularly frequently to revitalisation or restructuring through transfers of new technological advice.[10]

The second of these questions asked the subsidiaries that provided advice to UK suppliers to evaluate the relevance of three forms this might take (Table 8.4). By far the most prevalent of these was 'specification of component or input to be supplied', with 90.4 per cent of respondents who provided advice rating this as 'very' important and only 1.9 per cent considering it to be 'not important'. This confirms the view that the distinctive competitive basis of MNE subsidiaries usually precludes the possibility of using off-the-shelf parts from UK component suppliers, but also indicates that there are substantial elements of the input needs of these companies that can be added quite easily to the scope of local subcontractors. This is likely to be the most transaction specific of the types of advice, and least likely to provide useful externalities to the UK subcontractors and possible wider spillover benefits to local industry. Thus these new MNE-specific components are unlikely to be appropriate to the needs of the component manufacturer's existing UK customers, and even where this was the case the subcontracting agreement would probably preclude such externalised supply. Some insights from the new product technology acquired might strengthen the UK company's ability to support its established local customers (especially those where it is involved in shared development programmes) through adjustments to existing components. But where such potential spillovers were obviously and visibly strong, they might again be seen as compromising the important subcontracting agreement with the MNE and ultimately be played down in terms of practical implementation.

The second type of technical advice that might be transferred to local suppliers was described as 'details of the production process for the component or inputs to be supplied'. Here only 24.5 per cent of respondents rated this as a 'very important' component of their advice to UK subcontractors, with 46.2 per cent considering it to be 'quite important' and 29.4 per cent as 'not important'. This tends to confirm the view that those UK subcontractors that are accessed by subsidiaries are mainly accepted as having an existing capability in the relevant areas of component supply, so that they in fact need little additional information to secure effective production of the new input beyond details of its unique characteristics (that is, those specific to the MNE's needs). Although once again intrinsically transaction specific, this type of process knowledge might have more potential to enrich the wider production technology of the local suppliers in ways that could not clearly be

Table 8.3 Prevalence of provision of technological advice by MNE subsidiaries to UK input suppliers

	Provision of advice to input supplier[1] (percentage of respondents)					
	Freq-uently	Some-times	Rarely	Never	Total	Average Response[2]
By industry						
Food	44.4	44.4	11.1		100.0	3.33
Automobiles	33.3	44.4	22.2		100.0	3.11
Aerospace	66.7	33.3			100.0	3.67
Electronics and electrical appliances	34.0	44.7	10.6	10.6	100.0	3.02
Mechanical engineering	20.8	62.5	16.7		100.0	3.04
Instruments	54.5	27.3	9.1	9.1	100.0	3.27
Industrial and agricultural chemicals	8.3	66.7	20.8	4.2	100.0	2.79
Pharmaceuticals and consumer chemicals	63.6	27.3	9.1		100.0	3.55
Metal manufacture and products	20.0	50.0	10.0	20.0	100.0	2.70
Other manufacturing	20.0	40.0	26.7	13.3	100.0	2.67
Total	30.8	47.7	15.1	6.4	100.0	3.03
By home country						
USA	39.7	47.6	7.9	4.8	100.0	3.22
Japan	35.9	35.9	17.2	10.9	100.0	2.97
Europe	10.3	61.5	25.6	2.6	100.0	2.79
Total[3]	30.8	47.7	15.1	6.4	100.0	3.03
By subsidiary type[4]						
ESTPROD/UK	32.1	44.0	13.1	10.7	100.0	2.98
ESTPROD/EUR	35.9	43.5	8.7	12.0	100.0	3.03
COMPART	23.1	61.5	7.7	7.7	100.0	3.00
DEVELPROD	33.3	42.4	13.6	10.6	100.0	2.98

Notes:
1. Respondents who used UK input suppliers of component parts or other inputs were asked to grade the frequency with which they provided them with technological advice.
2. The average response was calculated by allocating the reply of frequently the value of 4, sometimes the value of 3, rarely the value of 2 and never the value of 1.
3. Includes subsidiaries of MNEs from Australia and Canada.
4. Covers subsidiaries that described themselves as 'only' or 'predominantly' each type. For definitions, see Table 3.1.

Source: Survey of producing subsidiaries.

demonstrated to breach any contractual stipulation that sought to preclude such spillovers. Where it occurs, therefore, modest externalised benefits to local industry could follow from such technology transfers. Indeed, the relatively constrained amounts of this form of advice offered by MNEs could reflect such fears of limited appropriability of its benefits to local suppliers (that is, extensive external benefits to transactions that do not involve the MNE). Furthermore, if this suggests that MNEs do tend to believe that process technologies are particularly hard to appropriate (compared to product technologies) once transferred to suppliers, then it would mean that more radical innovations of this type would be internalised (that is, only made available to intra-group suppliers) even if other factors favoured use of independent local input sources.[11]

The last type of knowledge transfer evaluated by subsidiary respondents was 'wider advice on industrial production processes', covering broad organisational practices and skills (for example, quality control, procurement and inventory control, and plant layout), whose improvement in a supplier's operation could enhance its service to the MNE customer. There appeared to be relatively little provision for the transfer of such generalised types of industrial expertise, with only 11.5 per cent of respondents rating it as 'very important' and 54.0 per cent saying it was 'not important'. Where needed, the supply of such troubleshooting types of advice could sharpen the efficiency of the UK component producers in ways that provide substantial spillovers to other parts of their activity (for example, to local firms purchasing other inputs), but in ways that are sufficiently diffuse (that is, not deriving explicitly from product or process technologies of the MNE) to cause little appropriability concern to the subsidiary. The limited transfer of these types of support by MNEs therefore seems more likely to reflect confidence in the existing capabilities of their UK input suppliers than any worries about the consequences of spillover gains that might accrue outside of the specific subcontracting relationship.

The latter two types of advice were rather more likely to be provided by ESTPROD/EUR operations, suggesting that these subsidiaries, needing to assert their position in a highly competitive supply network for standardised products, were concerned to ensure the optimal quality and cost of the inputs they secured from local subcontractors. Japanese subsidiaries also were most notably above average in their provision of these two forms of advice. This partly reflects their particularly strong commitment to the ESTPROD/EUR role, but is also likely to be related to a traditional expectation of reliability and precision in input sourcing.

Table 8.4 Prevalence of different types of advice to UK input suppliers by MNE subsidiaries

	Importance of advice[1] (average response[2])		
	A	B	C
By industry			
Food	2.89	2.11	1.67
Automobiles	2.94	1.88	1.81
Aerospace	2.75	2.00	2.00
Electronics and electrical appliances	2.90	2.18	1.70
Mechanical engineering	2.88	1.96	1.52
Instruments	3.00	2.00	1.38
Industrial and agricultural chemicals	2.86	1.47	1.35
Pharmaceuticals and consumer chemicals	2.88	1.67	1.60
Metal manufacture and products	2.86	1.57	1.00
Other manufacturing	2.79	2.25	1.60
Total	2.88	1.95	1.58
By home country			
USA	2.89	1.87	1.56
Japan	2.93	2.15	1.71
Europe	2.83	1.77	1.41
Total[3]	2.88	1.95	1.58
By subsidiary type[4]			
ESTPROD/UK	2.91	1.76	1.48
ESTPROD/EUR	2.95	1.90	1.57
COMPART	2.92	1.69	1.23
DEVELPROD	2.90	1.79	1.41

Types of advice
A Specification of component or input to be supplied.
B Details of the production process for the components or inputs to be supplied.
C Wider advice on industrial production processes.

Notes:
1. Respondents who provided advice to UK input suppliers were asked to grade both types as either (i) very important, (ii) quite important, (iii) not important.
2. The average response was calculated by allocating the reply of very important the value of 3, quite important the value of 2, not important the value of 1.
3. Includes subsidiaries of MNEs from Australia and Canada.
4. Covers subsidiaries that described themselves as 'only' or 'predominantly' each type. For definitions, see Table 3.1.

Source: Survey of producing subsidiaries.

CONCLUSIONS

Three broad types of input supplier emerge as playing roles in the component sourcing scope of MNE subsidiaries' operations in the UK. Two of these seek to extend to UK subsidiaries the use of parts of the MNE groups' existing supply network relationships. The first appears to replicate in the UK ties to independent component companies that have already been fully formulated elsewhere. Thus part of the motivation for the presence of these suppliers seems to be to retain reliable input sources for subsidiaries needing to produce established goods cost effectively for competitive market areas (notably in the ESTPROD/EUR role). In addition, however, where these UK-based intermediate goods companies are from a third country (and are, perhaps, themselves subsidiaries of leading component MNEs) they also have a strong connection to DEVELPROD subsidiaries, and thus may be providing creative attributes in ways that again build on extant understandings and shared knowledge from elsewhere in global supply programmes. Where leading intermediate goods MNEs locate in the UK, probably at the behest of an important final-product MNE customer, this may assist the competitiveness of UK-based industry in three ways. Firstly, by ensuring that MNEs supplying external markets (notably Europe) can do so in ways that fully reproduce their existing levels of competitiveness. Secondly, by providing part of the creative support needed by subsidiaries that aim to innovate new goods or derive major product variants (that is, by becoming part of a creative nexus built by the subsidiary). Thirdly, by establishing new supply relationships with UK-owned companies that can expand their scope and efficiency.[12]

The second type of input source that is likely to replicate existing supply arrangements involves imports from other parts of the same MNE group. Whether from within Europe (most strongly for subsidiaries of European companies) or from outside (mostly for US and Japanese companies) intra-group sourcing emerges as quite significant, but by no means dominant or overwhelming. These results suggest that the home country may well be the main source of such intra-group intermediate good supply which, as well as again seeking to retain a proven efficiency supporting relationship, may also provide part of a mechanism for the transfer of new centrally-derived product or process technologies. On this basis the relative reluctance of DEVELPROD subsidiaries to access intra-group sources may be interpreted as another part of their mechanism for moving into individualised scope (alongside, as already noted, independent third-country suppliers) as a way of asserting a unique status.

Independent UK companies are the third potential source of inputs investigated, and emerge as part of the supply network accessed by the vast majority of MNE subsidiaries. The quality and content of these local linkages is, then, an important issue. A negative possibility is that these local associations could be peripheral to the main input programmes of the MNEs, and involve only residual fulfilment of very mundane needs. A more optimistic interpretation, however, may derive from the extensive involvement of UK suppliers with DEVELPROD subsidiaries, which certainly seem to be setting up a supply nexus (including other independent companies) that emphasises their individuality and provides externalised sources of creativity. Here real opportunity would seem to exist for the UK companies to enhance and develop creative potentials in ways that should then provide extensive scope for the provision of spillovers that benefit parts of UK industry external to the original (MNE-related) transaction. In fact, the most sustained competitive gains to the UK industrial sector from the involvement of local supplier companies with subsidiaries may emerge from knowledge and competences *generated* dynamically and interactively within such relationships, rather than more static one-off gains *learned from* MNE partners in transaction-specific forms.

NOTES

1. Alternative possibilities with regard to such linkages have been clearly distinguished in two scenarios outlined by Turok (1993, pp.402-3). Firstly, a *developmental* scenario reflects positive aspects of flexibility in production where 'processes of vertical disintegration of large corporations and decentralisation of decision-making demand closer, more collaborative relationship between individual plants, suppliers and distributors within the value chain'. In addition to saving on transport and transaction costs, the geographical clustering that emerges facilitates 'high-level exchange of technical ideas, market awareness and corporate plans'. This perspective provides a clear emphasis 'on the potential of inward investment to induce all-round development', where MNEs 'get deeply embedded in the local economy through the creation of a network of sophisticated, interdependent linkages, which support the expansion of local firms and generate self-sustaining growth of the cluster as a whole'. In the process of such interaction, MNE subsidiaries may provide local firms with 'valuable technology and expertise' which could provide them with the basis to become 'specialist suppliers'. In the alternative *dependent* scenario, Turok perceives negative implications deriving from flexibility. Here 'local clusters are weak nodes within a wider network of powerful multinationals' whose 'direct global connections expose local economies to volatile world markets and make them vulnerable to forces of international competition'. Now local linkages 'are driven more by cost-cutting than by a desire to add value through the exchange of technology and information'. In these more hierarchical relationships, there is little scope for suppliers to participate in the development and technological evolution of products.
2. This may to some degree contrast with evidence for MNE subsidiaries operating in the US. Thus Kotabe and Murray (1996) found that use of intra-group supply sources by US-based subsidiaries was positively related to product innovation (just short of significance at 10 per cent). Also Murray, Wildt and Kotabe (1995) noted that intra-group sourcing was higher for

non-standardised components (which might be closer to the creative stage) than for standardised inputs. This is attributed (Murray, Wildt and Kotabe, 1995, p.322) to the fact that 'the ability to internally source non-standardised components with high-technology content or proprietary knowledge allows the firms to keep the technology within the corporate system, thus facilitating the firm's ability to protect the product's competitive advantage'. We suggest two circumstances that may, on occasion, transcend this logical imperative. Firstly, where the external (independent local) supplier can itself provide unique knowledge (embodied in non-standardised inputs) that assists the subsidiary's creative process (in line with our view that such DEVELPROD units benefit from a position in the local knowledge community including component producers – as well as that of the MNE group). Secondly, innovation-oriented subsidiaries may sometimes seek to assert their particular intra-group status through such individualised extra-group linkages.

3 . This particularly reflects the preferences of Japanese subsidiaries who are the strongest users of this input source. The limited use of this source by European subsidiaries may simply reflect easy access to suppliers from the home country, due to relatively short transport distances and low restraints in trade due to EU regulations.

4 . By the same logic, the strong accessing of such suppliers by those subsidiaries that themselves produce components (COMPART) suggests that where these companies extend the supply chain further back, to other independent companies, the main aim is to source their own inputs in a secure and cost-effective way from previous home-country associates of proven reliability.

5 . The relatively limited use of this supply source by the COMPART subsidiaries may indicate a desire to remain independent of other leading players in the intermediate goods sector, using instead more hierarchical associations with less powerful home-country suppliers.

6 . The overall suggestion that local (UK-based) supply sources predominate is compatible with Murray, Wildt and Kotabe's (1995) documentation of MNE subsidiaries in the US. In terms of value 73.7 per cent of these subsidiaries' inputs were sourced in the US, with 23.1 per cent of these respondents sourcing all their components locally and 35.6 per cent more obtaining between 76 per cent and 99 per cent of inputs (by value) from such domestic sources. Of the total foreign sourcing (Murray, Wildt and Kotabe, 1995, Table 2) 60.4 per cent were secured from the home country of the MNE, 28.9 per cent from other developed countries and 10.6 per cent from developing countries.

7 . Murray, Wildt and Kotabe's (1995, Table 3) analysis of input sourcing of subsidiaries in the US shows that of components sourced intra-group but outside the US 76.7 per cent came from the MNE's home country, 17.8 per cent from other developed countries and 5.5 per cent from less developed countries.

8 . The use of existing parts of the range of UK component suppliers might be more likely where these local companies take part in a product development programme of an MNE subsidiary. Thus a high-quality local-company component of proven success could be treated as a reference point in the product/process development project, with the characteristics of the final good and relevant elements of its engineering then designed to encompass it. Changes to existing MNE products or processes to embody local components might be more strongly resisted (given continued convenient access to those inputs already compatible with the final product).

9 . As, earlier, we suggested that those subsidiaries that produce intermediates (COMPART) are themselves frequently involved in the development process relating to final products to which they will supply inputs.

10 . Indeed, it is noteworthy in this context that two of these industries (aerospace and petroleum) are amongst those least likely to use UK independent suppliers (Table 8.1). Similarly, all three have an above-average propensity to sustain intra-group supply linkages. Thus from a survey of literature on global sourcing, Cavusgil, Yaprak and Yeoh (1993, p.151) note that 'products of high intrinsic value with sophisticated or special processing requirements and relatively short product lives which are subjected to frequent technological upgrading are generally sourced internally en route to final assembly'.

11. If a DEVELPROD subsidiary with a strong relationship with a local subcontractor discerns a powerful new process technology to be vulnerable within the existing agreement, it might choose to sustain the association, with greater security, by taking over (that is, internalising) the local supplier (that is, source B in Table 8.1). This could contribute to the relatively strong presence of source B for DEVELPROD subsidiaries, and especially for European subsidiaries where building a strong and secure localised creative nexus has been suggested as providing a means of trying to retain product development scope against centralising tendencies in these MNEs.

12. This may involve the displacement of less-effective or less-creative local suppliers.

9. Multinationals and national competitiveness

The investigation of the strategic dimensions of MNE operations in the UK in previous chapters endorses the modern view of these companies as dynamic differentiated networks. The individual subsidiaries of MNEs can now take one of several very different strategically-oriented roles, and these roles are permanently open to change as the forces of globalised competition alter the needs, priorities, strengths and weaknesses of the groups' worldwide networks. Thus one set of forces that could ultimately impinge on the positioning of individual subsidiaries may remain those that are predominantly exogenous to a particular MNE, in the form of intensification of the immediate competitive environment in reflection both of institutional change (freer international trade and crucial elements of deregulation in many leading nations or regions) and of the emergence of major new players in the worldwide market. However, we have also placed a vital emphasis on the fact that as MNE groups seek to position themselves for short-term and long-term survival in an environment that is increasingly conditioned by both strident current competition and evolutionary volatility (notably with regard to products, processes and organisational techniques) endogenous (that is, intra-group) forces can also be embraced in a positive fashion by subsidiaries taking a proactive view of their own competitiveness and development. These perspectives closely parallel another emerging perception, suggesting that the modern MNE cannot avoid a sustained, and globally-articulated, commitment to both the effective exploitation of its existing sources of competitiveness and to their renewal and revitalisation through (increasingly internationalised) programmes of creative activity.

As a starting point for the broad application of the preceding understanding of the strategic nature of the contemporary MNE to the investigation of a richer public policy basis with regard to 'inward investment', we can analyse the nature of the two key evolutionary transitions implied by the typology of subsidiary roles utilised in our research, that is, from truncated miniature replica (TMR) to rationalised product subsidiary (RPS) and from RPS to world or regional product mandate (WPM/RPM). Of course, this does not represent a unique or immutable process of subsidiary evolution, and other changes in status are obviously possible. Two that certainly have a high degree of contemporary plausibility would be a transition directly from TMR to WPM/RPM status, or a regression (as it would logically be perceived) from a PM role to that of RPS. The policy contribution (perhaps, in the second case, policy failure) of these transitions can, however, be deduced within the analysis of relatively gradualist progress of the more routine evolutionary process normally perceived as available to subsidiaries.

The transition process from TMR to RPS is, we have already indicated, one that is essentially part of an MNE's group-level response to exogenous changes. In the specific case of subsidiaries located in the UK, the most decisive element in this type of reformulation of their competitive approach has probably been the local economy's participation in the moves towards increasingly free trade within Europe. Although this institutional change of itself points to the reorientation of UK subsidiaries to an export-oriented positioning, it also provides the ideal context within which to grasp the general need to greatly revitalise efficiency, as the established MNEs face a further tightening of international competition with the emergence of major new rivals (using new technology and implementing new – more globalised – organisational strategies). Thus the RPSs pursue the efficiency-seeking imperative that has increasingly emerged in MNEs over the past three decades, and reconfigure their operations to eliminate the sources of inefficiency that are likely to be endemic to the market-seeking motivation of the TMR status.

Changes with regard to both ownership advantages (OAs) and location advantages (LAs) are central to the TMR to RPS transition. In fact, in the case of OAs the essential nature of these does not change since the RPS will still use its MNE's well-established and standardised technologies and practices to supply parts of the group's mature and proven product range. The crucial change is that the RPS now (compared to the TMR) uses a much smaller part of the MNE's current overall scope, with the OAs that it does activate being *selected* as those elements of the wider group menu whose input needs fit most closely those available from the local economy. It is, then, the change in LAs that is most radical and provides the defining impetus to the TMR to RPS transition. In the TMR environment, the relevant LAs determining the products manufactured locally (and therefore the OAs activated) were the size and characteristics (average income levels, income distribution, and so on) of the national market and the structure of protection (determining which goods could not be effectively supplied by trade). The lowering of trade protection (in defining the new RPS environment) allows the import of goods whose local manufacture had been inefficient and provides the initial impulsion towards the rationalisation of a subsidiary's product range. The concomitant opening of foreign markets to the subsidiary removes local-market conditions from a unique (or indeed substantial) influence on its supply profile. The crucial LAs that now motivate RPS decision making are the host country's sources of static comparative advantage, that is, the standardised inputs it can supply in the most cost-effective fashion. The optimising pursuit of an ideal match between the parts of the MNE's technology used locally and the availability of inputs is the first source of improved efficiency engendered by the TMR to RPS transition. Others include better realisation of economies of scale that become available with the wider market scope and diminished X-inefficiency in production and organisational procedures, provoked by the generally more strident competitive environment faced by the subsidiary (inside its group as well as in final product markets). Overall, then, the emergence of the RPS mode of behaviour in MNEs can be a key facet of the ways in which these companies can contribute to the refocusing and restructuring through which a host country (such as the UK) addresses a new free-trade-oriented competitive environment.

Our analysis also indicates, however, that a host country's enthusiasm for the undoubted cost-efficiency potentials of RPSs should be tempered by their innate lack of dynamism and of embeddedness. The OAs used by an RPS are those that have already been fully formulated elsewhere in the group and which have usually reached a degree of standardisation that makes them accessible (in a more or less public-good fashion) to most other subsidiaries of the MNE. The RPS is not expected to need any distinctive competences to assimilate the imported OA, nor is it permitted to impose any original localised dimensions on its use of the OA (apart, perhaps, from minor adaptation to the production process to allow it to supply the established product in the most cost-efficient and reliable way using the available local inputs).

The ability of a pure RPS to retain its position in the MNE's supply network derives not from any differential in-house competences (beyond the ability to perform routine administrative tasks at least as well as other 'competitor' RPSs elsewhere), but from the cost and effectiveness of the inputs it can secure from its host economy. The capacity of local inputs (that is, LAs) to support an RPS depends, therefore, on their ability to immediately (or with limited and inexpensive adaptation; most notably training of local labour to carry out new process-specific jobs)[1] fulfil roles dictated by the existing MNE technologies in a cost-effective fashion. There is, then, no plausible position for higher-quality, but more expensive, inputs or for more idiosyncratic attributes (notably creative capabilities, such as entrepreneurial drive in managers, marketing flair or R&D scope) in a pure RPS. In summary, local inputs to RPSs are not expected to require, or to provide the capability to achieve, any substantial alteration in the way the RPS carries out its externally-imposed role in the MNE's wider competitive programmes.

Although the interface between the MNE's OAs and the host country's LAs, which is secured within the pure RPS, may involve limited changes in the production process and/or routine training of labour, these would be expected to occur only to the extent that is needed to optimise effectiveness in the subsidiary's allocated role. They would involve no attempt to create distinctive new competences that could individualise its scope and point towards a dynamic and proactive status within the group's evolutionary processes. These factors also indicate a lack of embeddedness of a pure RPS in its host economy, in the sense that this role does not require, and from its cost-dominated imperative should not try to afford, the generation of capacities and competences that substantially differentiates it from other comparable facilities. This lack of locally-originated qualitative distinctiveness in an RPS means that its activity can be very easily replicated elsewhere in an MNE's current (or expanding) network, and only continued cost efficiency in an allocated role can sustain its position.

Two areas of host country policy seem to be of crucial relevance to the attraction and support of MNE RPSs. The first of these is the country's sustained commitment to participation in an evolving free-trade environment. Once the impact of freer trade has provided a sufficient exogenous stimulus to provoke the transformation of TMRs into RPSs (or to encourage the implementation of *de nuovo* subsidiaries of this type) it clearly behoves a host country to manifest a transparent involvement in the further progress of this environment. Where a country is confident that it has sources of comparative advantage that could be beneficially utilised by MNEs through RPS-type operations (noting that residual trade restraints may be rather more harmful to the price- and cost-competitiveness of these subsidiaries than the quality/originality that defines the PMs) it should work with other relevant countries (globally, through the World Trade Organisation, or regionally, as appropriate) towards the creation of an overall environment in which these companies feel able to generate internationally-coordinated networks of supply facilities. More specifically, it should avoid the provocation of trade disputes that could lead to retaliation in key markets for RPS exports. Low protection in a country can then facilitate an MNE's restructuring to RPS operations in two ways. Firstly, by allowing the free import (or at least at no higher level of restraint than in competitor countries) of capital goods, component parts, raw materials, and so on, that are not obtainable locally by the subsidiary. Secondly, by permitting the effective import of those final goods of the MNE that are demanded by local consumers, but which are not part of the RPS's product range (that is, which are likely to have been part of a TMR's range in the earlier trade-restrained situation). Our results provide clear confirmation that the crucial context for these aspects of policy support for MNE subsidiaries in the UK takes the form of the country's continued participation in the free-trade provisions of the European Union. In fact, this is reflected not only in the strong presence of subsidiaries playing the ESTPROD/EUR role, but also in the considerable European-market orientation of the DEVELPROD facilities.[2]

The second important area of host country policy affecting RPS operations lies in avoiding the imposition of inappropriate and unnecessary costs. One dimension of this lies in the institutional provision of flexible and administratively inexpensive factor markets (that is, avoiding unnecessary bureaucratic burdens), which allow subsidiaries to efficiently locate and employ those inputs that represent the host country's relevant LAs at prices that reflect their current availability and opportunity cost. Our understanding of the ways in which the dynamic potentials of subsidiary positioning in the modern MNE can be embedded within the changes implied by successful industrialisation and development indicate, however, that this aspect of cost consciousness should not involve attempts to suppress the upward pressures on factor prices that are a manifestation of a contribution to successful economic performance and growth.

Another much debated aspect in the avoidance of elements of costs that could compromise RPS competitiveness relates to the implication of possibly inappropriate overhead commitments. The issues that relate to the social-welfare content of such overheads are beyond the scope of our investigation. However, our analytical perceptions of the scope for harnessing MNE evolutionary processes to sustained host-country growth does suggest that a tendency to often characterise current expenditures on human-capital development and technological speculation as overheads may be damagingly myopic. The tendency, on occasion, of politicians and analysts to justify some of the more short-termist elements of public policy as being particularly necessary to attract 'inward investment' seems to reflect a perception of MNE operations as being uniquely of a cost-oriented RPS type, and therefore embodies a failure to comprehend the potential for their involvement in the qualitative upgrading in a country's knowledge scope that is crucial to progress into the medium and long term.

The preceding discussion defines not only the positive value of the RPS role as an MNE faces the need to reconfigure the use of its existing competitive attributes (OAs) in the face of freer trade and the increasing intensity in its global markets, but also the limitations of this form's static efficiency to a company that also seeks to address the dynamic medium- or longer-term needs of strategic competitiveness. Once a successful RPS has demonstrated the value of a country's sources of static comparative advantage, dynamic forces may emerge which provoke consideration of the possibility (or perhaps inevitability) of its mutation into a WPM or an RPM. Our analysis has indicated that the RPS to PM transformation may be a response to mainly endogenous forces (compared with the predominantly exogenous ones which lead to the TMR to RPS transition) which emerge within both the country's industrialisation and the MNE group's strategic evolution.

Within a host country, the process of industrialisation and growth (to which the RPS should have made a positive contribution) will have led to a rising quality, and a broadening, in the input base and thus to increases in the real incomes earned by these factors of production. It is the precise aim of economic development to upgrade an economy's sources of comparative advantage and thus to be able to support rises in real income. However, this then implies changes in a host country's LAs as perceived by inward-investing MNEs. Notably, general upward wage pressures in the labour market, as well as increased support for training to higher basic skill levels, means that the types of cheap unskilled labour that represented the LA originally needed by many RPSs will become decreasingly available. Given the lack of local embeddedness of RPSs, and the ease of comparing the relative cost efficiency of their performance with other potential sites, an efficiency-seeking parent MNE will very quickly begin to consider the future of such a subsidiary once the host country's LAs move significantly away from those that attracted its original establishment.

We can consider three options available to an MNE whose RPS is declining in effectiveness due to the forces envisaged above, with all accepting the inevitable diversion of supply of the subsidiary's current products to other (now more cost-efficient) sites. The first alternative is simply to close down the RPS. The indicated lack of embeddedness (and absence of intra-subsidiary dynamic factors that might point immediately to new potentials) means that this is usually a readily available option to an MNE targeting the short-term efficiency of a supply network. It might, however, prove damagingly myopic for two reasons. Firstly, the MNE would presumably still wish to derive profits from supply of the host country market and the loss of goodwill (with consumers and, perhaps, government) might significantly compromise that. Secondly, it may suggest an unwillingness to consider the ways in which the new configuration of host country LAs might be incorporated in other phases of the MNE's production and in the overall enhancement of its competitive scope.

The second alternative is to regenerate the capabilities of the subsidiary *within the RPS mode of behaviour*. This could be done through the provision of new higher-value-added parts of the MNE's OA scope that can utilise effectively (as LAs) alternative aspects of the host country's upgraded comparative advantage. The move here would normally be expected to be towards more skill-intensive and more capital-intensive modes of production. However, even where the use of the procedure of sequential upgrading of RPSs is accepted in principal in an MNE it by no means fully alleviates the technological dependency and intrinsic vulnerability of this subsidiary form. Thus the ability of a particular RPS to accede to a new higher-level opportunity within an MNE's efficiency-seeking imperative depends on the *group* possessing (or being able to swiftly generate) those production techniques (OAs) that could benefit from the host country's reformulated LAs, and being able to transfer them to the new location without disruptive knock-on effects elsewhere in its supply network. The continued dependence of an RPS on the import of its core knowledge from elsewhere in an MNE may seem increasingly inappropriate to such a subsidiary if it persistently needs to enhance its own in-house engineering resources and technological capabilities in order to be able to assimilate, implement and perhaps, to some degree, to adapt these acquired group attributes.[3] These limitations, vulnerabilities and stresses of the RPS role (even in its more dynamic formulation) in fact, then, point to the third available response to LA upgrading, in the form of the basic reorientation of the subsidiary's strategic position to the RPM or WPM role.

Independent of (though logically often ultimately supported by) the changes in host-country LAs, other endogenous (here intra-group) impulses towards the RPS to PM transition may be related to the dynamic tensions that are likely to be endemic in those MNEs that articulate global competitiveness through differentiated networks. Thus the management of a pure RPS, which is solely involved in the routine supply programmes of its group, will be well aware of the very limited degree to which any distinctive in-house competences it possesses, or feels it could readily derive from newly-emerging attributes of its host economy, can affect the prospects for its survival or allow for non-dependent dimensions of progress. Furthermore, its networked positioning will make it aware of the much greater self-determination and higher-value operating scope that accrues to those PM subsidiaries that it can observe and to which it may, indeed, be hierarchically subordinate and dependent. We noted above that the longer an RPS survived the first plausible fate (closure) the more in-house scope (in engineering, technology and increasingly entrepreneurial management drive) it was likely to generate to sustain its capability with regard to the second (upgrading within the RPS role). Eventually, we suggest, it will feel impelled to explore the potential for the reorientation of its in-house knowledge and skill competences away from merely assimilating and *applying* pre-existing group-level technologies (as an RPS) towards a much more individualised position in the MNE's programme for *generating* new products and scope (as a PM). Where a new WPM/RPM emerges in this way, its ability to implement its new role will be derived from the knowledge and capabilities it activated and used in the later stages of its RPS existence. It is on these antecedents that it will build the initial phases of its PM operation. This is then clearly compatible with the importance amongst the technologies operationalised by DEVELPROD subsidiaries (see Chapter 4) of those already embodied in existing products (ESTPRODTECH) and in the capabilities of engineers and shopfloor personnel (ENGUNIT). In turn this then underwrites the interdependent individualism of the emerging PM's status, allowing it to add very distinctive dimensions to the MNE's knowledge and product scope but by doing so in ways that assert crucial inter- dependencies with the wider progress of the group's technological trajectory.

The emergence of a WPM/RPM subsidiary in a particular country is a manifestation of the knowledge-seeking imperative that is a crucial facet of the expanded scope of the heterarchical MNE. Its aim is thus to derive subsidiary-level knowledge and product-development abilities that enhance the overall scope of the MNE group by internalising creative elements in the host country's labour force and acquiring distinctive new technologies emerging in the science base. To outcompete indigenous firms in securing these local attributes it must expect to be able to utilise them more effectively. Its ability to do that, we suggest, still derives from its access to particular OAs of its MNE group. Thus our analysis points to the PM subsidiary building on the existing core technologies of its MNE group, utilising transferred skills that represent key facets of its tacit knowledge and benefiting from access to the group's existing international marketing network and, most notably, from the use of a globally-respected trademark and established product reputation. Quite crucial as an OA supporting the emergence of a successful PM operation, we argue, is a central management capability that understands the diversity of a heterarchical MNE and develops procedures that facilitate both the individualism and the interdependencies through which such a subsidiary can fully realise its own potential and be able to articulate this in ways that also benefit (and benefit from) wider aspects of group performance and progress. The new dimensions invoked by a PM subsidiary are, almost inevitably, going to challenge the status of some established interests within an MNE group. For a subsidiary to commit its resources, and risk its intra-group goodwill, in propounding its case for PM status it needs to expect informed and fair judgement from a farseeing central management that is taking a flexible and dynamic view of group evolution. In this sense, the perceived availability of procedural justice within the group is a key OA activated by a WPM/RPM subsidiary.

Although inputs that allow a PM subsidiary to produce its goods competitively are clearly still very relevant to the success of such an operation, the defining LAs here are now, as indicated above, the access to local personnel with distinctive and creative talents (in management, technology, engineering, marketing, and so on) and the scope to tap into unique aspects of knowledge and research capacity emerging in the host-country science base. The emergence of specific sources of competitive advantage within a PM subsidiary (which not only support the success of its goods in final product markets but also underwrite its status in its parent group) therefore represents the creative synthesis, or partial overlap, of MNE-derived OAs and host country-originated LAs.

Ideally, an MNE is strengthened by the new knowledge and reinforced product range that it secures through a PM-type subsidiary, whilst that subsidiary's distinctive antecedent competences (derived from its group positioning) help develop those aspects of knowledge-related potential that now constitute LAs more effectively than would otherwise have occurred. By comparison with the arm's-length complementarity of unchanged OAs and LAs in the RPS, the intrinsic behaviour of WPMs/RPMs is predicated on dynamism and embeddedness. The continued progress (and indeed ultimate survival) of a PM operation depends on the sustained reinforcement of its unique competences, which it must secure through the deepening and enriching of its linkages with host-country scientific progress and the evolution of idiosyncratic talents in local personnel (that is, its interaction with sources of dynamic or created comparative advantage). A successful PM provides none of the migratory, footloose, dangers of the RPS. The embeddedness of a PM in its host country's national system of innovation not only directly strengthens explicit elements of this (for example, by securing an improved commercialisation, in international competition, of parts of the country's scientific knowledge) but provides crucial spillovers into its further development (for example, by enhancing the skills and perceptions of scientists it employs, through contractual research arrangements with local universities, and through mutually-supportive creative and knowledge-sharing programmes with local input suppliers).

We can characterise the RPS to PM transformation as one of a creative transition, representing the subsidiary's changing strategic status from one that involves a cost-based ability to supply existing products efficiently, to one that is driven by the imperative to create new products from an individualised scope that extensively reflects host-country knowledge inputs.[4] In broad terms it can then be expected that such subsidiary-level transition is interdependent with comparable upgrading in aspects of the host-country economy, where less emphasis is placed on sources of static comparative advantage and moves are encouraged towards dynamic or created forms of international competitiveness. A crucial element of host-country policy towards inward investment, therefore, needs to understand the dynamic processes available to MNE subsidiaries and that these allow such operations to be positively embedded, in a sustained fashion, in the changes implied by development rather than be challenged by them.

Thus in their detailed review of after-care programmes in the EU Young and Hood (1994, p.51) observe that the services supplied by government agencies should be 'designed to facilitate both the successful start-up and the continuing development of a foreign affiliate in a host country or region, with a view towards maximising the local economic development contribution of that affiliate'. Central to this is that 'after-care programmes are designed to exploit the opportunities and minimise the threats of highly dynamic [MNE] networks ... [so that] services of a strategic nature are designed to support an affiliate within its transnational corporate framework' (p.52).[5] The after-care services are here perceived as supporting the subsidiary in its 'strategy and planning' with help provided in, for example, presenting the case for new investment to corporate headquarters or assisting in intra-group bids for new projects and generally preventing adverse effects of rationalisation (p.53). In line with the likely content of the creative transition, Young and Hood also indicate that the after-care provision can also support the subsidiary in presenting its case 'for new activities at plant level, e.g. research and development, marketing'.

Alongside the general need for host-country policies to comprehend and respond to the scope for restructuring of MNE subsidiary roles is the complementary importance of a specific understanding of the crucial position of technology, knowledge and skill at the core of the implied upgrading process. The dangers of failing to address the need for technological deepening as a process of industrialisation moves away from origins in low-cost standardised inputs can be found in Lall's (1995, pp.11–15; 1996, pp.67–70) analyses of the Asian newly industrialised countries. This is exemplified quite decisively in a comparison of the cases of Singapore and Hong Kong. In the latter case, industrialisation 'started and stayed' with export-oriented, light, labour-intensive manufacturing industries, with no proactive support for technological upgrading and industrial deepening. With rises in wages and land costs, firms relocated their manufacturing to other countries (notably mainland China) so that Hong Kong suffered a significant loss of industrial activity. By contrast, Singapore 'has developed a far deeper structure (in terms of the sophistication of production and exports) and has continued to sustain high rates of industrial and manufacturing export growth despite having higher industrial wages'. Vital in this achievement, Lall argues, was intervention to induce MNEs to upgrade through the support of heavy investment in education (including an efficient, industrial targeted, higher education structure), training (notably 'one of the best systems in the world for specialised worker training') and in physical infrastructure. Efforts to induce MNEs to establish R&D units in Singapore were complemented by the setting up of several government-supported research centres.[6]

In more precise terms, one aspect of the growing importance of decentalised R&D in the modern MNE emerges, in our study, as being to take a key position in forming the ability of subsidiaries to play the product mandate role (DEVELPROD in our analysis). Furthermore, the willingness of MNEs to set up laboratories in the UK is seen to be strongly influenced by 'supply-side' factors in the form of the continued access to a notable technological tradition, encompassed within the scope of the ongoing work of the local scientific community, and the availability of a top-quality (and hopefully persistently reinforced) scientific labour force. Therefore it is an obvious and decisive policy prescription that support for the local science base, in terms of both its research capacity and the quality of its human capital (through education and training), is crucial to a country that seeks to involve itself with the technological progress of leading MNEs and, in particular, to retain, and benefit from the continued upgrading of, their most influential subsidiaries. Our analysis also indicates, however, that to benefit fully from the participation of parts of the *global* technology programmes of MNEs in the development of its *national* scientific scope, a particular country needs to understand the range of motivations that can underlie the MNE's involvement.[7]

Our overall interpretation of the positioning of decentralised technological activity in the contemporary MNE is that this contributes to their pursuit of strategic competitiveness in the forms of both the effective application of the group's core existing knowledge resources and the capacity to achieve their successful further evolution and regeneration. Both these dimensions of an MNE's technological trajectory logically benefit from the participation of overseas R&D units. Thus, as just noted, one role for overseas R&D is exercised within a product development subsidiary (a WPM/RPM), as a locally integrated laboratory (LIL), with the aim of facilitating the creation of a new good around an available source of original disembodied technology. The latter may either have emerged within the MNE's activity in the same country or have been acquired, for localised product development, from elsewhere in the group (perhaps to derive the regional product variant within a global innovation strategy).

Some reservations may then be appropriate with regard to the second of these variants of LIL/PM creativity (that is, where it applies group-originated knowledge for a limited market context) in that it may retain a degree of technological dependency within these higher-order activities, since the defining technology is still derived from outside the local science base. Nevertheless, even where MNEs address a dispersed approach to innovation in this way, securing the position of a local LIL/PM nexus within these groups' wider creative programmes is still likely to be a valuable means of operationalising elements of local knowledge and talent in support of the competitiveness of the national industrial sector. Ultimately, therefore, it would be expected that the emergence of an LIL reflects a key part of the way in which a PM subsidiary activates distinctive local creative resources (hopefully enhancing their contribution to local industrial competitiveness in the process) in conjunction with complementary group-level attributes and as part of the MNE's programme for expanding and differentiating its global product scope. Thus a high-quality contribution from an LIL helps to embed a PM subsidiary in the local economy and to secure its position within the creative and competitiveness-enhancing programmes of the group.

Our analysis also confirms the presence in the decentralised R&D portfolios of MNEs of laboratories that, in their pure form, operate independently of local producing units of the same group. Such stand-alone laboratories would be expected to do precompetitive work (basic or applied research), which does not seek to address any immediate commercial potentials or problems, but rather takes a more long-term and speculative approach to the extension of the core science available to the group. Often such laboratories consciously eschew any local integration with other functions of their MNEs and instead articulate their work more in terms of international interdependencies with other, similarly oriented, laboratories of the group. Thus such an internationally interdependent laboratory (IIL) may sometimes carry out work which is a specialised component of a wider programme that is conceived and coordinated from a central laboratory (perhaps a 'parent' or home-country unit). Even where this degree of formal organisation, or external supervision, is not present, the IIL will be expected to constantly communicate the content of its ongoing research projects to other sister laboratories, in pursuit of unexpected synergies and the scope to pull together complementary strands of progress. One interpretation is, then, that an IIL is likely to function as a conduit through which very distinctive research results, deriving from the work of top quality local scientists and building on a unique technological heritage that is currently manifest in those disciplines that define the country's 'scientific comparative advantage' (that is, its areas of world research leadership), may leave the country with no direct route into support of competitiveness in national industry.

Certainly the potentials just described need to serve as a strong warning against any policy bias towards an unquestioning welcome for very prestigious and well-publicised pure research projects of MNEs, which may serve to divert support or encouragement away from those more 'bread and butter' laboratories that have a more developmental orientation. With that said, it also seems likely that attempts to systematically exclude (or severely limit) IIL-type work may also be very short-sighted (or indeed a manifestation of the facet of those short-termist policies that might see basic research as an unnecessary cost). One relevant point here is that our results indicate that often the output of IIL-type activity (some basic research and substantial parts of applied research) *does* feed into local product development of MNEs. Where this is the case, the subsidiaries carrying out the innovations may create particularly distinctive new goods and secure worldwide market access for them (that is, operate as WPMs rather than RPMs) and thereby provide especially rewarding and dynamic new elements in the international competitiveness of local industry.

Even where an IIL does operate systematically in total independence of other MNE functions in its host country, there are likely to be plausible and distinctive spillover potentials available to the wider local science base within which it will seek to function as an integral part. This reflects the fact that the IIL articulates its programmes for development of local scientific capabilities and potentials within the technological trajectory of its MNE group. Since this specialised positioning of the IIL is thus derived from a different technological tradition, and therefore likely to target rather different research objectives (compared with local firms that will also activate parts of the science base) it should impart alternative and enriching dimensions to the evolutionary progress in local knowledge. This may occur at two levels. The MNE locates in the particular country because one of the key areas of science it feels a need to investigate is one where the host has a strong heritage and still evolving research competence. The IIL then provides reinforcing perspectives *within* the agglomerative development of the shared areas of scientific interest (that is, the point of overlap of the MNE's and host country's spectrums of technological concerns). But because the IIL is specialising in only one of several disciplines that comprise its MNE's overall research needs it exchanges information with other laboratories that are focusing on different, but potentially complementary, technologies. This speculative interdependence of the IIL's work with that of sister laboratories in other knowledge communities may benefit the host-country scientific scope by helping to prevent the agglomerative tendency from narrowing to a perhaps excessive degree of specialised introversion. In short, the IIL's participation may help to reinforce the country's area of revealed technological advantage whilst also asserting an awareness of the wider synergistic contexts with which they may have become usefully involved.[8]

The previous point relates to an IIL's ability to impart enriching and differentiating elements to an already healthy and vibrant science base. It may sometimes have an alternative value in salvaging areas of scientific strength that face atrophy and decline due to inadequate support from government and indigenous industry. It is probably reasonable to suggest that, on occasion, public and private funding in a country neglects some of its areas of quality research for reasons other than an objective evaluation of their scientific value and potential. The take-up of such opportunities by MNEs may thus sustain and reinforce aspects of the local science base, with longer-term spillover benefits that were being neglected or undervalued by local interests. An important facet of this may lie in the ability of IILs to provide employment opportunities that prevent the migration of top-quality individual scientists or the breakup of effective and well-balanced research teams. It can then be argued that, even if the direct results of their work in an IIL becomes the property of foreign companies, the retention of especially charismatic and influential personnel within a country's scientific community may have significant spillover benefits. The leadership qualities of such individuals may spread beyond their immediate research situation, and their continued presence may, in particular, support the development of local programmes and capabilities through their membership of government committees, scientific advisory authorities and funding bodies.

Our documentation of the assertive position of product development subsidiaries and of strategically proactive decentralised R&D operations in the modern MNE, has derived explicitly from the analysis of the UK situation. Yet ironically, in terms of our view of the policy bases needed to nurture and benefit from those higher-level stratas within MNE global activity, it is impossible to avoid a suspicion that the presence and persistence of such operations in the UK has been more a matter of luck than judgement. And the luck may be in danger of running out.[9] Over the past two decades, macro-policies conducive to deindustrialisation, short-termist public and private attitudes that often see R&D and innovation categorised as risky overheads, and 'inward investment' policies that then myopically focus on *attraction* of new FDI merely to fill the short-term gaps (notably in employment) that are generated by the first two elements, seem to be impervious to (and clearly to jeopardise) the wider dynamic potentials still revealed within the UK scope of MNEs. In a cogent characterisation, Sharp and Walker (1994, p.398) draw attention to the 'Thatcher government's economic daring or foolhardiness' with a 'medium-sized industrial nation liberalising its markets from a position of industrial weakness, and during a technological revolution in which it played only a minor part'. Certainly our analysis fully acknowledges the virtue of attracting cost-effective RPS operations to help sharpen industrial competitiveness, and this may have served the UK very well in asserting a position in European markets in sectors where local firms' presence is now limited (for example, electronics, motor vehicles). Less clearly detectable in UK policy has been an awareness of the need to upgrade industry around higher-value inputs, and a predominant low-cost perception of competitiveness has often been attributed, in particular, to the supposed needs of 'inward investors'.[10]

An ability to produce cost effectively *is*, of course, a key priority of MNEs utilising globalised approaches to competing in the current international marketplace, and the scope to supply efficient inputs to this phase of their operations may be crucial to a country's initial capacity to attract the companies. However, the same firms also need to have a comparably decisive commitment to the regeneration of their competitiveness, through new product innovation and the acquisition of new core knowledge competences.[11] Furthermore, globalised approaches to these phases of MNE development are also emerging as strategically crucial. Therefore, host countries that recognise the potential for subsidiary upgrading within the dynamic heterogeneity of MNE global programmes can themselves reorient policy away from emphasising mainly standardised cost-related attributes, which may take the lead in attracting these companies, towards those more created types of comparative advantage (technology, innovation-oriented skills) that can secure a more sustained and deep-rooted involvement within these companies' higher-value and strategically forward-looking concerns. Ultimately for the UK, and similar economies, it is an awareness of these aspects of the strategic nature of the MNE that is crucial. The changes in the costs and capacities of local inputs that are inherent to processes of growth, development and industrialisation should not be feared as likely to alienate inward investors, but instead be supported and enhanced as a means of securing a higher-level status in, and deeper involvement with, the differentiated networks of MNEs. Here we find a promising platform to build on in the current roles played within MNE operations in the UK, but with increasing intra-group competitive dynamism the ability to realise this potential is ever-more dependent on a supportive policy environment, in terms of education, training and a revitalised commitment to science and research. In such a policy context the operations of MNEs can be an integral component of the assertion of knowledge, talent and skill in the sustained development of national competitiveness.

NOTES

1. A necessity to train local labour in the more generalised and basic types of industrial skills, or even to inculcate the behavioural attitudes expected of an industrial labour force, would often be seen as an unnecessary overhead (which should have been achieved in host-country training systems) and would probably tend to mitigate against commitment to an RPS. Relating these basic capacities to specific techniques in the MNE's processes, however, would be accepted as a routine subsidiary-level responsibility. This would still only be expected to raise the capacities of these local workers to that level which could be equally easily achieved in other sites that are potential competitors for the locating of an RPS.

2. Although the propensity of the DEVELPROD subsidiaries to compete through the originality and distinctive quality of their goods means that they may well be somewhat less constrained by residual protective barriers than the more price-competitive RPS orientation of the ESTPROD/EUR units.

3. We noted in Chapter 4 that the RP type of subsidiaries in the UK (ESTPROD/EUR) appeared to possess an R&D unit more often than would be implied by its pure motivation. The need to apply upgraded technology inputs within the RPS role may then provide the formal rationale for possession of such laboratories, but we noted in earlier discussion that it will perhaps more decisively (from the subsidiary point of view) represent the attempt to create the competences required for metamorphosis to WPM/RPM status.

4. In a detailed review of the lessons that may be learned from the East Asian newly industrialised countries, Lall (1996, p.12) argues that an approach that emphasises technological capabilities offers 'a comprehensive and coherent view of policy needs [since] it explains why I-S [import-substitution] strategies failed and E-O [export-oriented] worked, not by "getting prices right" and realising static comparative advantage, but by promoting a healthy and dynamic learning process'.

5. In line with their earlier analyses (discussed here in Chapter 2) and the results of our own work in this book, Young and Hood (1994, p.52) indicate that these concerns of after-care services derive from the fact that 'foreign affiliates evolve and develop over time in response to a wide variety of variables, from global and regional strategies of the parent through the interplay of corporate networks in Europe to the performance and competitiveness of the affiliate'.

6. The spread of an understanding of the potential of embedding MNEs in sustained industrialisation is also to be found in Lall's (1996, pp.70 71) exposition of the case of Malaysia. Here, Malaysia's initial success in attracting electronics MNEs 'was based on targeting firms that were relocating the more labour intensive assembly activities from Singapore' and attracting them through 'good infrastructure, low wages, [and] literate and trainable labour'. Once established in Malaysia, MNEs 'responded to rising wages by increasing automation and process upgrading rather than by "footloose" behaviour', with the support of 'Singapore-style policies' that sought 'to induce [MNEs] to upgrade technologically by undertaking local design and development, and to strike deeper local supply linkages'.

7. From an investigation of the changing relative status of US technology in the post-war period, Nelson and Wright (1992) evoke the issues that emerge from their observation that 'it is increasingly difficult to create new technology that will stay contained within national borders for very long in a world where technological sophistication is widespread and firms of many nationalities are ready to make the investment needed to exploit new generic technology'. In addressing the issue of whether 'national technology policy' is obsolete in a globalised world, Fransman (1995) suggests that Japan's technology planners 'have responded by internationalising Japan's technology policy while retaining its national objectives'. For our earlier interpretation of these issues see, Pearce and Papanastassiou (1996a, pp.96–100) and Pearce (1997, Chapter 2).

8. The same types of benefits may, of course, also emerge when local MNEs extend and diversify their research programmes into the science bases of other countries.

9. In our open-ended interviews with research directors of MNE laboratories in the UK, a considerable majority confirmed that the quality and distinctive scope of the UK scientific community still represented a key reason for their presence, but also tended to express fears that recent neglect of public policy support for science and technological education was beginning to seriously undermine the viability of a sustained commitment to their operations.

10. This, at least, seems implied in general statements at government level. A more informed understanding of MNE needs and attitudes may be operated at the level of Regional Agencies. See the analysis of Young and Hood (1994) discussed earlier.

11. In recent years there has been an element in public debate in the UK that has articulated the avoidance of unnecessary costs as crucial in order to compete with the newly industrialised countries (NICs), whose virtuous performance is seen as stemming essentially from cost-efficient production. Our interpretation of Lall's analysis of the 'first wave' NICs is that this policy emphasis may be seeking to compete with the past rather than the present of these countries. Thus it may be that the crucial achievement of, and therefore the true lessons to be learned from, Singapore, Taiwan and perhaps Korea (setting aside its recent troubles) has been to secure the persistence of development as the sources of comparative advantage move away from low-cost standardisation of inputs.

References

Almor, T. and S. Hirsch (1995), 'Outsiders' response to Europe 1992: theoretical considerations and empirical evidence', *Journal of International Business Studies*, **26**(2), pp.223–37.

Archibugi, D. and J. Michie (1995), 'The globalisation of technology: a new taxonomy', *Cambridge Journal of Economics*, **19**, pp.121–40.

Bartlett, C.A. (1986), 'Building and managing the transnational: the new organisational challenge', in M.E. Porter (ed.), *Competition in Global Industries*, Boston, Mass.: Harvard Business School Press, pp.367–401.

Bartlett, C.A. and S. Ghoshal (1990), 'Managing innovation in the transnational corporation', in C.A. Bartlett, Y. Doz and G. Hedlund (eds), *Managing the Global Firm*, London: Routledge, pp.215–55.

Bartlett, C.A. and S. Ghoshal (1989), *Managing Across Borders: The Transnational Solution*, London: Hutchinson Business Books.

Bartlett, C.A. and S. Ghoshal (1987a), 'Managing across borders: new strategic requirements', *Sloan Management Review*, **28** (summer), pp.7–17.

Bartlett, C.A. and S. Ghoshal (1987b), 'Managing across borders: new organisational responses', *Sloan Management Review*, **28** (fall), pp.43–53.

Bartlett, C.A. and S. Ghoshal (1986), 'Tap your subsidiaries for global reach', *Harvard Business Review*, **64**(6), pp.87–94.

Behrman, J.N. (1984), *Industrial Policies: International Restructuring and Transnationals*, Lexington, Mass.: Lexington Books.

Behrman, J.N. and W.A. Fischer (1980a), *Overseas R&D Activities of Transnational Companies*, Cambridge, Mass.: Oelgeschlager, Gunn & Hain.

Behrman, J.N. and W.A. Fischer (1980b), 'Transnational corporations: market orientations and R&D abroad', *Colombia Journal of World Business*, **XV**, pp.55–60.

Birkinshaw, J.M. (1994), 'Approaching heterarchy – a review of the literature on multinational strategy and structure', *Advances in International Comparative Management*, **9**, pp.111–44.

Birkinshaw, J.M. and A.J. Morrison (1995), 'Configurations of strategy and structure in subsidiaries of multinational corporations', *Journal of International Business Studies*, **26**(4), pp.729–54.

Brockhoff, K.K. and A.W. Pearson (1998), 'R&D budgeting reactions to a recession', *Management International Review*, **38**(4), pp.363–76.

Buckley, P.J., Z. Berkova and G.D. Newbould (1983), *Direct Investment in the United Kingdom by Smaller European Firms*, London: Macmillan.

Cantwell, J.A. (1991a), 'A survey of theories of international production', in C.N. Pitelis and R. Sugden (eds), *The Nature of the Transnational Firm*, London: Routledge, pp.16–63.

Cantwell, J.A. (1991b), 'The theory of technological competence and its application to international production', in D. McFetridge (ed.), *Foreign Investment, Technology and Economic Growth*, Calgary: University of Calgary Press, pp.33–70.

Cantwell, J.A. (1991c), 'The international agglomeration of R&D', in M.C. Casson (ed.), *Global Research Strategy and International Competitiveness*, Oxford: Blackwell, pp.104-32.

Cantwell, J.A. and S. Iammarino (1998), 'MNCs, technological innovation and regional systems in the EU: some evidence in the Italian case', *International Journal of the Economics of Business*, **5**(3), pp.383–408.

Cavusgil, S.T., A. Yaprak and P. Yeoh (1993), 'A decision-making framework for global sourcing', *International Business Review*, **2**(2), pp. 143–56.

Chesnais, F. (1988), 'Technical cooperation agreements between firms', *STI Review*, **4**, pp.51–120.

Cohen, W.M. and D.A. Levinthal (1989), 'Innovation and learning: the two faces of R&D', *Economic Journal*, **99**, pp.569–96.

Contractor, F.J. and W.K. Narayanan (1990), 'Technology development in the multinational firm: a framework for planning and strategy', *R&D Management*, **20**(4), pp.305–22.

Cordell, A.J. (1973), 'Innovation, the multinational corporation: some policy implications for national science policy', *Long Range Planning*, **6**, pp.22–9.

Cordell, A.J. (1971), *The Multinational Firm, Foreign Direct Investment and Canadian Science Policy*, Science Council of Canada, Special Study No. 22, Ottawa: Information Canada.

Crookell, H. (1990), *Canadian–American Trade and Investment Under the Free Trade Agreement*, New York: Quorum Books.

Crookell, H.H. and A.J. Morrison (1990), 'Subsidiary strategy in a free trade environment', *Business Quarterly*, (autumn), pp.33–9.

D'Cruz, J. (1986), 'Strategic management of subsidiaries', in H. Etemad and L. Séguin Dulude (eds), *Managing the Multinational Subsidiary*, London: Croom Helm, pp.75–89.

De Meyer, A. (1993), 'Management of an international network of industrial R&D laboratories', *R&D Management*, **23**(2), pp.109–20.

De Meyer, A. (1991), 'Tech talk: how managers are stimulating global R&D communication', *Sloan Management Review*, (spring), pp.49–58.

Dosi, G. (1988), 'The nature of the innovation process', in G. Dosi, C. Freeman, R. Nelson, G. Silverberg and L. Soete (eds), *Technical Change and Economic Theory*, London: Pinter, pp.221–38.

Dunning, J.H. (1996), 'The geographical sources of competitiveness of firms: some results of a new survey', *Transnational Corporations*, 5(3), pp.1–29.

Dunning, J.H. (1995), 'Reappraising the eclectic paradigm in an age of alliance capitalism', *Journal of International Business Studies*, 26(3), pp. 461–92.

Dunning, J.H. (1993a), *Multinational Enterprises and the Global Economy*, Wokingham: Addison-Wesley.

Dunning, J.H. (1993b), *The Globalisation of Business*, London: Routledge.

Dunning, J.H. (1988), *Explaining International Production*, London: Unwin Hyman.

Dunning, J.H. (1977), 'Trade, location of economic activity and the multinational enterprise: a search for an eclectic approach', in B. Ohlin, P.O. Hesselborn and P.M. Wijkman (eds), *The International Allocation of Economic Activity*, London: Macmillan, pp.395–418.

Dunning, J.H. and S.M. Lundan (1998), 'The geographical sources of competitiveness of multinational enterprises: an econometric analysis', *International Business Review*, 7(2), pp.115–34.

Dunning, J.H. and A. Rugman (1985), 'The influence of Hymer's dissertation on the theory of foreign direct investment', *American Economic Review: Papers and Proceedings*, 75(2), pp.228–32.

Fors, G. (1996), *R&D and Technology Transfer by Multinational Enterprises*, Stockholm: Stockholm School of Economics.

Forsgren, M., U. Holm and J. Johanson (1992), 'Internationalisation of the second degree: the emergence of European-based centres in Swedish firms', in S. Young and J. Hamill (eds), *Europe and the Multinationals*, Cheltenham: Elgar, pp.235–53.

Forsythe, D.J.C. (1972), *US Investment in Scotland*, New York: Praeger.

Fransman, M. (1995), 'Is national technology policy obsolete in a globalised world? The Japanese response', *Cambridge Journal of Economics*, 19, pp. 95–119.

Freeman, C. and L. Soete (1997), *The Economics of Industrial Innovation*, London: Pinter.

Giddy, I.H. (1978), 'The demise of the product cycle model in international business theory', *Colombia Journal of World Business*, XIII(1), pp.90–7.

Multinationals, technology and national competitiveness

Granstrand, O. and S. Sjolander (1992), 'Internationalisation and diversification of multi-technology corporations', in O. Granstrand, L. Håkanson and S. Sjolander (eds), *Technology Management and International Business*, Chichester: Wiley, pp.181–207.

Gupta, A.K. and V. Govindarajan (1994), 'Organising for knowledge flows within MNCs', *International Business Review*, **3**(4), pp.443–58.

Gupta, A.K. and V. Govindarajan (1991), 'Knowledge flows and the structure of control within multinational corporations', *Academy of Management Review*, **16**(4), pp.768–92.

Hagedoorn, J. (1993), 'Understanding the rationale of strategic technology partnering: interorganisational modes of cooperation and sectoral differences', *Strategic Management Journal*, **14**, pp.371–85.

Hagedoorn, J. and J. Schakenraad (1991), *The Role of Interfirm Cooperation Agreements in the Globalisation of Economy and Technology*. The MONITOR-FAST programme – prospective dossier No. 2 'Globalisation of Economy and Technology', Vol. 8. Brussels: Commission of the European Communities.

Håkanson, H. and J. Laage-Hellman (1984), 'Developing a network R & D strategy', *Journal of Product Innovation Management*', **1**, pp.224–37.

Håkanson, L. (1990), 'International decentralisation of R&D – the organisational challenges', in C.A. Bartlett, Y. Doz and G. Hedlund (eds), *Managing the Global Firm*, London: Routledge, pp.256–78.

Håkanson, L. (1983), 'R&D in foreign-owned subsidiaries in Sweden', in W.H. Goldberg (ed.), *Governments and Multinationals. The Policy of Control Versus Autonomy*, Cambridge, Mass.: Oelgeschlager, Gunn & Hain, pp.163–76.

Håkanson, L. (1981), 'Organisation and evolution of foreign R&D in Swedish multinationals', *Geografiska Annaler*, **63B**, pp.47–56.

Håkanson, L. and R. Nobel (1998a), 'Technology characteristics and reverse technology transfer', paper presented at the Academy of International Business Annual Conference, Vienna, October 7–10.

Håkanson, L. and R. Nobel (1998b), 'Organisational characteristics and reverse technology transfer', paper presented at the European International Business Academy Annual Conference, Jerusalem, December.

Håkanson, L. and R. Nobel (1993a), 'Foreign research and development in Swedish multinationals', *Research Policy*, **22**, pp.373–96.

Håkanson, L. and R. Nobel (1993b), 'Determinants of foreign R&D in Swedish multinationals', *Research Policy*, **22**, pp.397–411.

Håkanson, L. and R. Nobel (1992), 'International R&D networks – managing dispersed capabilities', paper presented at European International Business Academy Annual Conference, Reading, December.

Håkanson, L. and U. Zander (1988), 'International management of R&D: the Swedish experience', *R&D Management*, **18**, pp.217–26.

Håkanson, L. and U. Zander (1986), *Managing International Research and Development*, Stockholm: Mekan.

Harrigan, K.R. (1984), 'Innovation within overseas subsidiaries', *Journal of Business Strategy*, **4**(4), pp.47–55.

Haug, P., N. Hood and S. Young (1983), 'R&D intensity in the affiliates of US-owned electronics companies manufacturing in Scotland', *Regional Studies*, **17**, pp.383–92.

Hedlund, G. (1993), 'Assumptions of hierarchy and heterarchy, with applications to the management of the multinational corporation', in S. Ghoshal and E. Westney (eds), *Organisation Theory and the Multinational Corporation*, London: Macmillan, pp.211–36.

Hedlund, G. (1986), 'The hypermodern MNC: a heterarchy?', *Human Resource Management*, **25**, pp.9–35.

Hedlund, G. and J. Ridderstråle (1997), 'Towards a theory of the self-renewing MNC', in B. Toyne and D. Nigh (eds), *International Business: an Emerging Vision*, Columbia, SC: University of South Carolina Press, pp.329–54.

Hedlund, G. and D. Rolander (1990), 'Action in heterarchies – new approaches to managing the MNC', in C.A. Bartlett, Y. Doz and G. Hedlund (eds), *Managing the Global Firm*, London: Routledge, pp.15–46.

Hewitt, G. (1983), 'Research and development performed in Canada by American manufacturing multinationals', in A.M. Rugman (ed.), *Multinationals and Technology Transfer – The Canadian Experience*, New York: Praeger, pp.36–49.

Hewitt, G. (1980), 'Research and development performed abroad by US manufacturing multinationals', *Kyklos*, **33**, pp.308–26.

Hirschey, R.C. and R.E. Caves (1981), 'Internationalisation of research and transfer of technology by multinationals', *Oxford Bulletin of Economics and Statistics*, **42**(2), pp.115–30.

Hood, N. and S. Young (1988), 'Inward investment and the EC: UK evidence on corporate integration strategies', in J.H. Dunning and P. Robson (eds), *Multinationals and the European Community*, Oxford: Blackwell, pp.91–104.

Hood, N. and S. Young (1980), *European Development Strategies of US-owned Manufacturing Companies Located in Scotland*, Edinburgh: HMSO.

Hood, N. and S. Young (1976), 'US investment in Scotland: aspects of the branch plant syndrome', *Scottish Journal of Political Economy*, **23**, pp. 279–94.

Hood, N., S.Young and D. Lal (1994), 'Strategic evolution within Japanese manufacturing plants in Europe: UK evidence', *International Business Review*, **3**(2), pp.97–122.

Howells, J. (1990a), 'The internationalisation of R&D and the development of global research networks', *Regional Studies*, **24**(6), pp.495–512.

Howells, J. (1990b), 'The location and organisation of research and development: new horizons', *Research Policy*, **19**, pp.133–46.

Hymer, S. (1972), 'The multinational corporation and the law of uneven development', in J. Bhagwati (ed), *Economics and World Order from the 1970s, to the 1990s,* London: Macmillan, pp.113–40.

Hymer, S. (1970), 'The efficiency (contradictions) of multinational corporations', *American Economic Review – Papers and Proceedings*, **LX**(2), pp.441–8.

Hymer, S. (1960/1976), *The International Operations of National Firms: A Study of Direct Investment*, PhD Thesis, MIT. Published 1976, Harvard: MIT Press.

Jarillo, J.C. and J.I. Martinez (1990), 'Different roles for subsidiaries: the case of multinational corporations in Spain', *Strategic Management Journal*, **11**, pp.501–12.

Johnson, J.H. (1995), 'An empirical analysis of the integration–responsiveness framework: US construction equipment industry firms in global competition', *Journal of International Business Studies*, **26**(3), pp.621–35.

Kim, C. and R.A. Mauborgne (1993a), 'Procedural justice, attitudes and subsidiary top management compliance with multinationals' corporate strategic decisions', *Academy of Management Journal*, **36**(3), pp.502–26.

Kim, C. and R.A. Mauborgne (1993b), 'Effectively conceiving and executing multinationals' worldwide strategies', *Journal of International Business Studies*, **25**(3), pp.419–48.

Kim, C. and R.A. Mauborgne (1991), 'Implementing global strategies: the role of procedural justice', *Strategic Management Journal*, **12**, pp.125–43.

Kobrin, S. (1991), 'An empirical analysis of the determinants of global integration', *Strategic Management Journal*, **12**, pp.17–31.

Kojima, K. (1978), *Direct Foreign Investment: A Japanese Model of Multinational Business Operations*, London: Croom Helm.

Kotabe, M. and J.Y. Murray (1996), 'Determinants of intra-firm sourcing and market performance', *International Business Review*, **5**(2), pp.121–35.

Kuemmerle, W. (1998), 'Strategic interaction, knowledge sourcing and knowledge exploitation in foreign environments – an analysis of foreign direct investment in R&D by multinational companies', in H.H. Michael (ed.), *Managing Strategically in an Interconnected World*, New York: John Wiley.

Kuemmerle, W. (1997), 'Building effective R&D capabilities abroad', *Harvard Business Review*, (March–April), pp.61–70.

Kumar, N. (1996), 'Intellectual property protection, market orientation and location of overseas R&D activities by multinational enterprises', *World Development*, **24**, pp.673–88.

Lall, S. (1996), *Learning from the Asian Tigers – Studies in Technology and Industrial Policy*, London: Macmillan.

Lall, S. (1995), 'Industrial strategy and policies on foreign direct investment in East Asia', *Transnational Corporations*, **4**(3), pp.1–26.

Lall, S. (1979), 'The international allocation of research activity by US multinationals, *Oxford Bulletin of Economics and Statistics*, **41**, pp.313–31.

Leong, S.M. and C.T. Tan (1993), 'Managing across borders: an empirical test of the Bartlett and Ghoshal organisational typology', *Journal of International Business Studies*, **24**(3), pp.449–64.

Levitt, T. (1983), 'The globalisation of markets', *Harvard Business Review*, (May–June), pp.92–102.

Lundvall, B.A., (ed.) (1992), *National Systems of Innovation: Towards a Theory of Innovation and Interactive Learning*, London: Pinter.

Manea, J. and R. Pearce (1997a), 'The potential role of Romania's technological and scientific capacity in attracting FDI: an exploratory analysis of its national system of innovation', in R. Pearce (ed.), *Global Competition and Technology*, London: Macmillan, pp.183–215.

Manea, J. and R. Pearce (1997b), 'Foreign direct investment in Romania and multinationals' strategies: an analysis of subsidiaries roles', University of Reading, Department of Economics, Discussion Papers in International Investment and Management, Series B, No. 241.

Mansfield, E.D., D. Teece and A. Romeo (1979), 'Overseas research and development by US-based firms', *Economica*, **46**, pp.187–96.

Martinez, J.I. and J.C. Jarillo (1991), 'Coordination demands of international strategies, *Journal of International Business Studies*, **22**, pp.429–44.

Molero, J. and M. Buesa (1993), 'Multinational companies and technological change: basic traits and taxonomy of the behaviour of German industrial companies in Spain', *Research Policy*, **22**, pp.265–78.

Molero, J., M. Buesa and M. Casado (1995), 'Factors in the siting and commercial behaviour of multinational companies in Spain', in J. Molero (ed.), *Technological Innovation, Multinational Corporations and New International Competitiveness*, Luxembourg: Harwood Academic Publishers, pp.237–63.

Murray, J.Y., A.R. Wildt and M. Kotabe (1995), 'Global sourcing strategies of US subsidiaries of foreign multinationals', *Management International Review*, **35**(4), pp.307–24.

Nelson, R.R. (ed.) (1993), *National Systems of Innovation: A Comparative Study*, Oxford: Oxford University Press.

Nelson, R.R. and S.G. Winter (1982), *An Evolutionary Theory of Economic Change*, Cambridge, Mass.: Harvard University Press.

Nelson, R.R. and G. Wright (1992), 'The rise and fall of American technological leadership: the postwar era in historical perspective' *Journal of Economic Literature* **XXX** (December).

Niosi, J. and B. Bellon (1996), 'The globalisation of national innovation systems', in J. de la Mothe and G. Paquet (eds), *Evolutionary Economics and the New International Political Economy*, London: Pinter, pp.138–59.

Ozawa, T. (1992a), 'Cross-investments between Japan and the EC: income similarity, technological congruity and economies of scope', in J.A. Cantwell (ed.), *Multinational Investment in Modern Europe*, Cheltenham: Edward Elgar, pp.13–45.

Ozawa, T. (1992b), 'Foreign direct investment and economic development', *Transnational Corporations*, **1**(1), pp.27–54.

Ozawa, T. (1991a), 'Japanese multinationals and 1992', in B. Burgenmeier and J. Mucchielli (eds), *Multinationals and Europe 1992*, London: Routledge, pp.135–54.

Ozawa, T. (1991b), 'Japan in a new phase of multilateralism and industrial upgrading: functional integration of trade, growth and FDI', *Journal of World Trade*, **25**(1), pp.43–60.

Papanastassiou, M. (1995), *'Creation and development of technology by MNEs' subsidiaries in Europe: the cases of UK, Greece, Belgium and Portugal'*, Thesis submitted for the Degree of Doctor of Philosophy, University of Reading.

Papanastassiou, M. and G. Anastassopoulos (1997), 'Aspects of Greek inward and outward foreign direct investment: the case of the food and drink sector', *Development and International Cooperation*, **XIII** (24–25), pp. 349–74.

Papanastassiou, M. and R. Pearce (1998a), 'Individualism and inter-dependence in the technological development of MNEs: the strategic positioning of R&D in overseas subsidiaries', in J. Birkinshaw and N. Hood (eds), *Multinational Corporate Evolution and Subsidiary Development*, London: Macmillan, pp.50–75.

Papanastassiou, M. and R. Pearce (1998b), 'The value-adding procedure of scientific inputs in the overseas R&D laboratory: from recruitment to the board of directors, an inter-functional process', in P.J. Buckley, F. Burton and H. Mirza (eds), *The Strategy and Organization of International Business*, London: Macmillan, pp.210–32.

Papanastassiou, M. and R. Pearce (1997a), 'Cooperative approaches to strategic competitiveness through MNE subsidiaries: insiders and outsiders in the European market', in P.W. Beamish and J.P. Killing (eds), *Cooperative Strategies: European Perspectives*, San Francisco: New Lexington Press, pp.207–30.

Papanastassiou, M. and R. Pearce (1997b), 'Technology sourcing and the strategic roles of manufacturing subsidiaries in the UK: local competences and global competitiveness', *Management International Review*, **37**(1), pp. 5–25.

Papanastassiou, M. and R. Pearce (1996), 'The creation and application of technology by MNEs' subsidiaries in Europe', in F. Burton, M. Yamin and S. Young (eds), *International Business and Europe in Transition*, London: Macmillan, pp.207–30.

Papanastassiou, M. and R. Pearce (1995), 'The research and development of Japanese multinational enterprises in Europe', in F. Sachwald (ed.), *Japanese Firms in Europe*, Luxembourg: Harwood Academic Publishers, pp.265–310.

Papanastassiou, M. and R. Pearce (1994a), 'Host-country determinants of the market strategies of US companies' overseas subsidiaries', *Journal of the Economics of Business*, **1**(2), pp.199–217.

Papanastassiou, M. and R. Pearce (1994b), 'The internationalisation of research and development by Japanese enterprises', *R&D Management*, **24**(2), pp.155–65.

Papanastassiou, M. and R. Pearce (1992), 'Firm strategies and the research intensity of US MNEs' overseas operations: an analysis of host-country determinants', University of Reading, Department of Economics, Discussion Papers in International Investment and Business Studies, No. 164.

Patel, P. and M. Vega (1997), 'Patterns of internationalisation of corporate technology: location versus home country advantages', paper presented at the seminar 'The internationalisation of corporate R&D', CIRST, Montreal, August.

Pearce, R. (1998), 'The evolution of technology in multinational enterprises: the role of creative subsidiaries', *International Business Review*, 7.

Pearce, R. (1997), *Global Competition and Technology*, London: Macmillan.

Pearce, R. (1992), 'World product mandates and MNE specialisation', *Scandinavian International Business Review*, 1(2), pp.38–58.

Pearce, R. (1989), *The Internationalisation of Research and Development by Multinational Enterprises*, London: Macmillan.

Pearce, R. and M. Papanastassiou (1997), 'European markets and the strategic roles of multinational enterprise subsidiaries in the UK', *Journal of Common Market Studies*, 35(2), pp.243–66.

Pearce, R. and M. Papanastassiou (1996a), *The Technological Competitiveness of Japanese Multinationals*, Ann Arbor MI: University of Michigan Press.

Pearce, R. and M. Papanastassiou (1996b), 'R&D networks and innovation: decentralised product development in multinational enterprises', *R&D Management*, 26(4), pp.315–33.

Pearce, R. and S. Singh (1992a), *Globalising Research and Development*, London: Macmillan.

Pearce, R. and S. Singh (1992b), 'Internationalisation of research and development among the world's leading enterprises: survey analysis of organisation and motivation', in O. Granstrand, L. Håkanson and S. Sjolander (eds), *Technology Management and International Business*, Chichester: Wiley, pp.137–62.

Pearce, R. and A.T. Tavares (1998), 'Strategies of multinational subsidiaries in a context of regional trading blocs', University of Reading, Department of Economics, Discussion Papers in International Investment and Management, No. 257.

Perrino, A.C. and J.W. Tipping (1989), 'Global management of technology', *Research and Management of Technology*, 32(3), pp.12–9.

Porter, M.E. (1990), *The Competitive Advantage of Nations*, New York: The Free Press.

Porter, M.E. (1986), 'Competition in global industries: a conceptual framework', in M.E. Porter (ed.), *Competition in Global Industries*, Boston: Harvard Business School Press, pp.15–60.

Poynter, T.A. and A.M. Rugman (1982), 'World product mandates: how will multinationals respond?', *Business Quarterly*, 47(3), pp.54–61.

Prahalad, C.K. and Y. Doz (1987), *The Multinational Mission: Balancing Local Demands and Global Vision*, New York: The Free Press.

Ronstadt, R.C. (1978), 'International R&D: the establishment and evolution of R&D abroad in seven US multinationals', *Journal of International Business Studies*, 9(1), pp.7–24.

Ronstadt, R.C. (1977), *Research and Development Abroad by US Multinationals*, New York: Praeger.

Rosenberg, N. and R.R. Nelson (1994), 'American universities and technical advance in industry', *Research Policy*, 23, pp.323–48.

Roth, K. and A.J. Morrison (1992), 'Implementing global strategy: characteristics of global subsidiary mandates', *Journal of International Business Studies*, 23(4), pp.715–35.

Roth, K. and A.J. Morrison (1990), 'An empirical analysis of the integration responsiveness framework in global industries', *Journal of International Business Studies*, 21(4), pp.541–64.

Rugman, A.M. (1983), 'Multinational enterprises and world product mandates', in A.M. Rugman (ed.), *Multinationals and Technology Transfer – The Canadian Experience*, New York: Praeger, pp.73–90.

Rugman, A.M. (1981), 'Research and development by multinationals and domestic firms in Canada', *Canadian Public Policy*, 1(4), pp.604–16.

Rugman, A.M. and J. Bennett (1982), 'Technology transfer and world product mandating in Canada', *Colombia Journal of World Business*, 17(4), pp.58–62.

Rugman, A.M. and S. Douglas (1986), 'The strategic management of multinationals and world product mandating', *Canadian Public Policy*, 12(2), pp.320–28.

Serapio, M.G. (1993), 'Macro-micro analyses of Japanese direct R&D investments in the US automotive and electronics industries', *Management International Review*, 33(2), pp.209–25.

Sharp, M. and W. Walker (1994), 'Thatcherism and technical advance - reform without progress?', in T. Buxton, P. Chapman and P. Temple (eds), *Britain's Economic Performance*, London: Routledge, pp.397–429.

Sleuwaegen, L. (1988), 'Multinationals, the European Community and Belgium: the small country case', in J.H. Dunning and P. Robson (eds), *Multinationals and the European Community*, Oxford: Blackwell, pp. 153–70.

Taggart, J.H. (1997a), 'Constituents of subsidiary strategy', in K. Macharzina, M.-J. Oesterle and J. Wolf (eds), *Global Business in the Information Age*, Proceedings of the 23rd Annual European International Business Academy Conference, Stuttgart, pp.622–41.

Taggart, J.H. (1997b), 'US MNC affiliates in the UK: a special relationship?', in P.J. Buckley, M. Chapman, J. Clegg and A.R. Cross (eds), *The Organisation of International Business*, Proceedings of the 1997 Annual Conference, Academy of International Business, Leeds, pp.31–64.

Taggart, J.H. (1997c), 'Mapping stability and evolution of subsidiary strategy on the integration–responsiveness framework', in P.J. Buckley, M. Chapman, J. Clegg and A.R. Cross (eds), *The Organisation of International Business*, Proceedings of the 1997 Annual Conference, Academy of International Business, Leeds, pp.1–30.

Taggart, J.H. (1997d), 'An evaluation of the integration–responsiveness framework: MNC manufacturing subsidiaries in the UK', *Management International Review*, **37**(4), pp.295–318.

Taggart, J.H. (1997e), 'Autonomy and procedural justice: a framework for evaluating subsidiary strategy', *Journal of International Business Studies*, **28**(1), pp.51–76.

Taggart, J.H. (1996a), 'Multinational manufacturing subsidiaries in Scotland: strategic role and economic impact', *International Business Review*, **5**(5), pp.447–68.

Taggart, J.H. (1996b), 'Evolution of multinational strategy: evidence from Scottish manufacturing subsidiaries,' *Journal of Marketing Management*, **12**, pp.535–49.

Taggart, J.H. (1993), 'Strategy conflict in the MNE: parent and subsidiary', paper presented at EIBA Annual Conference, Lisbon.

Taggart, J.H. (1991), 'Determinants of the foreign R&D location decision in the pharmaceutical industry', *R&D Management*, **21**, pp.229–40.

Tavares, A.T. and R. Pearce (1998), 'Regional economic integration processes and the strategic (re)positioning of MNEs' subsidiaries; a conceptual investigation', University of Reading, Department of Economics, Discussion Papers in International Investment and Management, No. 254.

Turok, I. (1993), 'Inward investment and local linkages: how deeply embedded is Silicon Glen', *Regional Studies*, **27**, pp.401–17.

Vernon, R. (1979), 'The product cycle hypothesis in a new international environment', *Oxford Bulletin of Economics and Statistics*, **41**(4), pp.255–67.

Vernon, R. (1966), 'International investment and international trade in the product cycle,' *Quarterly Journal of Economics*, **88**, pp.190–207.

White, R.E. and J.A. Poynter (1990), 'Organisation for world-wide advantage', in C.A.Bartlett, Y. Doz and G. Hedlund (eds), *Managing the Global Firm*, London: Routledge, pp.95–113.

White, R.E. and T.A. Poynter (1984), 'Strategies for foreign-owned subsidiaries in Canada,' *Business Quarterly*, (summer), pp.59–69.

Yamin, M. (1997), 'An evolutionary analysis of subsidiary innovation and reverse transfer in multinational companies', in K. Macharzina, M.-J. Oesterle and J. Wolf (eds), *Global Business in the Information Age*, Proceedings of the 23rd Annual European International Business Academy Conference, Stuttgart, pp.211–30.

Yamin, M. (1995), 'Determinants of reverse transfer: the experience of UK multinationals', in R. Schiattarella (ed.), *New Challenges for European and International Business*, Proceedings of the 21st Annual European International Business Academy Conference, Urbino, pp.193–213.

Yamin, M. (1991), 'A reassessment of Hymer's contribution to the theory of the transnational corporation', in C.N. Pitelis and R. Sugden (eds), *The Nature of the Transnational Firm*, London: Routledge, pp.64–80.

Young, S. (1992), 'European business and environments in the 1990s', in S. Young and J. Hamill (eds), *Europe and the Multinationals: Issues and Responses for the 1990s*, Cheltenham: Elgar, pp.3–17.

Young, S. and N. Hood (1994), 'Designing developmental after-care programmes for foreign direct investors in the European Union', *Transnational Corporations*, 3(2), pp.45–72.

Young, S., N. Hood and S. Dunlop (1988), 'Global strategies, multinational subsidiary roles and economic impact in Scotland', *Regional Studies*, 22(6), pp.487–97.

Zejan, M.C. (1990), 'R&D activities in affiliates of Swedish multinational enterprises', *Scandinavian Journal of Economics*, 93, pp.487–500.

Index

aerospace 69,70, 73, 79, 85, 126, 215
    222
Almor, T. 87
Anastassopoulos, G. 207
Archibugi, D. 142
assembly 23, 27, 31, 46, 208, 239
Australia 52
automobiles 58, 62, 70, 73, 79, 85,
    112, 126, 237
autonomy 21, 29, 31, 32, 36, 37, 40-
    42, 44, 46, 50, 51, 87, 90, 96,
    102, 128

Bartlett, C.A. 33-38, 46-48, 50-54
    95, 96, 118, 120, 143, 158
Behrman, J.N. 17, 120, 121
Belgium 87
Bellon, B. 18
Bennett, J. 52
Berkova, Z. 87
Birkinshaw, J.M. 45, 52, 53
Brockhoff, K.K. 188
Buckley, P.J. 87
Buesa, M. 143, 187
bureaucracy 2, 45, 228

Canada 23, 24, 52
Cantwell, J.A. 17, 118, 121, 188, 201
Casado, M. 143
Caves, R.E. 120-122, 142, 143
Cavusgil, S.T. 222
chemicals 19, 58, 69, 70, 71, 73, 79,
    85, 112, 119, 134-140, 166,
    167, 170, 171, 182, 192
Chesnais, F. 119

China 233
Cohen, W.M. 205
communications 3, 27, 37, 69, 78, 122
    148, 153, 178, 187, 194, 204
comparative advantage 1, 6-8
    12, 13, 17, 19, 49, 55, 87,
    226-229, 232, 238, 240
components 23, 27, 48, 58, 62, 70,
    78,102, 107, 126, 154,155,
    208-223, 227
consultants 3
Contractor, F. 118
control 5, 37, 45, 47, 121,
    188
coordination 27, 37, 41, 45, 47,
    95, 121, 147, 148, 178
Cordell, A.J. 120, 187
creative transition 42, 51, 96, 97, 101,
    117, 118, 232, 233
Crookell, H.H. 52

D'Cruz, J. 23, 24
De Meyer, A. 187
Dosi, G. 118
Douglas, S. 52
Doz, Y. 38, 52
Dunlop, S. 31
Dunning, J.H. 1, 2, 18, 119

economies of scale
  in production 5, 22, 25-28, 35,
    56, 58, 96, 208, 226
  in R & D 95, 121, 148, 178
economies of scope 25, 35, 56, 96
    207

education 10, 11, 25, 26, 97, 173,
    177, 186, 233, 234, 238
efficiency-seeking 2, 3, 6, 7, 18, 27,
    37, 47, 53, 79, 225, 229,
    230
electronics 19, 56-58, 62, 63, 69, 70,
    73, 79, 112, 126, 133-140,
    143, 167, 171, 173, 175, 182,
    184, 188, 238
engineering 13, 25, 30, 59, 94, 108,
    109, 118, 155, 156, 162, 163,
    188, 199, 204, 222,230
entrepreneurial management 25, 28,
    29, 52, 100, 226, 230
Europe, 16, 19, 25, 26, 31, 32, 41,
    42,52, 53, 56-59, 62, 63, 68,
    69, 73 76, 78, 79, 85, 87, 100-
    102, 108-113,117, 119, 124,
    128, 130- 140, 144, 151-154,
    162-166, 170, 171, 174, 175,
    182, 183, 185, 188, 192, 194,
    195, 208, 213-215, 220, 222-
    225, 228, 238, 239
exports 5, 24, 26, 28-30, 39, 47, 50,
    51, 55, 56, 59, 65-78, 121, 128,
    152, 153, 225, 233

Fischer, W.A. 120, 121
food 56, 62, 69, 70, 73, 79, 112, 119
Fors, G. 143, 188
Forsgren, M. 53
Forsythe, D.J.C. 52
Fransman, M. 239
Freeman, C. 188
free trade 4-6, 25-28, 37, 53, 56, 224-
    228

GATT/WTO 5, 25, 227
Germany 143, 187

Ghoshal, S. 33-38, 46-48, 50-54, 95,
    96, 118, 120, 143, 158
Giddy, I. 118
global innovation strategy 93-95,
    101, 110, 147, 148, 158,
    159, 161, 162, 165, 185,
    186, 234
global strategy 4, 27, 34, 35, 42, 49,
    224
Govindarajan, V. 35-37
Granstrand, O. 92, 93, 118
Gupta, A.K. 35-37

Hagedoorn, J. 119
Håkanson, H. 187
Håkanson, L. 121, 122, 142, 143,
    186, 187
Harrigan, K. 118
Haug, P. 52, 187
Hedlund, G. 43-45, 118, 142
heterarchy 15, 19, 29, 36, 43-46, 53,
    87, 97, 118, 187, 206, 231
heterogeneity,
  market 5, 37, 43, 90, 95, 96,
    151
  technological 6, 37, 43, 90,
    94, 103
Hewitt, G. 121-123, 142
hierarchy 3, 15, 18, 43-46, 53, 97,
    117, 211, 221, 222, 230
Hirsch, S. 87
Hirschey, R.C. 120-122, 142, 143
Holm, U. 53
Hong Kong 233
Hood, N. 30-32, 52, 87, 187, 233,
    239, 240
Howells, J. 187
Hymer, S. 2, 18

Iammarino, S. 188
import substitution 25, 49, 56, 76,239
innovation 2, 3, 8, 18, 22, 36, 46-48,
        54, 69, 90-96, 101, 119, 120,
        143, 146, 158, 165, 168, 185-
        188, 192, 194-196, 201, 204,
        221, 235, 237, 238
    approaches to innovation,
    centre-for-global 95, 96, 120
    globally-linked 96, 143, 158
    local-for-local 36, 95, 96
    locally-leveraged 96, 143
input costs 1, 3, 6, 12, 22, 58, 97,
        130, 225
instruments 62, 69, 70, 73, 85,
        112, 113, 119, 126, 215
integration 20, 37-40, 49, 53, 54, 95
interdependency 29, 30, 36, 39, 41,
        43, 44, 51, 59, 90, 97,
        101, 102, 123, 146, 148,
        151-158, 162, 171, 174,
        177, 178, 180, 194, 195,
        231
interdependent individualism 37, 40,
        181, 231
intermediate goods 70-73
intra-group trade 69, 70, 87
inward investment 1, 10, 14, 20,
        165, 221, 224, 228, 229, 232,
        237, 238

Japan 19, 26, 31, 32, 57, 58, 62, 63,
        68-70, 73, 76, 79, 85, 92, 93,
        100, 101, 107-110, 113,
        118, 126, 128, 130-139, 141,
        144, 164, 165, 170-175, 182,
        185, 188, 193, 214, 215, 218,
        220, 222, 239
Jarillo, J.C.38, 49, 51-53
Johanson, J. 53
Johnson, J.H. 52

Kim, C. 40, 53
knowledge 2, 26-30, 33, 35-37, 42-
        44, 46-48, 86, 90-92, 97, 98,
        101, 108, 122, 143, 147, 148,
        153, 158, 164, 170, 174, 185,
        187, 189, 195, 204, 208, 228,
        231, 232, 236, 238
knowledge-seeking 7, 27, 147, 231
Kobrin, S. 54
Kojima, K. 18
Korea, 240
Kotabe, M. 221, 222
Kuemmerle, W. 143, 144.
Kumar, N. 142

Laage-Hellman, J. 186
laboratories,
    age of 130-134, 144
    types of,
    internationally interdependent
        157-159, 164-168, 170,
        181-183, 185, 186, 192-196,
        198, 201-206, 235-237
    locally integrated 154-159,
        164-168, 170, 181, 186, 188,
        192-196, 198, 199, 201, 204,
        206, 234, 235
    support 149, 151-157, 164-
        167, 177, 181, 183, 188,
        192-196, 198, 201, 204
Lal. D. 31, 32
Lall, S. 122, 142, 143, 238-240
Leong, S.M. 48
Levinthal, D.A. 204, 205
Levitt, T. 37
local content requirements 208
location advantage 1, 5-7, 10-13, 18,
        28, 59, 225-232
Lundan, S. 18
Lundvall, B-A, 188

Malaysia 239
management 2, 9, 11, 24, 28, 29, 33,
    34, 43, 57, 59, 109, 155, 156,
    231
Manea J. 52
Mansfield, E. 142, 143
marketing, 2, 3, 11, 13, 21-24, 28-30,
    33, 34, 39, 52, 57, 63, 94, 95,
    100, 109, 110, 123, 155, 156,
    162, 168, 199, 204, 226, 231,
    233
market-seeking 1-3, 5-7, 24, 27, 28,
    53, 87, 225
Martinez, J.I. 38, 49, 51-53
Mauborgne, R.A. 40, 53
mechanical engineering 56, 62, 69
metals 56, 70, 71, 73
Michie, J. 142
Molero, J. 143, 187
Morrison, A.J. 45, 52, 53
multidomestic strategy 4, 18, 24,
    26, 27, 36, 79
multinational enterprises,
  as differentiated networks 8,
    10, 15, 224
  types of,
  global organisation 38, 46-48,
    95
  horizontal organisation 53
  international corporation 47,
    48, 54, 118
  multinational corporation 38,
    46-48, 95
  transnational 46-48, 53, 54, 95,
    96, 143
  see also, heterarchy
            hierarchy
Murray, J.Y. 221, 222

Narayanan, W.K. 118

national system of innovation 6, 18,
    187, 206, 232
Nelson, R.R. 118, 188, 206, 239
Netherlands 143
new protectionism 25, 26
Newbould, G.D. 87
newly industrialised countries 26,
    233, 239, 240
Niosi, J. 18
Nobel, R. 122, 143, 187, 188

ownership-advantage 2, 3, 6, 7, 10-
    13, 18, 225-232
Ozawa, T. 19

Papanastassiou, M. 24, 52, 53, 62, 68,
    87, 88, 93, 95-97 100, 106,
    109, 118, 123, 142-144, 175,
    207, 239
Patel, P. 143
Pearce, R. 24, 25, 52, 53, 62, 68, 87,
    88, 93, 95-97, 100, 106, 118,
    119, 123, 142-144, 146, 148
    149,160, 175, 187, 188, 206,
    239
Pearson, A.W. 188
Perrino, A.C. 146
pharmaceuticals 19, 57, 58, 62, 63,
    69, 70, 73, 79, 85, 112, 119,
    121, 133, 134, 138, 143, 166,
    170,171, 180, 181, 183, 184,
    192, 193, 215
Porter, M.E. 4, 18, 24, 36
Poynter, T.A. 21-24, 30, 52, 53
Prahalad, C.K. 38, 52
procedural justice 21, 40-42, 50, 53,
    87, 231
process adaptation 28, 39, 41, 56, 97,
    112-117, 120, 143, 149, 151,
    152, 154, 163-167, 184, 192,
    199, 222, 226

product adaptation 22, 25, 28, 37, 39, 41, 42, 46, 56, 57, 62, 68, 97, 112-117, 120, 143, 149, 151-155, 163-168, 170, 177, 182, 184, 198, 199, 201, 204, 222

product development 6, 7, 13, 22-25, 27-31, 36, 37, 41-43, 46, 58, 62-64, 68, 70, 78, 87, 90, 94, 95, 98, 100-103, 108-112, 123, 126,130, 143,146,147,151-158,162-168,170,171,181, 182-188,190,192,194-199, 201-204,206,209,211,213-215, 220, 222, 231, 234, 236-238

product life cycle 2, 3, 7, 8, 54, 118

R & D 11, 12, 21, 24, 28-34, 38-41, 52, 63, 93-98, 102-112, 118-188, 192-199, 201-206, 226, 233-237, 239

R & D collaborations 11, 107, 108, 189-207, 231

R & D funding 180-183

regional integration 5, 25, 52, 62

regulations 57, 63, 113

research

applied 13, 94, 123, 147, 148, 155, 157, 159, 160, 167, 171, 181, 182, 184-186, 190, 192-199, 201, 202, 204-206, 235, 236

basic 13, 93, 94, 123, 147, 148, 157-160, 162-167, 170,171, 180-182, 184, 186, 190, 192-199, 201-206, 235, 236

resource seeking 28

responsiveness 20, 37-40, 46-53, 94, 95, 148, 153, 188

Ridderstråhle, J. 142

Rolander, D. 44, 45

Romeo, A. 142, 143

Ronstadt, R. 120, 187

Rosenberg, N. 206

Roth, K. 52, 53

Rugman, A. 17, 52, 122

Schakenraad, J. 119

science base 11, 12, 26, 27, 30, 91 97, 158, 163, 166, 173, 180, 185, 186, 189, 190, 201-205, 231, 234-237, 240,

Scotland 31, 32, 38, 52

Serapio, M. 188

Sharp, M. 237

Singapore 233, 234, 239, 240

Singh, S. 119, 146, 149, 160, 187, 206

Sjolander, S. 92, 93, 118

Sleuwaegen, L. 87

Soete, L. 188

Spain 38, 143, 187

stand-alone laboratories 14, 107 149, 155, 158, 159, 171, 185, 186, 190, 235

strategic asset-seeking 18

strategic competitiveness 16, 96, 123, 140, 142, 148, 149, 157, 160, 167, 182, 204, 228, 234

strategic technology alliances 119, 194

subsidiaries

age of 78-81, 142

individualism in 29, 30, 36, 38, 41, 43, 44, 87, 90, 91, 98, 102, 123, 178, 197, 206, 211 220, 227, 231

size of 79, 82, 83

types of,
actives 39, 40, 51, 52, 54
autonomous 39, 40, 49, 54
black hole 35, 54
branch plant 23
collaborator 41, 42
contributor 34, 35, 51
global innovator 35, 36
globally rationalised 24
implementor 35-37, 50
integrated player 35, 36
local innovator 36, 37
local service business 23
marketing satellite 21, 22
militant 41, 42
miniature replica 22, 24, 30-32,
    52
partner 40, 41, 51, 53, 87
product mandate 8, 24, 28-30,
    36, 38, 40, 45, 48, 50-
    54, 58, 59, 62-64, 78, 87, 90,
    92, 94, 110-112, 224, 225,
    229-236, 239
product specialist 22, 23, 30-
    33, 52
quiescent 38, 40
rationalised manufacturer 22,
    30-33, 52
rationalised product subsidiary
    27-29, 37, 39, 41, 42, 45, 50,
    52, 54, 56-58, 63, 64, 79, 112,
    124, 126, 128, 144, 224-
    232, 237, 239
receptives 39, 50
satellite business 23
strategic independent
    23, 30-32, 52
strategic leader 34, 35, 38, 51
truncated miniature replica
    24-28, 37, 41, 42, 49,

    50, 52, 54, 56, 63, 79, 85, 112,
    124, 224-228
vassal 42, 50
supply networks 20, 29, 36,
    42, 48, 53, 54, 57, 59, 72,
    102, 153, 229
Sweden 92, 93, 118, 121, 142,
    143,188

Taggart, J.H. 32, 33, 37-42, 49-53
    87, 121, 122
Taiwan 240
Tan, C.T. 48
tastes 4, 24, 26, 29, 37, 43, 47, 57,
    62, 63,68, 73, 78, 94, 113,
    128,152-154
Tavares, A.T. 52
technology monitoring 90, 91, 188,
    201, 202, 206
technology trajectory 16, 30, 62, 91,
    92, 98, 108-110, 118, 139,
    140, 143, 148, 157, 160, 17
    186, 188-190,204, 206, 231,
    234, 236
Teece, D. 142, 143
Tipping, A.C. 146
trade protection 1, 22-26, 73, 225,
    239
training 10-12, 25, 26, 186, 226, 229,
    234, 238
transition economies 9, 34
Turok, I. 221

Universities 11, 107, 143, 160, 162,
    189, 190, 192, 193, 199, 201-
    206, 232
USA 2, 19, 25, 31, 32, 53, 56-59, 62,
    63, 68, 69, 73, 76, 79, 85, 87,
    92, 93, 100, 101, 109, 110,
    113, 118, 128, 130-139, 141,

142, 144, 163, 164, 170, 171,
175, 182, 185, 192, 206, 214,
215, 220, 221, 239

Vega, M. 143
Vernon, R. 2, 3, 19, 54

Walker, W. 237
White, R.E. 21-24, 30, 52, 53
Wildt, A.R. 221, 222
Winter, S.G. 118
Wright, G. 239

Yamin, M. 17, 143
Yaprak, A. 222
Yeoh, P. 222
Young, S. 30-32, 52, 87, 187, 233,
239, 240

Zander, U. 121, 187
Zejan, M. 143